D0812318

"ASPECT" GEOGRAPHIES

A GEOGRAPHY OF SETTLEMENTS

"ASPECT" GEOGRAPHIES

A GEOGRAPHY
OF SETTLEMENTS

F. S. HUDSON, B.A., F.R.G.S.

*Deputy Headmaster, and Head of Geography
Department, King James's Grammar School,
Almondbury, Huddersfield*

MACDONALD & EVANS LTD
8 John Street, London W.C.1.
1970

First published October 1970

©
MACDONALD AND EVANS LIMITED
1970

S.B.N: 7121 0710 X

This book is copyright and may not be
reproduced in whole *or in part* (except for
purposes of review) without the express
permission of the publishers in writing.

HD
111
H45

Printed in Great Britain by Fletcher & Son Ltd, Norwich

NMU LIBRARY

Introduction to the Series

THE study of modern geography grew out of the medieval cosmography, a random collection of knowledge which included astronomy, astrology, geometry, political history, earthlore, etc. As a result of the scientific discoveries and developments of the seventeenth and eighteenth centuries many of the component parts of the old cosmography hived off and grew into distinctive disciplines in their own right as, for example, physiography, geology, geodesy and anthropology. The residual matter which was left behind formed the geography of the eighteenth and nineteenth centuries, a study which, apart from its mathematical side, was encyclopaedic in character and which was purely factual and descriptive.

Darwinian ideas stimulated a more scientific approach to learning, and geography, along with other subjects, was influenced by the new modes of thought. These had an increasing impact on geography, which during the present century has increasingly sought for causes and effects and has become more analytical. In its modern development geography has had to turn to many of its former offshoots—by now robust disciplines in themselves—and borrow from them: geography does not attempt to usurp their functions but it does use their material to illuminate itself. Largely for this reason geography is a wide-ranging discipline with mathematical, physical, human and historical aspects: this width is at once a source of strength and weakness, but it does make geography a fascinating study and it helps to justify Sir Halford Mackinder's contention that geography is at once an art, a science and a philosophy.

Naturally the modern geographer, with increasing knowledge at his disposal and a more mature outlook, has had to specialise, and these days the academic geographer tends to be, for example, a geomorphologist or climatologist or economic geographer or urban geographer. This is an inevitable development since no one person could possibly master the vast wealth of material or ideas encompassed in modern geography.

This modern specialisation has tended to emphasise the importance of systematic geography at the expense of regional geography, although it should be recognised that each approach to geography is incomplete without the other. The general trend, both in the universities and in the school examinations, is towards systematic studies.

This series has been designed to meet some of the needs of students pursuing systematic studies. The main aim has been to provide introductory texts which can be used by sixth formers and first-year university students. The intention has been to produce readable books which will provide sound introductions to various aspects of geography: books which will introduce the students to new ideas and concepts as well as more detailed factual information. While one must employ precise scientific terms, the writers have eschewed jargon for jargon's sake; moreover, they have aimed at lucid exposition. While, these days, there is no shortage of specialised books on most branches of geographical knowledge, there is, we believe, room for texts of a more introductory nature.

The aim of the series is to include studies of many aspects of geography embracing the geography of agriculture, the geography of manufacturing industry, biogeography, land use and reclamation, food and population, the geography of settlement and historical geography. Other new titles will be added from time to time as seems desirable.

H. ROBINSON
Geographical Editor

Author's Preface

LITTLE justification is required for writing this book. Its subject-matter is of particularly wide concern at the present time when the world is undergoing what has often been called a "population explosion." Individual settlements in virtually all countries are growing rapidly both in number and in size, and it is not surprising therefore that in 1965 the World Society for Ekistics (*i.e.* the science of human settlements) was founded. Its birthplace was London, one of the world's giant cities, its headquarters are in Athens, in a country which saw the origin and growth of some of the world's earliest urban settlements. Planners, sociologists, architects, historians, economists and others besides geographers are concerned with settlement study, for the places people inhabit are at once a synthesis of material structures, economic units and, not least, living organisms.

Where people live and where they spend both their working and leisure hours, the nature and grouping of their dwellings and factories and offices, are of the utmost relevance to geographical studies. Recently, there has been a great upsurge of interest at the universities and in the schools in urban geography, but much less attention has been paid to man's smaller settlements, even though the bulk of the world's people still live in them. This book is an attempt to cover, at G.C.E. "A" and "S" Levels, the whole content of settlement study. The point of view is that of a human geographer, who selects material from other disciplines but organises it and uses it in his own way. Had the work been written by a local or regional planner, a traffic consultant, historian or sociologist, much of the same material might have been embodied in it, but the result would have been a different book, with a different emphasis and outlook as well as a different approach.

In composing and arranging my materials, I have been very conscious of my debt to a large number of other writers, especially but by no means exclusively geographers. Among them are R. E. Dickinson, J. H. Johnson, Emrys Jones, Lewis Mumford, R. E. Murphy and A. E. Smailes, some of whose works on the subject are listed in the bibliography at the end of the book.

I should also like to thank the many government agencies, tourist offices and industrial firms who have been generous enough to allow me to borrow photographs for incorporation in this book. Many of my sixth-form pupils have also been helpful, both as guinea-pigs and as field-workers in the Huddersfield area; one of them has been kind enough to print for me several of the photographs I wished to include. Finally, I should also like to express my gratitude to my wife, not only for her encouragement but also because she has made so few demands on me during my many writing hours.

August 1970   F.S.H.

Contents

List of Illustrations

Part One

INTRODUCTION

Chapter I

An Introduction to Settlement Geography

THE GEOGRAPHER AND SETTLEMENTS

THERE are as many ways of looking at geography as there are of bowling a cricket ball. To some writers, teachers and students "areal differentiation" is the most meaningful, though brief, description of what geography is about; to others, an examination of the inter-relationships of two or more environmental factors may provide a satisfactory viewpoint. Some geographers demand a more complete synthesis and find the most worthy aim lies in the description and interpretation of complete natural and cultural landscapes, while others tend to regard their discipline as human ecology, and, by insisting on the pre-eminence of Man, seek to elucidate his active and passive relations with the natural environment. A world point of view is adopted by the systematic geographer, who often tends to regard his field as the "science of distributions," but the interpretation of a small area with its own individuality is looked upon as the core of the subject by the regional geographer.

Whatever one's point of view, the study of settlements is accepted as an integral part of the subject by all except the narrowest of geographical specialists. Whether the unit of settlement is the individual farm, the village, town, city or conurbation, there is plenty of variety in its spatial setting. The settlement is central to all human geography, modifying as it does the natural environment by intruding a cultural element. Any settlement can be studied in either a world or a regional context, but any settlement, if it is to be adequately appreciated, must be correlated with other facets of geography, e.g. relief, climate, geology and social and economic conditions.

The Diversity of Settlements

Every settlement is unique, and has a personality of its own. Among cities, there is only one London, one Melbourne, one New York. Each village and farm, too, is a distinctive item in the landscape, and has no precise duplicate even among its near neighbours. All large cities, however, have certain common attributes. Villages often occupy similar sites, share the same form and perform similar functions, and individual buildings— though varying regionally from an Eskimo igloo and a Kazak *yurt* (*see* Fig. 1) to a Manhattan skyscraper and a Hebridean black-house—are, in a particular area, generally built of identical materials and assume the same shape. It is therefore possible to adopt a comparative treatment and to

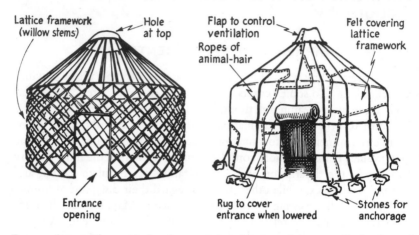

FIG. 1 —A *yurt*. The *yurt* is the characteristic habitation of the nomadic herders of the Central Asian steppes. The first sketch shows its lattice framework, the second the completed dwelling. The felt used as a covering is made chiefly from sheep's wool, the ropes from horse-hair. The whole is easily and quickly assembled, and its materials are readily portable.

attempt some classification. The latter may be based on size, site and situation, function, age, building materials, cultural characteristics or the layout of streets and buildings.

Temporary and Permanent Settlements

Most settlements have some degree of permanence, even though their buildings may have to be replaced from time to time, or their functions altered. Some settlements, however, are temporary. They may be occupied seasonally and then left untenanted, or they may be so transient that they occupy a particular site for only a short time, and are then either abandoned or shifted elsewhere. Cities, towns and most villages are relatively permanent elements in the landscape, but some villages and many individual dwellings are temporary features only.

People engaged in hunting and gathering may use natural caves as shelters, as some aboriginal tribes do in the Australian desert. But most of their dwellings are man-made: they are erected in a very short time and are made out of locally available materials. The very simple *wurleys* of the Australian aborigines and the crude wind-breaks of the Central African pygmies are examples. These shelters, at best, consist merely of a partial circle of tree boughs driven into the ground, bent over to form a half-dome and lashed together by a lattice of strong grasses or other fibres.

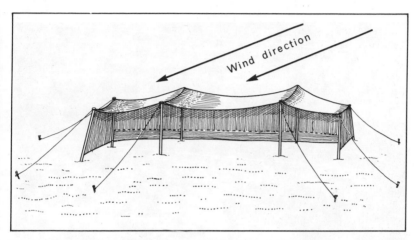

Fig. 2.—A large Bedouin tent. The Arabian Bedouin (or Badawin) erect their tents in a rough circle within which they often impound their herds at night. Each tent is made from lengths of black goat-hair cloth sewn together by women and supported by poles and guy ropes. The back strip, forming a valance, can be reversed if the wind-direction changes, and in the coldest weather additional strips of cloth may be used to cover the front of the tent. Most Bedouin tents are much smaller than the one illustrated.

They provide some protection against the sun, wind or rain, especially when covered with leaves or bark. The Eskimoes, on their hunting expeditions, find snow the most convenient material for building; their igloos are as quickly made as the wurley, and are equally impermanent.

The dwellings of nomadic pastoralists are rather more elaborate than those of hunters because herders usually possess some form of animal transport which they can use to carry constructional materials, provided these materials are not too bulky, too heavy or too fragile. Thus the Kirghiz, Kazak and kindred people of the Central Asiatic steppe and desert zone make their *yurts* (*see* Fig. 1) out of willow-stems and felt, the Bedouin of Arabia their tents from goat-hair cloth (*see* Fig. 2), the East African Masai their huts out of plaited stakes covered with grass, usually coated with cow-dung, hides or mud, and the northern Tungus of the Siberian tundra their conical tents from reindeer skin or birch-bark.

The homes of nomadic herders are generally assembled in groups to ensure protection against marauding animals or human predators, and are usually sited close to water-holes. The same is generally true of other socially cohesive people (*e.g.* shifting cultivators) whose villages, however, are commonly more substantially built as they are designed to last

[*Courtesy: South Africa House*

Fig. 3.—A South African *kraal*. In the grassland zone of South-east Africa, the typical Zulu village or *kraal* consists of a number of beehive-shaped huts built on a framework of poles interlaced with grass and generally covered with sun-dried mud. In the *kraal* illustrated here the nearest building is probably a maize granary, and the dark-coloured enclosure may be a cattle-pen for use at night. The outer, circular stockade, originally erected as a defence against human enemies and wild animals, has been abandoned.

for at least a few years. Shifting cultivators are also less dependent upon building materials furnished by animals, and more often use vegetable products and bricks. Thus the dominant house in the African savanna is a small beehive or conical hut, the walls of which are of light timber plastered with mud, the roof thatched with grass. A number of huts are usually erected close together to form a roughly circular *kraal*, surrounding which is a strong thorn fence enclosing and protecting cattle which are brought in at night (*see* Fig. 3).

The use of temporary settlements is not confined to primitive hunters and food gatherers, wandering pastoralists and shifting cultivators. Numerous examples may also be found among more advanced peoples, *e.g.* in Europe. Here, in many mountainous areas, for instance Scandinavia and the Mediterranean lands, the practice of transhumance has led to the erection of two dwellings, a summer one on the high pastures, and a winter one, generally larger and better furnished, in the valleys below. The typical valley settlement forms a compact, permanent village while the summer shelters are dispersed. Even in advanced areas where transhumance is not practised, temporary settlements are not necessarily unusual. Thus in England there are numerous caravan sites and motels, post-war pre-fabs (originally built to tide over an expected ten-year period of housing shortage) and war-time military camps.

Most settlements, however, are more permanent. They include dispersed houses and farmsteads, hamlets, villages, towns and cities. On paper, and in common parlance, this ranking of settlements according to their size is generally acknowledged, but terminology presents a problem. There is, for example, no exact definition of a village compared with a town, nor of a hamlet compared with a village, and the significance of the word "city" varies from country to country. Even the terms "rural" and "urban" lack precision.

RURAL AND URBAN POPULATION

Some writers tend to regard a rural settlement as one whose inhabitants depend for their livelihood upon the exploitation of the soil, and an urban settlement as one whose people in the main are engaged in non-agricultural occupations. Acceptance of this unqualified distinction would exclude from the category of rural settlements many small fishing, quarrying and mining villages as well as forestry camps, none of which can be properly regarded as towns. Even in the typical farm village there are many people who are not strictly rural in their mode of life. They include: (*a*) secondary workers supplying services to the primary group of farmers and farm labourers, *e.g.* shopkeepers, teachers, clergymen, the publican, postmaster and smith or garage proprietor; and (*b*) an "adventitious" element, consisting in part of retired people and in part of younger persons who live in the village but go to work in a neighbouring town. The proportion each of these classes bears to the total village population varies, of course, with the kind of farming characteristic of the locality, the quality of the soil, the attractiveness and accessibility of the site, and its place within the general settlement pattern. In much of the

English Plain, the secondary population is about half the primary, and the adventitious element may account for about a quarter of the whole.

The United States Census Bureau divides the non-urban population into two groups: (*a*) rural-farm, and (*b*) rural non-farm. In the United Kingdom no such division is officially recognised. Here, the rural population is regarded for numerical purposes as embracing the people who reside in the administrative areas known as "rural districts"; the urban population lives in boroughs and urban districts, which may well include rural tracts. Several decades ago, the urban population of England and Wales, as defined by the Census, reached 80 per cent of the whole. This percentage is declining slightly as the growing number of private cars is enabling many urban people to live just outside town areas, *i.e.* in rural districts, and therefore to be officially classed as part of the rural population.

VILLAGES AND TOWNS

Towns have been described as "villages which succeeded," but not all towns began their careers as villages. Many—including Britain's New Towns—were planned *ab initio* as towns. The rigid division between town and country, so often referred to as if they were in direct contrast, is becoming increasingly elastic due to the spread of "suburbia," and the increasing tendency for urban areas to grade almost imperceptibly into rural. Nevertheless, most nucleated settlements retain in large measure a separate identity not only on the map but also in the field. To which should the name "village" be applied, to which the name "town"?

As with the terms "rural population" and "urban population," there is no consensus about what is a village and what is a town, and it is therefore not surprising, though hardly satisfactory, to find some writers seeking refuge in the statement that "only a town possesses urban functions." Further to confuse the issue, some geographers refer to small settlements of miners and quarrymen as "urban villages."

In trying to elucidate the differences between a village and a town size is certainly no criterion: some settlements may have populations of up to 5,000 without possessing the attributes of a town, while a number of market towns may support perhaps only 2,000 people and yet enjoy urban status. There does, however, exist some relationship between the type of settlement and the way in which people are clustered together. Though population densities vary greatly from one town to another, and from one part of the same town to another, they are almost always higher in towns than in villages, and not only houses, but other buildings, too, are usually more close-knit. Towns also possess a more marked community organisation, and many historians would claim that a town is a place enjoying "borough status," *i.e.* a considerable measure of self-government. Functional contrasts between towns and villages are not always clear-cut. For instance, Russian and Hungarian "agrovilles" are usually regarded as towns: they may house several thousand inhabitants, but a high proportion of their working populations devote themselves to farm production. In parts of southern Europe, too, many towns have a significant agricultural element, and in Western Europe during the Middle Ages farming was always an important occupation of townspeople. More distinctive urban functions include manufacturing, retail and wholesale trade, and professional and office work, which normally play a very small part in village life but dominate at least the inner parts of most urban settlements. In most towns, even in small ones, at least two-thirds of the employed people follow non-agricultural occupations, and there is usually a variety of shops, some of which sell such durable goods as furniture and jewellery, at least one bank, commonly one or more residential hotels and perhaps also a cinema, a secondary school, hospital and weekly newspaper office. Small towns no longer necessarily possess an agricultural market because improved transport facilities have reduced the number of weekly markets in most countries.

In a town the man-made scene predominates over the natural much more than in a village. The pace of life is quicker and in many cases more people enter it for daily work than leave it for employment outside, *e.g.* in field, forest, mine or quarry, at sea, or in larger nucleated settlements. Socially, townspeople follow a way of life foreign to the villager. In fact, it has been claimed that a town is more a social unit than an economic one, more a distinctive grouping of people than of buildings. Though, as an element of the geographical landscape, it may be defined, for instance, as "a concentration of dwellings in a recognisable street pattern, where people live in some social and economic interdependence, enjoying common administrative, cultural and social amenities" (J. I. Clarke, *Population Geography*), it is perhaps no less realistic to say that a settlement is a town simply when its inhabitants regard it as such.

TOWNS AND CITIES

As with towns and villages, so with towns and cities: there is confusion about what constitutes the difference between these two types of settlement. Broadly speaking, a city may be regarded purely as a leading town, *i.e.* one which has outstripped its local or regional rivals, as the cities of Leeds and Bradford have forged ahead of the towns of Huddersfield and

Halifax. In Lewis Mumford's words: "the city is in fact the physical form of the highest and most complex types of associative life" (*The Culture of Cities*). It exemplifies to a greater extent than a town the dominant elements of the cultural realm in which it lies and usually displays the most monumental architectural forms.

As R. E. Dickinson pointed out (in *City and Region*), the Latin *civitas* is the common etymological root of both city and civilisation, and other writers have emphasised that cities are not only the chief repositories of a country's civilisation but also the main sources from which further cultural advances spring.

While most cities in the United Kingdom are large, a number, *e.g.* Cambridge and Wakefield, are small. Most cities have cathedrals, but no single attribute is common to all of them. In fact they are simply towns which for a variety of reasons, many of them historical, have been deliberately designated as cities by the award of a charter by the country's rulers. In the British Commonwealth, during recent years, such dominant towns as Singapore and Nairobi have been officially endowed with the title of "cities." The custom is different in other countries. In the United States, for example, the legal city is normally a corporate unit with a minimum population of at least 2,500, though the required size varies somewhat from state to state.

VILLAGES AND HAMLETS

It is usual to regard hamlets as no more than small villages; many are in fact included in parishes belonging to villages, but it is impossible to state with conviction the point at which a hamlet becomes a village, for the latter has no given minimum number of buildings or people. It may be said, however, that in a hamlet the buildings are usually fewer and more loosely clustered than in a village, there is more rarely a church, inn, shop or school, and the site and communications are generally inferior. Strict definition, especially on a population basis, is feasible only when the pattern of settlement in a particular area is examined. Thus the population of a hamlet in an area dominated by large villages may reach as much as 500, while in a poorer area it may amount only to 10.

THE SUBJECT-MATTER OF SETTLEMENT GEOGRAPHY

Settlement geography is an offshoot of social geography, itself a branch of the main tree of human geography. The major part of the subject is concerned with urban geography, for towns and cities are the most striking man-made features on the earth's surface. Indeed, urban settlements may be described as the hall-marks of contemporary civilisation. Yet in many parts of the world, even in highly urbanised countries, people continue to live in villages, dispersed farmsteads and other single dwellings, and some attention must be paid to these minor seats of habitation. To present a rounded account of settlement geography, therefore, it will be necessary to describe and try to interpret the site and situation, building materials, form and function of small rural settlements and the pattern they make on the map, as well as the characteristics of urban settlements. The links which join villages and single dwellings to their immediate environment are usually closer than those of towns and cities, and if the reasons for the establishment and early growth of such small settlements are to be understood, such topics as relief, initial water supply and former defensive requirements must not be overlooked. Even in considering towns, however, it is found that the past is usually the key to the present, and again, therefore, a historical as well as a purely geographical perspective is needed.

In studying an urban settlement it is desirable to adopt two approaches: (a) the study of a town as an entity, and (b) the study of a town as an amalgam of interconnected but disparate areas. When adopting the former approach, the student must take into account the entire townscape and its relations with both the natural and cultural environment. Towns vary greatly in size, function and morphology, they are composed of people as well as of bricks and mortar, and they face a number of common problems. Hence, *inter alia*, the following subjects of study present themselves: the urban hierarchy or ranking, the spacing of towns in their local and regional settings, their dominant functions and social characteristics, and the nature of their problems and how they are handled. All towns and cities exert an influence upon the areas around them: urban spheres of influence, or what are sometimes called urban fields, therefore provide another fruitful field of inquiry.

In considering towns as collections of distinct but related parts, urban geographers must pay close attention to their areal arrangements. They must plot their functional zones and social tracts, and be able to distinguish and investigate those parts of a town which are organised to serve residential needs, those used mainly for business or industrial purposes, and those providing recreation and entertainment. They must also scrutinise the circulation patterns (often intricate) which allow the town as a whole to function efficiently as an economic and social unit.

Geographers have made many detailed studies of individual towns, and it is obvious from their researches that each town has its own individuality and makes its own contribution to the life of the region in which it is situated. Detailed comparative studies are rarer despite their undoubted value, but it is well known that the forces stimulating urban expansion or compelling decline are by no means unique to individual places. Out of these comparative studies (which have been attempted in both geographical and historical contexts) have come limited but helpful classifications based on site and situation, function, age and culture. In this book, references to selected towns will be introduced where appropriate, but attention will also be focused on comparative studies and on the value and limitations of suggested methods of urban classification.

As urbanisation becomes a more marked feature of demographic change, the field of settlement study intensifies and becomes more complex. Growing numbers of cities are now reaching "million" or "millionaire" status as population clusters, and many are expanding sufficiently of themselves or in conjunction with their neighbours to form continuous urban meshes or conurbations. As individual cities and polynuclear conurbations multiply and enlarge, and as educational and economic standards rise and people come to demand and expect better homes and more congenial conditions for both work and leisure, more attention is being paid by society at large to the quality of towns as living spaces. It behoves the urban geographer to take note of the numerous recommendations now being made by town-planners and others whose aim is to improve this quality.

METHODS OF SETTLEMENT STUDY

The scientific study of settlements clearly demands much of the geographer. He must be prepared to read books, examine documents and maps, and, above all, to observe and assess buildings and streets and the people who use them. He must be at once a historian, cartographer, artist, market researcher, sociologist and mathematician. The essence of his work is field study, followed by mapping, correlation and interpretation, and when comparative studies are being undertaken there is a place for quantitative as well as cartographic techniques.

Among the documentary evidence of assistance to the settlement geographer are early surveys like the Domesday Survey of England, town charters and terriers. Books include not only local histories but also town and rural guides; official publications include census returns and trade and telephone directories. Among useful maps and plans are early cadastral plans (which may well date from the sixteenth century), terrier plans (from the eighteenth century) and ordnance and other governmental or official survey maps (from the nineteenth century). Tithe maps, estate plans and parliamentary enclosure award maps are often valuable for detailed studies.

Current official survey maps suggest the shape, extent and general ground-plan of villages and towns, and they also indicate much of value regarding site, situation and accessibility. Land-use maps and geological maps repay study; place-names may provide evidence of early factors affecting settlement and the lands from which the original settlers came, but they require wary and knowledgeable evaluation. The geographer's own maps, drawn by himself and incorporating data derived from his personal field study, add greatly to his understanding of a settlement, for official maps, whatever their scale, do not, for instance, show the heights of buildings and therefore ignore the urban "skyscape." They do not normally incorporate traffic flows along their roads, nor do they mark the use of every small parcel of ground or the precise distribution and social character of the population. They possess a high degree of accuracy but they omit to provide many of those local details in which the settlement geographer is particularly interested.

Part Two

RURAL SETTLEMENTS

Chapter II

Single Dwellings and Other Individual Buildings

THE VARIETY OF INDIVIDUAL BUILDINGS

A WALK round any English town will reveal even to a casual observer a great diversity of buildings. One street in a poor residential area, for instance, may be lined with drab rows of early nineteenth-century stone-built back-to-back houses or improved brick-built terrace houses of a somewhat later date; another street, in a better-class area, may be bordered by large, opulent, stuccoed Victorian villas; a third by twentieth-century semi-detached dwellings or post-war bungalows, each with a larger garden than the older properties. Here, an old half-timbered dwelling may survive, its ground floor converted into a café. There, a tall block of modern flats constructed of ferro-concrete, and displaying many more windows, may dominate the townscape. In another part of the town there are likely to be factories: generally many-storeyed if of early design, but low and wide-spreading if of recent origin More scattered are churches and schools, "corner shops" and public-houses, each having its own individuality and a distinctively functional architecture. Even in a village many different kinds of buildings may be noted, and not even in an area where the settlement is dispersed is there much architectural uniformity.

If a visit is paid to another country, not necessarily in another continent, contrasts multiply, for not only do individual buildings again contrast with each other but also they differ severally and collectively from those in the homeland. Just as languages and customs change from country to country, so does the traditional appearance of houses and other structures and the way in which they are grouped together.

The appearance, both external and internal, of a single building is clearly a result of its particular size, shape or form, function, and the structural materials used in erecting its roofs and walls. Each of these factors may be examined in both a regional and in an historical or cultural context: obviously a formidable task. Because of the complexity of the undertaking, we shall in the main limit ourselves in this chapter to a consideration of dwellings rather than other buildings, the more stable rural rather than the rapidly changing urban landscape, and the typical and traditional rather than the unusual and recent.

THE SHAPES AND FORMS OF SINGLE DWELLINGS

In his paper, "L'habitation rurale en France" (*Annales de Géographie*), the French geographer Demangeon attempted for his own country a classification of rural dwellings based on their shape, which he found varied with the kind of agriculture practised by their inhabitants. He recognised the following types: (*a*) the rudimentary house, solid and heavy in appearance, characteristic of the small cultivator of Lorraine who tends to keep everything under one roof and at one level; (*b*) the compact house, typical of a more advanced farm economy and associated with more fertile areas, and marked by the grouping of the essential farm buildings round an enclosed farmyard; (*c*) the straggling house, more typical of a cattle economy, and with fairly close parallels in England, the farm buildings being separated from each other; (*d*) the vertical house, common in southern France, including the Alps, where cattle are housed on the ground-floor, people on the next, and grain is stored above. Demangeon's pupil, Brunhes, felt—as others since have done—that this classification is too rigid, and that in most rural areas at least the first three types of farm settlement may all be found within a small compass.

While, however, it may be difficult, perhaps impossible, to adopt a satisfactory classification of houses based on their distinctive shapes, it is true that in most cases their form and to some extent also their dimensions do tend to show regional variations. Such variations are due to a number of causes. Any kind of shelter must give protection against extremes of climate and weather—against excessive heat and sunshine in some areas, against heavy rain, snow, strong wind and even earth tremors in others; some dwellings must provide special protection against predatory animals and obnoxious insects, others against human raiders. Changes in architectural fashion and improvements in building techniques, adopted in some areas, but not until much later in others, and the availability of structural materials, capable of bearing different stresses and varying in their flexibility and degree of resistance to shaping: all these factors induce changes in both the exterior and interior character of dwellings.

It has often been pointed out, for example, that in many tropical areas the interiors of dwellings are kept cool and shaded by a limited use of wall-openings or a generous use of shutters, while in wet areas steeply-pitched roofs provide a more effective means of shedding rain than more gently inclined ones. In Australia, New Zealand and the Argentinian pampas, ranch-houses are equipped with verandahs which act as open-air sitting rooms shaded from the sun's heat (*see* Fig. 4). Japanese homes are typically flimsy, the walls in places consisting of little more than light bamboo frames covered with paper so that little harm is done if the whole

[*Courtesy: High Commissioner for New Zealand*

FIG. 4.—A modern farmhouse, New Zealand. The farm bungalow shown here, with its generous windows, wide verandas, timber walls, brick chimneys and spacious gardens, is typical of many in New Zealand. It is situated at Te Aroha, Auckland, in a setting of hill and plain divided into well-ordered farms, each concerned with dairying and with the production of fat lambs and beef. Horses and ponies still have a place on these farms, but the motor-car is now even more ubiquitous.

structure collapses during an earthquake. Until 1963, the height of Japanese buildings was restricted by law to a maximum of 102 ft (31 m) in order to minimise potential earthquake damage, but a protracted study of advanced building techniques has since shown that, provided a more flexible structure of ferro-concrete is adopted, much higher buildings can be erected with safety. A building of thirty-six storeys, 482 ft (147 m) high, has now been raised in Tokyo.* Not only is it believed capable of resisting even intense earth tremors, it is also fitted with glass thick enough to withstand the violent typhoons which from time to time assail Japan.

* The world's first skyscrapers were made possible only after the invention of the electric lift in 1857: a revolution in the internal equipment of a building.

On the coasts of Malaya, Indonesia, Borneo and the Philippines—as in most parts of the world—the diverse shapes, dimensions and plans of individual dwellings cannot be altogether accounted for in terms of either physical environment or economic efficiency, but owe much also to varied ethnic influences. The habit of erecting pile-dwellings, however,

[*Courtesy: Malaya House*

FIG. 5.—A Malayan house. This house—of a type common in the better-kept Malayan villages or kampongs—is built of timber, has a pent, thatched roof to shed the heavy rains, and is raised off the ground as a protection against damp, insects and snakes. There are sliding doors and a shady veranda. Behind is the Malayan forest, in front the garden.

is persistent. This custom may be partially due to folk memories of earlier tree-shelters, but it also answers the need for protection against damp, vermin and noxious snakes and other animals. In fact, the piles on which the buildings are raised are often fitted with wooden discs to prevent rodents from ascending them (*see* Fig. 5).

In an interesting article entitled "Thoughts on Housing for the Humid Tropics" (*Geographical Review*) D. H. K. Lee puts forward a model of the kind of house best fitted to suit the environment of the humid tropics and which would also provide comfort and efficiency and be aesthetically pleasing. For protection against excessive sunlight he recommends tall, leafy trees, for shelter from rain a steeply-pitched roof, and to protect the walls from undue heat he suggests broad projecting eaves on the south side and low shade trees on the east and west sides on to which the lower morning and evening sun shines. Openings in opposing walls would ensure air movement within, and a floor of cheap, semi-absorbent material laid down above ground level would be cool, easy to clean, and dry. Many tropical dwellings measure up to these ideal requirements though, until recently, few have been constructed consciously on scientific principles. Though their builders' knowledge of microclimates is often limited, climatic excesses have generally been minimised by rule-of-thumb methods which include the erection of windbreaks and shade trees and *ad hoc* experiments with the spacing and frequency of wall-openings and verandahs.

The need for defence against human enemies has often, like climate, led to a particular form of building. In England and France, for example, medieval castles and fortified manor-houses are almost invariably equipped with look-out towers, solid walls of abnormal thickness and narrow windows. In some parts of Albania, where blood-feuds were rife until very recently, the typical house has thick walls of stone or hard red brick, strong wooden doors, a few very small windows and a blind side facing the road.

BUILDING MATERIALS

In the past, only monumental buildings—religious edifices, imperial palaces, lordly mansions—were constructed of exotic materials brought from afar. Such buildings, as much through their structural materials as through their conspicuous size and form, conferred prestige upon their owners and helped them to assert and maintain their dominance over the societies they controlled. Nowadays, this ascendancy has waned, and modern transport allows building materials—though still heavy and bulky—to be moved more economically over greater distances. Moreover, a number of mass-produced articles, *e.g.* concrete, glass and metal sheets, are now widely available. Consequently, in advanced countries, urban building forms are coming to bear a more common stamp despite continued regional variations in climate and in the cultural heritage. There are imitations of Paris and New York even in some rural places, but it is mainly here—in the villages and hamlets of the more conservative agricultural areas—that we must look for those erections, especially houses and farm buildings, where man and his immediate environment still come close together.

Variations in climate and relief, diverse agricultural economies, social history and the ethnic influences to which societies have been subject all help to account for the detailed design of rural dwellings. Regional changes in geology and vegetation, however, go far towards explaining why house-types in one part of a continent or country differ from those in another. Thus in his *Human Geography* Brunhes emphasised the widespread use of timber in the coniferous forest areas of northern Europe, *e.g.* in Sweden, Finland and northern Russia, and also in many mountain areas, where most trees have straight trunks and can therefore be easily placed one upon another as logs or sawn into planks to make wooden houses. The stone house is more typical of Mediterranean Europe, where few forested areas now exist. Stone is also a common building material in many parts of "deciduous Europe," where geological conditions are favourable, because deciduous timber is normally hard and comes from trees which are only rarely supported on straight trunks; such trees, however, in the past, have been adequate for the making of half-timbered houses. Where the native rock is clay or alluvium rather than, for example, sandstone, limestone or granite, dried earth or mud, usually in the form of bricks, has tended to be the chief building material in areas which carry little timber, *e.g.* the Po Plain.

In England, as in Europe as a whole, there are sufficient regional contrasts in both geology and vegetation to furnish a wealth of building materials, and therefore a great diversity of house-types, as Fig. 6 shows. Good building stone is not so widespread as to be available everywhere, and it shows considerable regional variations. Forests and woodlands differ in density and in their characteristic trees, especially in the size and distribution of the pedunculate oak, the main wood used for timber framing. Areas floored with clay, though lacking in stone, offer the possibility of brick manufacture, and may also be well wooded.

Jurassic limestone can be squared up for building purposes without much difficulty, and mellows very well. For this reason alone it is not surprising that some of England's finest domestic and ecclesiastical architecture is to be found within the Jurassic belt, notably at Bath and in the Cotswolds (*see* Fig. 6). Hard, crystalline rock such as granite has been widely used by Cornish builders, but its intractable character offers less scope to masons, and dark, rugged, rather unbeautiful dwellings have usually resulted. The ease with which grey Welsh slate may be split provides a main reason for the distinctive village landscape of northwest Wales. In the south-western part of the West Riding, the almost ubiquitous use of the native millstone grit and Lower Coal Measure sandstones has enabled many villages round Bradford and Halifax to accord satisfactorily with geological surroundings, though many of their buildings here have been blackened by industrial grime. The use of the much whiter, less easily shaped, Carboniferous Limestone has been largely responsible for a very different settlement landscape in north-west Yorkshire. In all these areas of stone-built houses, the several villages and farms appear like the exposed bones of the earth itself.

FIG. 6.—Traditional building materials in England and Wales. This map should be studied in relation to both the text and a geological map. Observation of farm and village buildings during journeys by road and rail will amplify the generalised information the map conveys.

Many localities within the English clay vales, densely forested until relatively recent times, are punctuated with villages which are either dignified by the appearance of "black and white" architecture or warmed by the colour of the native reddish brick. In the former case, hewn out trunks have formed the traditional framework of the houses, and the spaces between uprights and beams have been filled in with woven twigs or slender laths of poorer timber, and then plastered over with mud to produce "wattle and daub" (*see* Fig. 7). Brick dwellings came gradually to replace half-timber as forest-clearing was intensified, and as knowledge of brick-making filtered in from the Low Countries in the fourteenth century. Brick buildings had the advantage of being more proof against both vermin and fire than half-timbered structures, and they often show more elegance, if greater simplicity, in their design. In some villages, timber and brick have been attractively allied by a device known as "bricknogging," *i.e.* the filling up of the timber frame by bricks, often laid diagonally. In others, "rough casting," *i.e.* the dashing of small pebbles against a plaster surface, has been employed.

[*Courtesy: Unilever Research Lab.*

FIG. 7.—Housing in Port Sunlight, Cheshire. These houses in Port Sunlight—a model village founded by W. H. Lever in 1886—are in the Cheshire "black and white" tradition. Even before they were built, half-timbering had given way to brick building. They illustrate one aspect of the Romantic architectural style which still finds favour.

Like stone, bricks vary considerably in both texture and colour. In the eighteenth and early nineteenth centuries brickfields round London were sited on various clays from which bricks could be made in diverse shades of grey and yellow. By contrast, the clays round Exeter in south Devon produced a rusty-red brick, and those near Leicester a salmon coloured one. Hence there are many local variations in the appearance of "brick villages." "Cob" is a building material traditional to parts of south-west England. It consists of a mixture of soil, dung, straw and

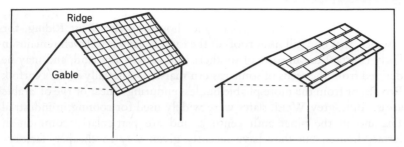

Pitched roofs: *(left)* for thatch or tiles, *(right)* for slates or stone-slats.

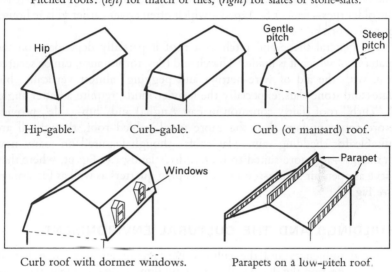

Hip-gable.　　　　Curb-gable.　　　　Curb (or mansard) roof.

Curb roof with dormer windows.　　　Parapets on a low-pitch roof.

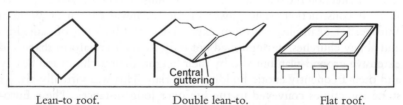

Lean-to roof.　　　Double lean-to.　　　Flat roof.

FIG. 8.—Typical house-roof shapes. These simple diagrams reveal part of the rich variety of roofing which may be seen in England and elsewhere. The shapes delineated are a reflection of architectural materials, wall structures and styles, and of the social and natural environment.

water, rammed solid and dried out. To prolong its life, it is often coated with coloured lime wash or tar, and raised on stone foundations.

Roofing materials are just as distinctive as the substances used in

NMU LIBRARY

England for constructing walls. Stone slats continue to be made in the Cotswolds, but it is only in the older houses of the West Riding, for instance, that one still finds roofs of the local flagstone. Thatch remains in fairly constant use in parts of southern and eastern England, and may be derived from the reeds of some eastern marshes, especially in the Norfolk Broads, or from the more pliable but less enduring wheat or rye of arable areas. Blue-grey Welsh slates were widely used for roofing in industrial England in the nineteenth century, and are particularly common in terrace houses, but they have recently given way to cheaper, factory-made red tiles. The latter are much more garish in their appearance than the older tiles—flat- or S-shaped—which often cover earlier village houses of native brick.

The general shape and pitch of a roof is partially dependent on the material of which it is made. Thatch and tiles, for instance, can be secured (*e.g.* with the aid of wire-netting and pegging) almost vertically, but slates and stone-slats, expecially the heavier kinds, require a flatter angle. A "curb" roof (fairly common in East Anglia) and "hip-gable" provide more room upstairs than the more usual gabled roof, though all are suitable for shedding rain. Flat roofs—though featured on many new buildings—are more suited to hotter, drier lands, *e.g.* Egypt, where they serve as open-air sitting-rooms and sleeping quarters as well as for storage (*see* Fig. 8).

BUILDINGS AND THE CULTURAL ENVIRONMENT

Social influences and the cultural heritage of an area often have a marked effect on the shape and size of buildings and on the materials used in their construction. The power of the medieval church in Western Europe, for example, was often expressed in the building of cathedrals and abbey churches, distinguished not only by their cruciform shape and extensive ground-plan but also by their height, their architectural beauty and their frequently exotic building material. This was virtually always stone sometimes conveyed to the site over long distances. These European cathedrals and abbey churches are, however, quite dissimilar in their appearance from the mosques of the Moslem world and the Hindu and Buddhist temples of India and the Far East, though these buildings may equally dominate the settlements of which they form a part.

On a more humble scale, quite ordinary dwellings owe at least something to social conditions. We have already seen that the Flemings reintroduced into England the art of brick-making, virtually lost with the departure of the Romans. The Spaniards carried to the New World the idea of the patio or enclosed courtyard as well as the Baroque church (*see* Fig. 9), though in their new physical environment both underwent some modification and adaptation. The houses of the Moslem Slavs in some mountain and forest areas of south-eastern Europe, while broadly resembling those of local Christians, are often distinguished from them by having fewer windows and higher garden walls. This is because of the

[*Courtesy: Pan American World Airways*

FIG. 9.—A Baroque church in Lima, Peru. This church (of San Marcello) was built by the Spaniards in 1584. It provides a good example of the Baroque style of architecture introduced into Latin America from southern Europe. Like many other such buildings in the New World, it is alien to the native environment and tradition.

women's secluded habits coupled with their need for unobserved open-air exercise. In certain Greek islands, *e.g.* Chios and Crete, Italianate as well as native influences are apparent in house-types, and in parts of Epirus Albanian influences seem to be responsible for the occurrence of towered, houses resembling fortresses.

In England, as H. H. Swinnerton has pointed out,★ agriculturally

★ "The Biological Approach to the Study of the Cultural Landscape," *Geography*, Vol. 23, 1938.

prosperous times have often produced well-built, substantial farm build-ings, on to which, in poorer days, ramshackle structures may have been added. In the early nineteenth century, when the community as a whole felt no responsibility for the conditions of the poor, many tiny cottages were built, sometimes by the farm labourers themselves. Later, when the public conscience was awakened, local authorities were empowered to make by-laws controlling such items as the capacity of rooms in dwelling-houses, the size of windows and the width of streets. Gardens became a feature and even the more humble houses became larger and more airy.

ARCHITECTURAL STYLES AND BUILDING FORMS

How far are buildings the product of their environment, physical and social, how far a product of man's artistic sense and technical ability? Why do buildings, like paintings, change from period to period when at least the physical, if not the cultural environment remains virtually the same? Is the effect of climate, geology and other physical attributes really minimal, and is the style of buildings determined rather by changing human needs? Is there not also scope for man as an artist, constantly striving to express himself in new terms, never content to be a mere copyist?

Undoubtedly, changes in architectural style or fashion do have a genuine effect on the design of buildings, viewed both externally and internally. Though the main purpose of a house is to satisfy the human need for shelter, the details of its shape, even if basically only a box, seem to be governed at least partially by the force of current taste and the prevailing architectural fashion. In England, for example, the broad European traditions of Classical and Romantic styles are both evident. Most towns and some villages show in both their domestic and public buildings elements of each, though neither took root in England without undergoing some insular modification, the Romantic style in particular containing many home-bred ideas. The Classical tradition, introduced by the Romans, brought in again briefly by the Normans, chiefly penetrated England during the Renaissance period. The Romantic tradition, originally emanating from northern Europe, but with a distinctive English patina, became dominant in the later medieval and early modern period, and right up to the present day has presented a challenge to the pre-eminence of the Classical.

The appearance of Classical houses—built with geometrical accuracy— satisfies the intellect and man's appreciation of good order and proportion, while that of Romantic buildings appeals more to his imagination and emotions, and evokes his love of the countryside and the less formal harmony of nature. The irregular, picturesque character of fifteenth-century and early Tudor buildings in England—well displayed at Laven-ham in Suffolk, where gables, large dormers and roof-lines at right-angles to the street are common—was followed by the rather more strict outlines of Elizabethan and Jacobean buildings, which gave way in their turn to the even more disciplined symmetry of Queen Anne and Georgian houses, so well seen, for example, in Bloomsbury. In Victorian and Edwardian times, though the Classical tradition remained, and is splendidly exempli-fied in many Lancashire cotton mills, in a number of public buildings such as town halls and art galleries, and in the model village of Saltaire, near Bradford, Romanticism reasserted itself strongly in the neo-Gothic, and in garden suburb and garden city movements, the former being particularly evident in ecclesiastical architecture and in Victorian villas, the latter at Hampstead, Letchworth and Welwyn Garden City. The numerous rows of cheap terrace houses erected in Britain near collieries and factories in the nineteenth century to house industrial workers represent a debased form of Georgian architecture, lacking the dignity and proportion of the true Georgian residences. They tend to look alike in all industrial towns except that in some areas they were built of the local stone, in others of mass-produced bricks.

Today, the Romantic notions of builders and house purchasers, expressed, for example, in contemporary bungaloid growth and in what Osbert Lancaster described as "by-pass variegated," vie with the geo-metrical severity of the new, towering slab blocks of offices and flats, becoming so common near city centres. Architects are no longer bound by local traditions and materials, and are less and less restricted by technological limitations. The result is that the harmony between build-ings and their setting is in danger of being lost in favour of the greater convenience and efficiency which purpose-built structures are expected, above all else, to bring. In urban areas the world over the rich variety of regional building traditions is gradually being reduced to a less attractive uniformity, though of course differences, at least in scale, persist.

TYPICAL DWELLING-PLACES

To conclude this chapter, details of typical dwellings in a number of widely separated settings are given in order to stress more firmly the relationship between domestic buildings and their physical and cultural environment. Our first examples will be from Egypt.

Dwellings in Egypt

Jean Brunhes (in *Human Geography*) draws a contrast between the houses of upper Egypt, made from regular cubes of Nubian sandstone, and the sun-hardened mud houses of lower Egypt, where stone is not readily available. He admits, however, that as both house-types are occupied by people of the same ethnic group, the differences are only

[*Courtesy: Aerofilms, Ltd.*

FIG. 10.—Houses in Sakkara, Egypt. This village, about 30 miles (48 km.) south of Cairo, shows the typical Egyptian skyline with tall palms and flat-roofed houses. The houses are of sun-dried bricks or stone. Where the window openings are large and numerous, they occupy the shady side of the walls.

superficial: houses in both areas possess fundamentally the same shape and other attributes. Roofs are typically flat and often used for storage (*see* Fig. 10), but here and there one meets, especially in the delta, a small dome, and in the valley above Cairo a vaulted roof. Harry Robinson goes further.★ He stresses the simple geometric forms, horizontal lines and large wall surfaces of domestic buildings and compares them with the vast, stern, monotonous, flattish landscape which surrounds them. He regards the ubiquity of the thick walls, with few apertures, as an obvious

★ "The Influence of Geographical Factors upon the Fine Arts," *Geography*, Vol. 34, 1949.

response to the intensity of the summer sun, and he thinks that the widespread use of sharply-cut, geometric forms may have been generated by the appearance of the sharp shadows cast by early structures. He also suggests that the abundance of date-palms may have inspired the design of the columns, whose capitals seem often to be derived from the shape of the native lotus of papyrus.

In the desert, beyond the cultivated strip of Egypt, the typical dwelling is the nomadic tent, easily assembled and transported, made from cloth derived from the herders' flocks of goats but usually purchased from village weavers, and well suited to a hot, arid environment. The cover, made up of several lengths of material sewn together, is supported (*see* Fig. 2) by a number of poles, and further secured by long ropes. To catch the breeze and obtain protection from blown sand, the open face of the tent—generally on the shady side—may be quickly reversed.

Dwellings in Western Norway

Timbered buildings remain typical of rural areas in western Norway, but as old buildings decay concrete is beginning to make its appearance, as in most advanced countries. Since there is little level ground for either building or tillage, most dwellings are isolated, compact and often lofty, the lower floor being used chiefly for farm animals and stores, the living quarters reached directly from the slope above. Most of the houses are of weather-board and are painted in pastel shades to relieve the dark monotony of the surrounding forest (*see* Fig. 11). Protection against rodents, ground rot, and winter snow is afforded by erecting the house on a base of stone, brick or concrete, and shelter from rain is ensured by the provision of a steeply pitched roof, often decorated with an ornamental gable. Detached storage sheds, often well built of logs, may well be thatched with turves, from which hay sometimes springs, to form a useful supplement to the crop of the meagre farm pastures. On the *saeters* (the high summer pastures), the practice of transhumance is declining and some of the wooden huts are now used to accommodate tourists from the coastal towns.

Greek Houses

In an article in *Geography* ("Traditional Houses in Modern Greece") J. M. Wagstaff points out that only since the 1920s has the harmony between Greek buildings and the environment been threatened, mainly by the construction of box-like dwellings of hollow-fired bricks and tiled roofs. The older, more traditional house was generally built of limestone, the dominant rock of Greece's mountainous terrain. The stone is often

[Courtesy: Aerofilms, Ltd.

FIG. 11.—Norwegian houses. On gently sloping ground, between fjord and forested mountain side, this group of modern, timbered buildings is characteristic of Norway. The foundations of the houses—usually of stone—are substantial, and may provide room for storage, as in the painted house in the foreground.

unhewn and gives rise to rather austere dwellings of a uniform grey, relieved somewhat by the whitewash used for outlining the windows. Roofs are typically of split stone or slate except in the plains where curved tiles or thatch (of reed or bamboo) are common, and where unfired mud bricks covered with plaster may replace the stonework of hillier areas. Both in the plains and mountains, and also in the mountains of Crete and in the Ionian Islands, pitched roofs are usual, but in the drier and hotter parts, *e.g.* the Aegean Islands, the Cyclades and the lower parts of Crete, flat-roofed houses predominate. For environmental reasons, the latter have thick roofs, often with corbelled domes and few windows.

Foreign, as well as native traditions, have had a bearing on architectural styles. In Chios, Crete and the Ionian Islands, the Italian custom of using hewn stone has been adopted; in western Thrace, there appears a Turco-Oriental house with an overhanging upper storey; and in Epirus, where towered fortress houses appear among the buildings, an Albanian intrusion is evident, as we saw on p. 27.

Some Houses in India

India is much more complex in its physical and ethnic character than Egypt, Norway or Greece. Consequently its house-types are more varied, even if we discount British intrusions. In a paper on "The Indian Village" (*Geography*), O. H. K. Spate summarises some of these types. He notes, *inter alia*, that the flat-roofed house of south-west Asia, with its thick blank walls, has not surprisingly invaded the dry north-west of the

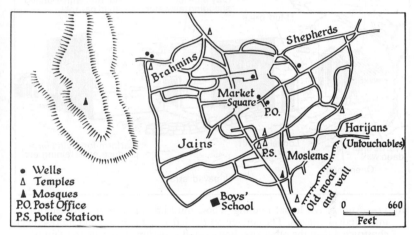

FIG. 12.—Aminbhavi, India: the village. Aminbhavi, a large village of more than 4,000 people, lies south-east of Bombay. This sketch-map shows the village clustered round the market-place, the position of the wells and important buildings, the haphazard arrangement of the winding streets, and the quarters in which the main elements of the population reside. It is typical of many Deccan villages.

sub-continent, while thatched gables are more characteristic of most of the wetter parts of the country. In Uttar Pradesh the richer farmers favour elaborate courtyard houses with decorative doorways and cool arcades, in the Maratha country one finds white bungalows with low gables of semi-cylindrical tiles, and in the Telugu-speaking parts north of Madras there are round huts with bold, vertical stripes of white and rusty red, interpreted by Spate as a cultural trait. Many Bengal houses have high, thatched gables and are walled with bamboo netting, which in hot weather allows draughts through but in wet weather swells to close up the cracks. Near the railways, the use of corrugated iron is now spreading (as in tropical Africa). This material—though unbecoming in appearance and doing little to check the penetration of external heat—is fire-proof, sheds rain well and, unlike thatch, does not harbour vermin.

In Spate's paper, C. D. Deshpande contributes a short survey of a sample Deccan village, Aminbhavi, about seven miles north-west of Dharwar in the south of the former province of Bombay (shown in Figs. 12 and 13). Here, the house roofs have rounded parapets; they are made of mud laid on a framework of crude beams and acacia branches. The

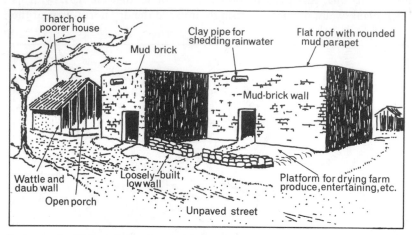

FIG. 13.—Aminbhavi, India: housing. These mud-brick houses are characteristic of many Indian villages. The cottage on the left is less spacious and more crudely constructed than the other two houses, and is occupied by a poorer family.

walls, also of mud brick, are thick and have few or no windows. Many habitations have a verandah in front which serves as a drying-place for farm produce, a reception room for visitors and a dormitory on hot summer nights. Raised up above a space at threshold level which may serve as a cattle pen is the large living-room, partially occupied by handicraft equipment and grain bags. Behind it is a kitchen (with a bath), which leads to a backyard containing a manure-pit and stacks of straw. Richer villagers possess houses with more rooms and separate bedrooms but the poorest people have only one-roomed hovels built of either wattle and daub or thin mud bricks and having crudely thatched roofs. The diversity of religious beliefs and social customs is not reflected in the shape of the house, but it is noteworthy that among most of the Hindus and Moslems—who generally occupy separate streets—the houses are either built on to each other or have contiguous compound walls, while the Jains and Brahmins, the culturally dominant groups, live in less tightly packed conditions.

Chapter III

Villages

WHAT IS A VILLAGE?

IN Chapter I it was pointed out that there is no clear-cut distinction between a hamlet and a village nor between a village and a town. It is generally assumed that a hamlet is smaller and less compact than a village and that it lacks some of its amenities, just as a village in its turn is less built up than a town and is without some of the facilities a town provides. But there is no legal definition of either village or hamlet, and neither size nor population will serve as exact criteria.

A village is more closely related to its immediate surroundings than a town and it more completely typifies the kind of region in which neither manufacturing industry nor commerce are highly significant. In most villages a majority of the workers are occupied in farming, but it is generally agreed that besides agricultural villages there also exist forest villages, mining and quarrying villages, fishing villages, villages chiefly supported by the tourist industry, dormitory villages serving nearby towns, and even industrial villages. Each has its own character: many industrial and mining villages are dirty and unprepossessing and suffer from ugly or drab surroundings; fishing and tourist villages are more attractively situated and in many cases possess the charm and interest of historic buildings, while most of the dormitory villages are either wholly new or consist largely of modern housing estates. In all such settlements, occupations are much more specialised than in towns and such typical urban functions as administration and wholesaling are rarely present.

Few villages are shown on atlas maps. Nevertheless, the number of villages in a country and the role they play in its social and economic life should not be underestimated. India, 80 per cent of whose people live outside towns, has well over 600,000 villages, most of them with populations of less than 500. England, whose rural population is only about 20 per cent of the whole, still has nearly 1,500 villages with greens and thousands of others without. In the world as a whole it is estimated that two out of every three people still live in villages or else in hamlets and scattered dwellings.

We noted on page 7 that even in the typical English farm village there are many people whose mode of life is not strictly rural. Similarly with buildings: only the majority are farmhouses and auxiliary structures. Most villages possess a garage (probably on the site of a former smithy), most have at least one general shop, a post office, inn, church and chapel, and many still support a primary school. There are often other buildings in which the community spirit is fostered, *e.g.* a village hall.

In Negro Africa, a large number of villages are diversified by a maize or millet granary. They support, besides peasant farmers, a blacksmith and tanner, and in some cases at least one potter and weaver. In India, also, villages commonly maintain a number of craftsmen and artisans—blacksmiths, carpenters, cotton spinners and weavers, and workers in leather. The pounding of rice, the making of *gur* (*i.e.* crude sugar), and the preparation of cooking oils are also undertaken by hand, though small-scale factory industries, *e.g.* mechanical spinning and weaving, are now being stimulated by the Government. Prominent features in Indian villages normally include the public well or irrigation tank, the large house of the headman or landowner, a moneylender's premises, a few small shops with open fronts, a market-place where a weekly bazaar is held, a police station, post office, grain warehouse, and Hindu temple or Mohammedan mosque, or both if the community is mixed. In a large rural settlement, as in parts of Negro Africa, there may be separate occupational as well as social quarters, and in South India segregation may go so far that the former 'untouchables' may even now be confined to sub-villages.

THE ORIGINS AND *RAISON D'ÊTRE* OF VILLAGES

Man's gregarious instinct reveals itself in some parts of the world, *e.g.* the East Indies and parts of Amazonia, in his habit of living, not simply with his immediate family, but with a number of inter-related families, in a large, communal dwelling. In south-east Colombia, for instance, the houses of the Tukano Indians, known as *malocas*, are seldom occupied by less than twenty people (B. Moser and D. Tayler, "Tribes of the Piraparana," in *Geographical Journal*). Built by the menfolk out of local timber and thatch, they may be 70 ft (21 m) long and 50 ft (15 m) wide (*see* Fig. 14). They have entrances at either end, one for men, one for women, and within are tall palm screens which separate the women's and children's quarters from the men's. The "long-house" of the Dyaks of Borneo, also built of wood and thatch, is even larger: it may exceed 650 ft (198 m) in length and house 600 persons, *i.e.* the whole com-

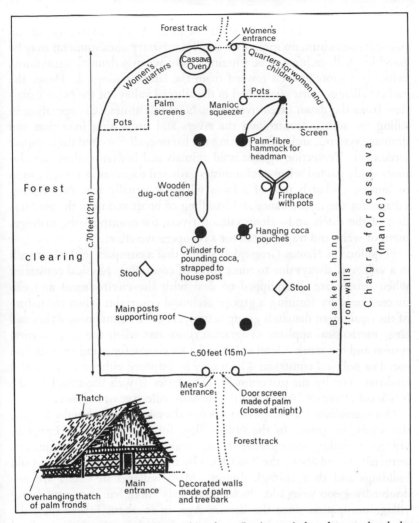

FIG. 14.—A *maloca* in Colombia. This plan of a house is based on a sketch by B. Moser and D. Tayler. Such a dwelling is designed to accommodate an extended family of Tukano Indians in the rain-forests of south-east Colombia. All the domestic equipment is home-made and derived from forest and river-bank materials. The women make most of the pottery, hammocks and baskets.

munity (C. Robequain, *Malaya, Indonesia, Borneo and the Philippines*). Each household has its own compartment, generally opening on to a corridor running the length of the building.

Man's herding instinct more commonly leads him to settle in a compact village, consisting of individual family houses, but under a primitive economy, for example, one based on hunting and collecting, or on pastoral nomadism, no more than small temporary encampments may be possible. Village life can be sustained only when sedentary agriculture, bringing a more assured reward from the land, is adopted. Hence the earliest villages—first established in the alluvial valleys of the Near East—date from the dawn of cultivation in Neolithic times. Co-operation in tilling the soil, in controlling the rivers and organising irrigation and drainage systems, and in distributing the harvest, all favoured the compact settlement. Protection against wild animals and human raiders was also more easily gained when communities gathered together in a fixed group of houses. What is true of a farm village is equally true of a fishing village, for the maintenance and handling of boats and nets, the preparation of the catch, and—along salmon rivers, for example—the management of weirs and traps, all call for a co-operative effort.

Perpillou (in *Human Geography*) argues that a compact settlement such as a village is always due to some form of constraint: physical constraint when people are ill equipped to deal with the environment and can succeed only by forming a group; technical constraint when the nature of the equipment demands group activity, *e.g.* for maintaining dykes and large mechanical appliances; agrarian constraint when the crop rotation system and the work calendar demand a set course for using the soil, and social or political constraint which may be imposed either by a powerful landowner or by the government. The latter is well illustrated by the Israeli collective or *kibbutz* and the Russian collective or *kolkhoz*.

Once established, a village may occupy the same site for hundreds, even thousands, of years. In the Nile valley, for example, most Egyptian villages, including some probably 6,000 years old, stand on low eminences artificially raised above the flood-level by the superimposed layers of old buildings and their rubbish dumps. Many villages in China are undoubtedly 4,000 years old. In southern Italy there has been continuous village occupation since the Bronze Age, in southern France since the days of the Romans and in England at least from Anglo-Saxon and Scandinavian times.

THE GROWTH OF THE ENGLISH VILLAGE

Prehistoric man in England first sought out the better drained upland pastures and light soils which could be satisfactorily worked with no more equipment than a digging stick or hoe, and later a light plough. He selected for his settlements defensive sites, mostly on the tops of slightly wooded chalk downlands and the Jurassic limestone uplands. Iron-using folk, notably the Belgae, were better able to deal with the valley forests and were able, with their stronger ploughs, to turn over the deeper, heavier soils of more low-lying areas. But it was the Anglo-Saxons in the fifth and sixth centuries A.D.—following the Roman interlude—who in large numbers first colonised the lowlands. Once they had made a forest clearing they were ready to embark on the task of building their villages and dividing up the land round them into the two or three large open fields for which they are best remembered. With the aid of ox-teams and the adoption of a simple rotation system they managed to produce from their arable strips and common pasture most of the food they required. Other supplies were obtained from marshes and streams, which yielded fish and fowl, and from the retreating forest, which furnished other game. Both forest and marsh provided building materials, *e.g.* timber and reed-thatch. Thus the typical Anglo-Saxon village, benefiting from the profitability of communal labour, was almost self-sufficing.

The existence of early Anglo-Saxon village sites is partially revealed to us today by the frequency with which place-names ending in "-ing" (people), "-ham" (farmstead) and "-ton" (village) occur in lowland England. They are specially characteristic of areas which remained relatively undisturbed by later immigrants and where a supply of water (from spring, stream or shallow well) and a sufficiency of fertile land were available.

As the population grew, more and more forest was cleared. The farm-land expanded, and villages multiplied. The Danes and Norsemen, who succeeded the Anglo-Saxons, first as raiders, later as settlers themselves, continued the protracted operation of converting England from forest to farm. The Danes sometimes took over existing English villages, at other times they established themselves on adjacent sites or built new villages on freshly cleared ground. Their influence on the landscape is indicated in part by the occurrence of the place-name element "-by" (village). The Norse, who entered England mainly from the western approaches, were more accustomed at home to a highland environment which favoured pastoral farming rather than cultivation. They tended in the main to carry settlement into the higher and more remote parts of England (*see* Fig. 15). Many small villages and hamlets in the Pennines and Lake District owe their origin to Norse colonisers; they are sometimes betrayed by the place-name elements "-thwaite" (enclosed land) and "-beck" (small stream).

The Norman aristocracy who followed William the Conqueror to England, and were awarded grants of land by the monarchy, added many fine churches, abbeys and manor-houses to the English village scene.

Round these new buildings, not always erected in existing settlements, fresh villages grew, some blossoming into market towns, and most bearing Norman-French names.

In succeeding centuries, the English woodlands were further reduced in area and many of the previously "waste" lands were gradually colonised

FIG. 15.—Great Britain: Main place-name elements. Prior to the Norman Conquest, Britain was periodically occupied by people emanating from the European mainland. All have left a legacy of place-names, the chief of which owe their origin to Anglo-Saxon, Danish and Norse invaders. This simplified map largely conceals the fact that most regions furnish examples of place-names derived from a number of different groups. It is, however, evident, that lowland Britain was chiefly settled by Anglo-Saxon and Danish people from the European Plain, Highland Britain by pre-Roman populations and invaders from the Scandinavian Highlands.

to make way for further farms and settlements. Following the dissolution of the monasteries and other religious establishments, offensive to the monarchy, in the sixteenth century, new landlords arrived who not only built themselves costly new habitations, often set in private parklands, but also extended their property by enclosing much common pasture. To secure a labour supply for tilling their land and tending their flocks and herds, many of them created model villages, planned *ab initio* and not growing spontaneously as most of the older settlements had.

The Industrial Revolution witnessed a fresh spurt in village building and the rise, especially on the coalfields, of new villages (as well as towns), whose inhabitants came to devote themselves increasingly to manufacturing and mining. Since then, the main developments have been the growth of seaside and dormitory villages, and the swallowing up of many farm villages by the rapidly expanding urban centres.

VILLAGE SITES

Village sites were originally much less carefully selected than those round which towns have grown, for they are related simply to the needs of small communities. The physical feature concerned may indeed be quite modest: a diminutive hillock scarcely raised above the level of the surrounding land, a level terrace of gravel just beyond the normal flood-plain of a river, or part of a slope with a southerly aspect and a local spring. In the case of the ordinary farm village, the essential needs are a supply of water—even now water is not always piped—a patch of land suitable for cultivation or affording good pasturage, and a trackway (in later times, once purely subsistence farming had ceased), providing access to a market town. In troubled times, a position with some natural defence is also very desirable, but even in that case proximity to water and to land which is worth developing is essential if the village is not to decay. Fishing villages, of course, have different site requirements: an inlet sheltered from storms and high winds, perhaps also from pirates, and access to productive fishing grounds. Mining villages, often beginning simply as camps, grow up as close as possible to the pit-head or other mineral working, but need contact with an outside market; industrial villages are usually sited in the vicinity of an industrial town. Seaside villages may take root near the place where a river or creek reaches the sea, where there is a broad stretch of sandy beach, or where a spectacular landscape leaves just sufficient level ground for building, as on a narrow raised beach or at a fjord head.

Valley villages are very numerous, especially in highland areas where compact settlements usually avoid the higher ground because of its excessively steep slopes, thin, often acid soils, and—in temperate lands—its bleak, windswept, generally rainy climate. Valley sites are usually well provided with flat, fertile agricultural land, and also with water, the latter perhaps a source of fish and a routeway as well as a source of drinking water for man and livestock. Running water may also provide opportunities for milling corn or wool with the aid of a water-wheel. In the Pennine area, for instance, wool manufacturing was early favoured by the numerous sites for fulling mills beside the swiftly flowing hillside becks. These mills formed the nuclei round which villages developed as early as the thirteenth century.

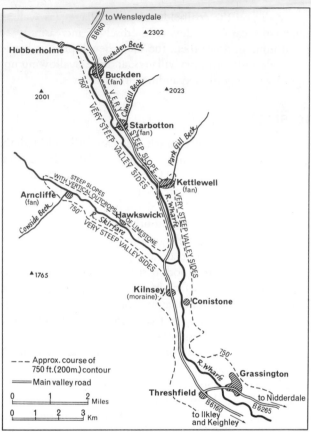

FIG. 16.—Village sites in the upper Wharfe valley. Most of Littondale and Wharfedale between Hubberholme and a point about half-way between Conistone and Grassington underwent marked glacial erosion during part of the Pleistocene period, and were later the sites of moraine-dammed lakes which have left them very flat and still liable to flood. Their sides—cut in horizontally-bedded limestone—are marked by a succession of limestone scars which rise in steps (generally to more than 1,500 ft (450 m)) before ascending more gradually to the summit levels (of Millstone Grit). Geomorphology has had a remarkable effect on the siting of village settlements, a number of which stand on gravel fans laid down by swiftly flowing side streams. Their houses are nearly all built of the local limestone.

To avoid floods, villages generally cling to the lower parts of the valley sides, or occupy dry, gravelly terraces. They are often built round tributary streams, not uncommonly on fans, and are usually strung together by a road parallel to the main river. There is a series of such villages along the eastern side of the flat-bottomed, glacially eroded Wharfe valley between Grassington and Hubberholme. In Fig. 16 it will be noted that the lowest villages are paired on either side of the Wharfe. Where valleys run from east to west, as in the Engadine and upper Rhône valleys in the Alps, villages hug the south-facing (*adret*) slopes and avoid the more shaded north-facing (*ubac*) ones.

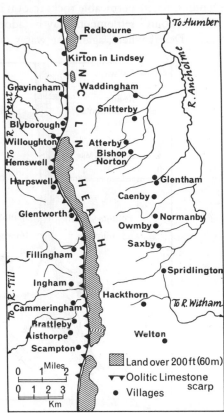

FIG. 17.—Scarp-foot and dip-slope villages in Lincolnshire. Lincoln Heath, or Lincoln Edge, reaching in places 400 ft. O.D. (120 m), is a Jurassic limestone *cuesta* sharply dividing the villages on its western side (all except Brattleby and Aisthorpe standing above 100 ft (30 m)) from those on the more gently sloping eastern side (all lying between 40 and 90 ft (12–27 m)). Glentham provides an example of a "double" village.

England provides many examples of spring-line villages. They have a dual advantage: access to a permanent water supply, and proximity to different kinds of agricultural land. Each margin of Lincoln Heath or Edge, for example, carries a line of villages, about a mile apart, those on the west side beside springs emerging from the scarp face, those on the east either on dip-slope streams or at points where water could be reached by shallow wells. Each village became the centre of an elongated parish which bore towards its upper end a stretch of dry, upland sheep pasture, an intermediate strip of well-drained ground well suited to cultivation, and, at the lower end, a patch of lowland based on damp, heavy clay soils best used for cattle pasture (*see* Fig. 17). There are similar strings of compact villages and long parishes south of the Thames estuary, where the Chalk and Lower Greensand ridges abut on clay vales. In south-west England, too, there are spring-line villages, *e.g.* Cheddar and Axbridge, along the foot of the Mendips, where permeable rocks rest on impermeable. To these examples of "wet point" settlements may be added the oases of areas such as the Sahara Desert where, again, the water supply is spatially restricted.

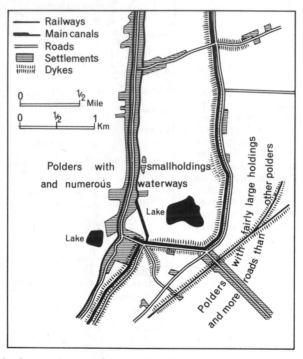

Fig. 18.—Settlements in part of the Dutch polders. This area, a short distance east of the coastal dunes, and north of Alkmaar, was reclaimed in the fourteenth century. More than a quarter of it is still occupied by water. The main economic activity is the growing of fresh vegetables. Transport is chiefly by water. Settlements are predominantly linear: they are strung out along the roads and the higher drainage canals.

Elsewhere, however, water may be too plentiful, as in the Dutch low-lands, where the early settlers looked for "dry points," or built them by raising artificial mounds locally known as *terpen*. Such flood refuges may be found today in the northern parts of the present provinces of Groningen and Friesland, and also in Zealand and other areas liable to inundation.

Modern drainage facilities, however, now allow the dykes and levees of the polder lands to be used for settlement (*see* Fig. 18) and many *terpen* have been abandoned. In Bengal, in the Ganges delta, many inhabited places occupy the sites of artificially banked alluvial islands only a little higher than the distributary waters. Such settlements are divided from each other at flood-time by swirling water, but at other periods by plots of rice and jute threaded by creeks.

England is not without "dry point" villages, *e.g.* Haddenham in the Fens, Upperthorpe in the lower Trent valley, Holme-on-Spalding-Moor

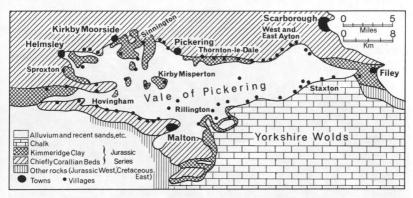

FIG. 19.—Village sites in and around the Vale of Pickering. The Vale of Pickering is the drained bed of the pro-glacial Lake Pickering, and is still prone to inundation. Hence most Vale villages are small, and—as in the Fens—occupy "dry points" on the slightly higher ground. There is a marked concentration of nucleated settlement on the drier ground surrounding the floor of the Vale. The market town of Malton provides a link between this area and the larger Vale of York.

in the Vale of York, Othery and Glastonbury in the Plain of Somerset, and Kirby Misperton in the Vale of Pickering. In all these naturally marshy areas, still liable to inundation despite a wealth of modern field drains and ditches, villages cluster along the higher, drier, firmer margins. There is, for example, a loop of such villages round the Vale of Pickering, *e.g.* Ayton, Thornton-le-Dale and Sinnington on the northern side, Sproxton on the west, and Hovingham, Rillington and Staxton on the south (*see* Fig. 19).

When the early English settlers moved up the lower Thames valley they found the river banks generally under marsh, but here and there a few isolated islands (*eys*) of gravel rose above the low-lying land to present firm foundations for village building. Among them was Thorney, which grew into Westminster, Bermondsey, Chelsea, Battersea and Hackney.

Before this time, of course, the Romans had founded Londinium on a similar patch of gravel. Similar terrace villages were founded in Germany in the Rhine rift valley and alongside the river Elbe.

Once settlements ceased to be self-sufficing, and trade routes began to spread, as in Europe in the Middle Ages, many hamlets swelled into villages because of their favourable location on early tracks. But even earlier it had

[*Courtesy: United States Information Service*

Fig. 20.—A Hopi village, south-western U.S.A. The cultivating Hopi Indians built their villages (*pueblos*) on *mesas*. They were difficult of access but highly defensible against their traditional enemies, the nomadic Navajo. The houses, of sun-dried mud or stone, are, typically, communal and are raised up to form a skyscraper group, the higher storeys being reached by external ladders.

often been necessary for peasant farmers to cross streams and rivers on their way to and from their fields. Hence the value of fords and bridging points as village sites, attested for by the number of place-names embodying these words. Other villages were built at minor cross-roads and along important long-distance routes, *e.g.* along the early Icknield Way, the prehistoric "Old Road" along the North Downs (the medieval Pilgrims' Way), and along the Roman roads, where the place-name "street" may be incorporated in a village (or town) name. Many such villages—commanding bridges and cross-roads, and occupying staging-points on important lines of communication—have, of course, grown into towns.

Hill-top villages, lacking the advantages of less elevated sites, are more numerous than current conditions warrant. They date from periods when raids by land and sea were more frequent than today, and when a naturally defensive position might provide a safe refuge. Such sites also provided firm ground for building, and rock for constructing dwellings. The Mediterranean countries, which were long in danger of piratical raids from both sea and land, furnish numerous examples of hill-top villages whose sites differ from each other only in detail. In the Central Massif of France, many small castles, with villages at their feet, crown the old volcanic necks of the Auvergne, while in New Mexico the Hopi Indians took advantage of residual buttes or *mesas* for the erection of their embryonic skyscrapers (*see* Fig. 20).

In England, most hill-villages are located on relatively low ridges, spurs or plateaux. Nearly all are below 1,000 ft (300 m), the largest and most compact being considerably lower than this height. For these villages to be successful, water had to be available (either from streams or from reasonably shallow wells), the slopes needed to be gentle enough, the soils deep enough to allow of satisfactory cultivation or stock-raising, and some communication with the lower ground was desirable to prevent future decay. In some areas, *e.g.* Cornwall and Devon, where most valleys form deep ravines, it was possible for hill-villages to be located on the more important routeways, but in general they remain isolated, and many of them are now in decline.

Dorothy Sylvester claims (in "The Hill Villages of England and Wales," *Geographical Journal*) that there are well over 1,000 hill-villages and hamlets in England, and over 200 in Wales, most of them agricultural, some devoted to quarrying and mining. She quotes, among numerous examples, Mow Cop in Derbyshire (a quarry village), Halton in Cheshire (a defensive centre, now being incorporated in Runcorn New Town), Appleton-le-Moors in Yorkshire (a mixed agricultural village), Brill in Buckinghamshire (a former market village) and Middlesmoor in Yorkshire (an old pastoral village).

THE SIZE OF VILLAGES

The size of a village reflects its natural, social and economic environment. Where land is flat and fertile and agriculturally rewarding, villages are generally quite large, as, for example, in the *limon* areas of northern France, but where the ground is hilly, the soils thin and sterile, or the natural resources as niggardly as they usually are on desert borders, villages —if they exist at all—are generally small.

People's skill in utilising their resources has a bearing on the size of their villages. In The Sudan, for instance, those tribes who are most apt at growing cassava and bananas and gathering food from the bush are concentrated together in greater numbers than other groups.

Most English villages are fairly small compared with many in other countries, *e.g.* China, partly because in England farming in earlier times was less labour intensive than in China and because now greater reliance

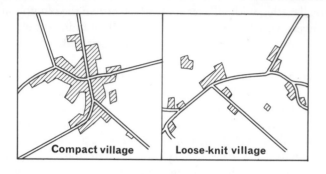

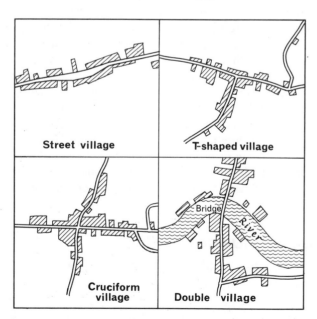

FIG. 21.—Typical village forms. While some villages appear to be formless, many adhere to one of the forms illustrated here. Most Ordnance Survey maps provide examples.

is placed on farm machinery than on human field labour, and also because fewer craftsmen live in English villages.

Villages are not static. They may rise and fall both in population and extent. Those which remain small have often suffered from either the continued poverty of the surrounding land or their isolation from modern traffic routes. Some mining villages have died altogether and become "ghost" villages following the exhaustion of a mineral deposit. Some fishing villages have decayed because of the economic pressures exerted on them by larger, well-equipped ports, while others have become re-vitalised by the expansion of the tourist industry. Near large cities many country villages have recently expanded into dormitory villages or even towns, and lost their traditional character. But in fully rural areas, the majority of villages and their buildings remain superficially almost the same as they were a century ago, for in all countries it is only in and near towns and cities that social and economic changes are rapid.

THE SHAPE AND FORM OF VILLAGES

The shape of a village is influenced by a number of factors, some geographical (*e.g.* position with respect to relief, rivers and roads), some historical (*e.g.* the early need for defence), some economic (*e.g.* the system of farming practised when the village was first established). Moreover, while most villages have probably grown up naturally or spontaneously, some were planned from their inception. Hence some forms are much more regular than others.

Although all villages are in some measure nucleated settlements, some have their buildings much closer together than others. Therefore we may at the outset contrast compact and loose-knit (or spread) villages (*see* Fig. 21). The former, unfortunately, are the only ones to be called "nucleated" by some writers. Whether compact or loose-knit, many villages have grown under the influence of roads. They include the following types:

1. *Street villages.* In such villages, the buildings stand side by side along a single highway. They are common in England and include, among Yorkshire examples, Coxwold, Long Preston and Hatfield. In France, besides many examples in Lorraine, they often take an extreme form, especially in Normandy, where, as Brunhes (*op. cit.*) reminds us, there are in the Aliermont district, the houses of four villages strung out along a 10-mile (16-km) stretch of road, almost without a break. Fig. 22 shows a street village in Derbyshire.

Other linear villages have been built along river terraces, along drainage canals (as in the Fens), along very narrow valleys (like the mining villages of South Wales), or along a line of springs. Such settlements often thread the sides of roads today, and it is tempting to call them "street" villages. However the elongation of these villages was originally due to the fact that their sites permitted little lateral development.

FIG. 22.—A Derbyshire "street" village. Chelmorton, about five miles east of Buxton, is at once a hill village and a street village. The houses at the end of the street (a minor motor road) reach 1,200 ft (366 m). The walls bordering the street, and many of the village houses, are built of the local Carboniferous Limestone, their roofs of either stone slats or Welsh slates. Rising in the background is Chelmorton Low (1,450 ft (440 m)).

2. *T-shaped, Y-shaped and cross-roads or cruciform villages.* These villages, of course, have buildings strung out along more than one road. They include modern service centres, generally with few houses but possessing such amenities as a garage, shop and café. Among old villages of this type are Waddesdon, a large village in the Vale of Aylesbury, partially built on either side of the Roman Akeman Street, and, on the other side of the Thames valley, Stone, a smaller, cruciform village.

3. *Double villages.* These are settlements standing at either side of a ford, or, more often in modern times, at either end of a bridge. Bourton-on-the-Water, in the Cotswolds, commanding an early ford across the Windrush, and now several bridges, furnishes a very picturesque example.

"*Green*" *villages* form a class of their own. They probably had their origins in forest clearings, the greens in Anglo-Saxon times, and in many cases later served to pasture farm animals at night and to safeguard them from human marauders. In this respect they resemble Bantu *kraals* and other settlements in Africa, most of which, to this day, shelter the village stock at night within their brushwood fences.

L. Dudley Stamp (in "The Common Lands and Village Greens of England and Wales," *Geographical Journal*) has recorded 1,475 village greens in England. Though he noted a marked concentration in the Home Counties, he admitted their wide distribution. Harry Thorpe has found nearly 100 in Durham, and claims that the "green" village is the commonest village form in that county ("Some Aspects of Rural Settlement in County Durham," *Geography*). Professor Stamp suggested that while many greens certainly acted as pastoral centres, some at least were valued for other purposes: as social centres, often laid out for sports and used for games; as market centres where periodic stalls could be mounted; as defensive centres, especially in vulnerable areas such as northern

FIG. 23.—Bamburgh, Northumberland. Bamburgh is an example of a fortified village near the Scottish border. The green is triangular. The cottages date from the eighteenth century. The castle, largely reconstructed, was erected in the twelfth century on a coastal outcrop of the Whin Sill, and was preceded by Saxon, and possibly, Roman fortifications.

England where the flanking buildings form an almost continuous barrier designed to protect people and stock against border raiders (*see* Fig. 23); and, following the enclosure movements, as a late provision for landless farmers, who might find there room at least for a few hens and other animals.

"Green" villages, like road villages, are by no means exclusive to England, though in continental Europe they have more often been built over or paved and used, for example, as car parks. Wherever they occur, they may often be distinguished from each other by the shape of their green. It is not unusual to find a small triangular green near a road junction. Square greens are generally larger: for example, in Heighington,

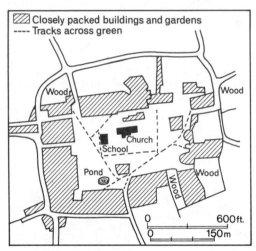

FIG. 24.—Heighington, Co. Durham. The whole of this "green" village is virtually square, and was probably built in this way for defensive purposes, the church tower providing a useful look-out and the green a refuge for man and animals. A number of buildings have encroached on the green since defensive needs ceased to be important.

Durham, where a church, school and pond find room (*see* Fig. 24), and in East Witton, in Yorkshire's Wensleydale. Circular greens, very common in Kent, Surrey and Middlesex, have a wide provenance, and, like square greens, usually have a road or path round them. Lens-shaped greens, leading to the growth of cigar-shaped villages, *e.g.* Trimdon, Durham, have tended to disappear in recent years and have been replaced by a broad central street, the former green perhaps acting as a bus park.

Villages may be square or round, and they may have a disused market-place, a church compound or a pond in the centre. The stone-built Blanchland, in Northumberland, sturdily set within an old stockade, is one of the best known of several border villages of this kind. Square villages, often walled, are common in the Balkans and are in most cases a legacy of Turkish rule. In the Fezzan oases (Libya) the round or elliptical and the quadrangular village are both found. Each type is compact and walled; the former, with Berber affinities, more frequently has a central fortress for protection than the latter, which is of Tuareg origin.

Many villages do not fit into any of the categories outlined above. They are indeed formless, and are especially common where neither important roads nor any marked physical features are present. They have no real centre, the church, post office, smithy or garage each gathering round itself a few houses. Like some more regular clusters, however, these amorphous villages may have been extended by the addition of new buildings.

PLANNED VILLAGES

Many villages are deliberately designed to conform to a particular architectural style or shape. They include, for example, certain late nineteenth-century English villages designed by humanitarian industrialists for their own employees, *e.g.* the "model" village of Saltaire, near Bradford, Port Sunlight, near Birkenhead, and the "garden" village of Bournville, near Birmingham. Others have been planned, often by governments, with a particular agricultural system in mind, *e.g.* the *kolkhozy* of the U.S.S.R., the communal villages of Israel, and the canal colony villages of the Punjab. Local authorities and colliery owners have been responsible for many modern colliery villages, *e.g.* in the concealed coalfields of east Durham and Derbyshire. Another group of villages, more gracefully designed, but usually following symmetrical principles, owe their planned character to individual landowners or village squires. These include Lowther, in Westmorland, a Georgian type; Milton Abbas, in Dorset, an old village rebuilt by the lord of the manor in the eighteenth century; and Ripley in Yorkshire, mostly built between 1780 and 1860 in a pleasing balance of Gothic and Tudor elements.

SOME TYPES OF GERMAN VILLAGE

German villages have been the subject of much research: those established by German colonists beyond the Elbe as well as those built by Germans prior to their eastward spread. Names given to various types of village by the Germans have often been applied elsewhere, for instance in Britain.

In north-west Germany, on the poor morainic country of the German *Geest*, one finds a number of small open clusters, often hamlets rather than large villages. They are known individually as *Urweiler* (literally, "primeval hamlet"), or *Drubbel*. They often contain less than twelve houses, though some have expanded into larger, but still formless, clusters. Another village type is the *Haufendorf* (literally "heaped-up village"), common west of the Elbe, but extending also into the loess

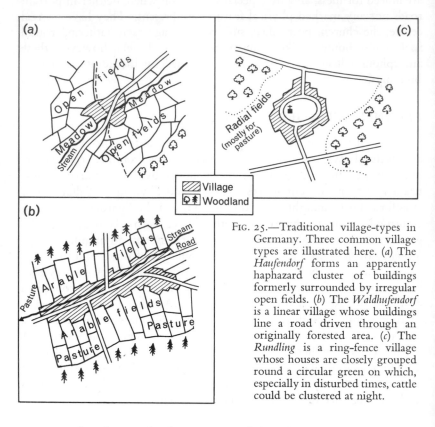

FIG. 25.—Traditional village-types in Germany. Three common village types are illustrated here. (*a*) The *Haufendorf* forms an apparently haphazard cluster of buildings formerly surrounded by irregular open fields. (*b*) The *Waldhufendorf* is a linear village whose buildings line a road driven through an originally forested area. (*c*) The *Rundling* is a ring-fence village whose houses are closely grouped round a circular green on which, especially in disturbed times, cattle could be clustered at night.

country of southern Poland, Hungary and the Ukraine (*see* Fig. 25). The form was transmitted into Slavonic lands (which at that period had only a rudimentary settlement pattern) by German colonists penetrating east in the thirteenth and fourteenth centuries both as military conquerors and as intending settlers. The *Haufendorf*, like the old three-field village of the English lowlands, consists of an irregular cluster of buildings suited to a communal type of strip farming. It is sometimes referred to as a *gewanndorf* (literally "furlong village"), when the pattern of the open-field strips is clearly marked.

Along the banks of drainage canals cut in the reclaimed marshes of the Weser and Elbe estuaries, and, later, further east in the former marshes of the Havel and the Spree, the more regular *Marschdorf* or *Marschhufendorf* was laid out. Where forest was encountered, the *Waldhufendorf* (literally "forest village") was favoured. This was a village—still common in upland forest areas, for instance, the Black Forest, Böhmerwald, Erz Gebirge and Thuringia—in which the farms were usually strung out on both sides of a stream or forest track, the fields running outwards (generally upwards) from each farm-house towards the surrounding forest. Similar is the *Strassendorf* (literally "street village") type, occurring mainly in lowland areas both west and east of the Elbe.

Especially noteworthy in the former zone of contact between Germans and Slavs (*i.e.* roughly along the line of the Elbe), is the *Rundling* (literally "round village"), perhaps initially a Slav form. It is sometimes called a "ring-fence" settlement: from its houses, open fields formerly radiated outwards towards the enclosing forest which formed a ring round the whole. There was a protective fence nowadays often replaced by a circular road. Somewhat similar is the *Angerdorf* (literally "green village"), a lancet-shaped settlement embracing, within an ellipse of buildings, a lacuna of common pasture just as the *Rundling* often enclosed a circular green. The *Angerdorf* remains a common village type in eastern Germany and Poland, but in some instances the lens-shaped green has now been built over.

SAMPLE STUDIES

Though the site and form of a village help to give it a particular character, its regional setting is also significant. Hence the value of studying examples of village types and of individual villages from different cultural and physical milieux. A few sample outlines are given below.

Villages in Bas Languedoc

In a paper in *Geography* entitled "Rural Settlement in the Coastal Plain of Bas Languedoc," S. Agnew discusses some geographical aspects of those villages which lie west of the lower Rhône and are penned in on the north by the Central Massif of France and on the south by the Mediterranean. The writer suggests that in the Middle Ages the self-sufficient agrarian system, while providing for individual freedom of cultivation and common grazing rights, determined as suitable village locations either the spring-line at the junction of the limestone scarps and plateaux above and the coastal and riverine plains below, or else various 'facets' between the floodable river flats and the first river terraces. The flood-plain was used for meadows and some field crops, the terrace face for vines, olives and almonds, and the terrace step for cereals and perhaps fruit. A few villages were also built on drove roads (*drailles*) used by transhumant sheep passing between the summer pastures on the Cevennes or the Great Causses and the winter pastures of the coast plain.

Defensive needs recommended hill-top or hill-flank sites, where these were available, and the erection of artificial fortifications, where they were absent. If springs or streams were lacking, well water could be drawn from the permeable sands and gravels of the plains. Sites near littoral swamps and lagoons—a prey to both mosquitoes and pirates— were avoided. The *mistral*, though not very fierce in Bas Languedoc, presented an occasional threat and encouraged most people to give their dwellings a southerly aspect with a ridge or valley flank at the rear, and also to build (for defensive purposes too) close agglomerations, whose narrow streets and alleys could provide coolness and shade in summer. The abundance of grey-white limestone in Bas Languedoc made it the favoured structural material. The walls of the houses are generally white-washed, the roofs covered with red tiles.

Today, the villages of this part of France are regularly spaced, the houses generally so compact that there is rarely room for gardens or open spaces. With increasing rural security, there has been some tendency to erect, away from the villages, some isolated rural settlements, and the coming of the railway and the expansion of monocultural viticulture have led to the establishment of new villages near the railway stations and the development of large, disseminated vineyard estates on some of the most fertile lowland tracts.

Some Villages in Mainland Tanzania

In the former territory of Tanganyika, the village is a common settle-ment feature, but where there is no serious threat from human or animal predators, there exist, throughout the cultivated lands, but more usually on knolls and spurs, small groups of habitations, housing extended families and their cattle pens. Mrs G. Milne informs us (in "Some Forms of East African Settlements," *Geography*), that in the fertile area situated on the rim of the West Usambara plateau large villages were erected as defensive points of concentration at the time of the Masai raids from the steppes below, while on the plateau itself and on the southern slopes of Mt Kilimanjaro, where there was less danger, family clusters rather than villages are characteristic. On the cultivated grasslands south of Lake Victoria family nuclei are concentrated very close together under granite *kopjes* and are often enclosed by hedges, which help to give them the appearance of small villages. Houses with stout earthen roofs are gathered into true villages among the Wabena of Njombe in southern Tanganyika, but with the decline of raiding many houses are becoming more scattered and crops are consequently in greater danger from wild game. In the Kasulu district, near Kigoma in western Tanzania, E. A. Leakey and N. V. Rounce tell us (in "The Human Geography of the Kasulu District, Tanganyika," *Geography*), that the typical settlement of the Muha tribe is the small sedentary village surrounded by a rough thorn fence within which the cattle are kept at night. Streets are lacking and the huts—bee-hive shaped, and made of woven bamboo—are set down indiscriminately. On higher ground, the dwellings are erected below the brow of a hill, for drainage purposes, and in the lowlands they are set close to a supply of water.

The establishment of mission stations, with churches, schools and clinics, has introduced a new village form to which many artisans and Indian shopkeepers have been attracted. Other compact settlements, in some cases townships, have recently arisen round the headquarters of the district administration, and round some of the railway stations and cotton ginneries. Mines and plantations (of coffee and sisal mainly) have workers' estates attached to them.

An Anatolian Village

W. C. Brice has made a study of Harran, a village in southern Turkey ("The Anatolian Village," *Geography*), one of several such in the Jullab valley between the Kurdish Hills and the high plains of northern Syria (*see* Fig. 26). Each of these villages is clustered near a water-hole or well, often close to a mound created by the remains of former settlements. Typical is one of about 500 people, whose houses are supported by walls of mud-brick with simple shuttered openings. The roofs are usually flat and made of mud resting on wooden beams. At Harran, however, and some other villages, where there is an absence of local timber, the roofs are adorned with a series of small, corbelled cupolas. Each house has its own walled compound, within which the family's sheep and goats are confined at night.

Most of the village workers are farmers, but there are also a few store-keepers and builders, a miller, prayer-leader, schoolmaster, district governor, and a police detachment. As well as the houses, therefore, there are other, detached, buildings, many comparatively new and some containing gabled roofs made from imported sheet iron and timber. They include a mosque, school, coffee-shop, post office, governor's office and

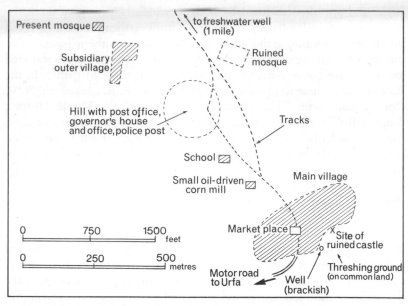

Fig. 26.—Harran, Anatolia. This village in southern Turkey is typical of many between the Kurdish Hills and the high plains of northern Syria. Buildings are scattered, the fresh-water supply position difficult. As in most Old World arid regions, relations between village farmers and nomadic herders are close.

police post. There are two wells: one for drinking water, one (more brackish) for the use of the farm animals and for washing. Round the village are small, family-worked plots, including a few cotton fields, irrigated by the River Jullab, and the grazing grounds. Periodically, a few Bedouin families come in from the surrounding dry pastures, erect their tents on the outskirts of Harran, and exchange the products of their herds for straw and improved grazing facilities.

THE CHANGING ENGLISH VILLAGE

It has already been noted (p. 49) that a village is not static. It is constant-ly changing, both in its material make-up and in its population. However despite the occurrence of deserted villages in parts of England, mostly dating from the enclosure movements of the late medieval and Tudor periods, when much arable land was converted to sheep pasture, it is a remarkably persistent landscape feature.

Even in a highly urbanised country such as Britain some additional housing is still being provided in some villages. Most of these villages are located on good roads near large towns and are increasingly valued as homes for commuters (who are not easily integrated into the village community). Others are becoming out-of-town shopping centres and in a few cases the sites of new factories. Other rural settlements—generally at some distance from urban areas but again benefiting from the rise in motor-car ownership—are expanding as tourist centres, perhaps because of a favourable situation with respect to the sea or the countryside, or because of their historic buildings. Recently, in Cheshire, it has been decided to extend certain villages as a means of catering for a growing county population, a move which raises the question of how to design new buildings sensitively and imaginatively so that they do not harm the existing village landscape.

Some farm villages—even a few in rather isolated areas—are growing a little as a result of agricultural intensification, improved farm employment conditions, a rising rural birth-rate, better utility and social services, and perhaps an influx of forestry workers. Though most English villages, however, now possess a piped water supply and benefit from electric lighting and heating, they still offer little excitement to young people. Moreover, in well-situated, attractively laid-out villages, young married couples are now finding difficulty in buying a house of their own even when they wish to remain in the village. There has recently been such an influx of retired and executive people, in search of quiet and solitude, that house prices have risen phenomenally. Wealthy townsfolk take a pride in reconstructing old village cottages for their own use, thus squeezing the villagers themselves out of the market.

In keeping with this changing population, a new type of village squire is appearing: one drawn largely from the class of executives. The traditional squires, generally members of the landed gentry are, in many cases, due to the burden of death duties, selling their village properties and going elsewhere to live.

In many villages, a smaller labour force is now required. Except in certain tourist villages, small-scale home industries have declined in favour of large, mechanically-powered factory industries, and increased farm mechanisation has reduced the demand for agricultural labour. Small schools are being closed. The advent of the travelling-shop is putting village storekeepers out of business. A parson nowadays—less exalted socially than formerly—often has to serve two or three villages, and the village "pubs" are now entering the better-class catering trade and attracting visitors from without instead of concentrating, as before, on a local clientele. The nucleus of middle-class people—doctor, minster of religion, schoolmaster, village squire—who had strong village roots and regarded it as their duty to lead the social activities of their community are in some danger of disappearing, to the detriment of the village spirit and tradition.

In the more remote areas, the decay of the village seems inevitable. To support a good primary school, shop, church, chapel and an inn, a settlement nowadays probably calls for a population of 1,000 people, but few villages support more than 500 people. If the small village is to survive, it will be as a less independent community. Nearby towns are bound to act more and more as village service centres.

Chapter IV

The Distribution and Patterns of Rural Settlement

THE DISTRIBUTION OF RURAL SETTLEMENT

WHETHER villages or single farmsteads or tiny hamlets, settlements tend to be numerous and fairly evenly distributed where the land is flat or fertile, *i.e.* where physical conditions (of relief, climate and soils) vary little. In the Ganges Plain, for example, water from rivers or wells is widely available, the ground slopes almost imperceptibly, and the alluvial soils are very productive. Here, large villages stand within a short distance of each other with few settlement gaps. The same is true over most of East Anglia and in little differentiated counties such as Rutland, though English villages are usually smaller. Over considerable parts of the Canadian Prairies individual farmsteads are in the same way and for similar reasons fairly uniformly spread.

In areas where water supplies are restricted and concentrated only here and there, and in areas of marked topographical variety, where abrupt changes of slope are frequent, rural settlements are usually confined to certain parts only, *e.g.* to oases, spring-lines and river terraces, and are absent from others. In many Mediterranean countries, chiefly for defensive reasons, villages crowd the hill-tops and avoid the low ground. In the Pennines, villages cluster in the dales (sheltered valleys), and shun the moors and mosses above, whereas in Cornwall and parts of Devon, where valleys are in many cases deep and narrow, villages take to the plateaux where the ground is flatter and therefore more convenient for agriculture, building and transport.

In wet, marshy areas, as we have seen (p. 45), man has sought out dry points for his villages, and in arid areas, wet points, and so has created distributional mosaics which vary with the hydrography.

PATTERNS OF RURAL SETTLEMENT

The distribution of settlements must not be confused with the pattern of settlements. The former, as we saw above, is concerned with the spread of settlements (*i.e.* where they are and where they are not), while the latter deals with the spatial relations between one dwelling and another (*i.e.* whether they are close together as in a village or town, or whether they are further apart, as in a hamlet or in single, more isolated homesteads).

The major patterns in rural areas, then, are either (*a*) nucleated, composed of villages, each more or less compact, or (*b*) dispersed, consisting of single homesteads at some distance from each other (*see* Figs. 27 and 28).

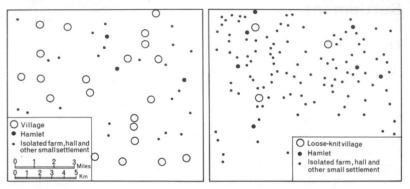

Fig. 27.—Nucleated settlement north of Grantham, Lincolnshire. This pattern of settlement—predominantly nucleated—has been characteristic of most of the English Plain ever since it was settled by the Anglo-Saxons and Danes.

Fig. 28.—Dispersed settlement east of Llanrwst, North Wales. Predominantly dispersed settlement is characteristic of Highland Britain, and in areas such as Wales may well date from early medieval times. Above 1,000 ft (300 m) there is little settlement of any kind, but in the valleys a structure of market towns (such as Llanrwst) came into being as farming became more commercialised.

An intermediate pattern, generally regarded as a kind of dispersal, is made up of scattered hamlets. The pattern may be complicated by the occurrence of both nucleated villages and scattered homesteads. Also, as times change, *e.g.* with improvements in technical efficiency or with the replacement of one agrarian régime by another, patterns are modified. In seeking to explain a pattern as it exists today, therefore, it is often necessary to recall the history of the area concerned. In general it may be said that a particular pattern may be related to local variations in relief, climate and soil fertility, to different methods of working the land, to diverse ethnic customs and traditions, to regional changes in the availability of water, and to the varying needs of defence.

In 1895, August Meitzen published his *Siedlung und Agrarwesen der Westgermanen und Ostgermanen* (*Settlement and Agrarian Systems of West and East Germany*), oft-quoted since, in which he argued that two settlement patterns were early recognisable in western Europe: the nucleated type, characteristic of which was the agglomerated village, and the dispersed type or *Einzelhof*, *i.e.* the isolated dwelling. He believed that each could be attributed to a particular agrarian régime: the nucleated village to communal cultivation as practised under the open-field system, and the dispersed homestead to individual cultivation. While this generalisation has some validity, Meitzen begged the question as to the motives which prompted farmers in some areas (he instances most of Germany) to undertake communal agriculture while in others (notably France) they favoured a more individual approach to farming. He went on to aver that dispersion goes back to the Celtic mode of land occupation, nucleation to the spread of Germanic people (*e.g.* the Anglo-Saxons to England). Whatever the original pattern in Germany, France, England and other old countries was, it must be remembered that as land holdings have become consolidated into individual ownership there has been, at least in some areas, a measure of secondary dispersion, or of intermediate (or intercalated) dispersion. Daughter settlements have hived off from older villages, small hamlets have been planted in woodland, moor or marsh not previously cleared or reclaimed, and isolated farmsteads have been established on land taken in from the open fields and common pastures following enclosure. (Enclosures were already common in England, especially in the Midland counties, in Elizabethan times; the Parliamentary enclosures of the late eighteenth and nineteenth centuries merely completed a process begun in the Middle Ages.)

It has been claimed by some economic historians, in opposition to Meitzen, that the original unit of even Celtic settlement was the compact village; the isolated farmstead or hamlet resulted, albeit at an early period, from the break-up of nucleated settlements largely through the operation of inheritance laws. They agree, however, that primary dispersion is characteristic of most of the new, extensively farmed areas of the North American Prairies, Australian grasslands and Argentinian Pampas.

FACTORS FAVOURING NUCLEATION

Man is a gregarious animal and to achieve very close social contiguity he may, as we saw on p. 36, prefer to inhabit a large communal dwelling. More usually, he chooses to live in a compact village or a town. In densely populated urban areas, nucleation takes an extreme form, and even in some rural areas people may live cheek by jowl, *e.g.* in the valleys of the Hadhramaut (southern Arabia), where dwellings often tower six to eight storeys high above the cultivated plots of the valley floor (*see* Fig. 29), or in China, where as much as half the area of a village may be roofed over, or in

Persia where surrounding walls pen up the villages into excessively crowded quarters.

The practice of living in compact settlements was fostered among newly settled communities (*e.g.* the Neolithic cultivators of ancient Egypt and China, and the early Anglo-Saxon immigrants into Roman Britain)

[*A Shell photograph*

FIG. 29.—High-storeyed houses in southern Arabia. Towering above the petrol pump, oil cans and tanker in the foreground are some of the high-storeyed, mud-brick buildings of Shibam, a large village in the Wadi Hadhramaut, southern Arabia. The very small wall-openings are typical of houses in hot, sunny, arid environments.

by the necessity of dealing effectively with a somewhat hostile environment, *e.g.* a forested or marshy landscape, and by the advantages of organising a permanent system of cultivation. In areas of fertile soil, such people could be in close touch with the fields which they worked and could also enjoy the social benefits of village life. Social advantages still exist: it is easier to obtain education and medical care, and easier to organise clubs and societies, in a nucleated village than in an area of dispersed settlement.

Certain land tenure systems and methods of organising labour lend themselves more than others to a nucleated pattern. The medieval open-field system of farming, with its emphasis on communal field labour, clearly favoured nucleation just as much as certain modern systems, *e.g.* those established for ideological reasons in the Soviet Union, China and Israel. In the U.S.S.R., successive Communist governments have aimed at maintaining full political control over the peasantry and at ensuring the prompt delivery of full agricultural quotas to the State. Their trust in the collective farming system as a means of fulfilling these purposes, boosted by the extensive use of motorised machinery, has perpetuated and emphasised the nucleated pattern of rural settlement already characteristic of Russia before 1917. Some Soviet villages, however, have smaller satellite settlements round them, chiefly devoted to pastoral farming. In Israel, there are both carefully planned co-operative villages, organised by smallholders and facing inwards to a community centre, and also collective villages (*kibbutzim*) where everything is held in common. The people have no private possessions, and they live, eat and farm communally, and share the total income. Many of these Jewish settlements are based on earlier defensive villages appropriate to a strongly united people clustering together for protection against external aggression.

Nucleation, of course, has always had a defensive value, as is shown, for example, by the walled villages of the Hausa tribes in northern Nigeria, and the "acropolis" villages perched on hill summits in the Mediterranean coastlands, *e.g.* in Roussillon, at the eastern end of the Pyrenees (*see* Fig. 30). Here, nearly a hundred lowland villages were abandoned for higher sites during the corsair raids of seven or eight centuries ago.

Largely for protection against Indian attacks, the early New England colonists established themselves in large compact villages, as did the Mormon settlers of Utah in the nineteenth century. During the Mau Mau uprising in Kenya in the 1950s, and at about the same time in Malaya (when Communist guerrilla activity was rife) and in Algeria (during the independence struggle), many people who had previously inhabited isolated farms and scattered hamlets sought out the sanctuary of villages.

A nucleated settlement pattern is also the obvious response to certain types of physical environment. Where water is scarce and hard to get, for example in deserts where deep wells may have to be dug for drinking water and cultivation, compact villages generally result. There are, however, exceptions which suggest the operation of factors favouring dispersion, *e.g.* in the limestone Causses of France, where, despite hydrological problems, dispersion is characteristic, and in certain other areas where technical advances in the provision of water supplies have permitted recent dispersion.

Trends from dispersion to nucleation are becoming evident near large

[*Courtesy: French Government Tourist Office*

FIG. 30.—Durban, southern France. This fortified village in the Pyrenean foothills of Aude, southern France, has many counterparts in Mediterranean Europe. The hill, with its ruined castle, is encircled by the homes of the village's 700 inhabitants.

cities and conurbations and along much-used motor roads where urban sprawl is devouring agricultural land and traffic growth is promoting ribbon settlement. Thus many erstwhile farmsteads and country hamlets are being incorporated into dormitory villages or else becoming part of the expanding townscape.

FACTORS FAVOURING DISPERSION

Dispersed settlements are normal in many unrewarding highland and forested areas, *e.g.* the Vosges, Black Forest and Carpathians, where agricultural opportunities are limited by a difficult terrain, a harsh climate and sterile soils. Uplands suited to little but sheep-rearing or extensive cattle-raising usually fall into this category: some of the flocks and herds would be too far from the stockman's home if it were in a village, and the value of the agricultural product is not enough to support a large community. In such areas, *e.g.* in the Pennines and Welsh Highlands and in parts of Norway (where, due to the practice of transhumance, small, isolated, upland farms are often economically attached to a village below) dispersed settlement—where any settlement exists at all—is a common feature.

An area where water supplies are virtually ubiquitous, provided it is also reasonably productive, may be expected to favour a dispersed pattern. This is certainly the case in Bengal, where there is a very high population density and the pattern, though dispersed, is very close. It is also true of parts of south-west Aquitaine and Kent (where some historians have attributed dispersion primarily to the Jutish land-holding system), of most of northern Belgium, and of many irrigated areas, *e.g.* the *huertas* of Spain. But in Hungary, for example, where water is also abundant, nucleation in the form of very large villages is characteristic.

Fertile lowlands in many of the newer parts of the world are marked by a dispersed settlement pattern, especially where they are devoted to extensive farming (*see* Fig. 31). In these regions, mainly temperate grass-

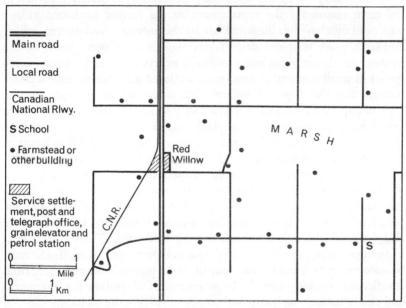

FIG. 31.—Dispersed settlement in part of Alberta. In areas of extensive commercial agriculture, whether based on cultivation or stock-raising, the dispersed settlement pattern, such as is shown here, is characteristic. Roads are generally straight on recently surveyed, unoccupied land, and most farmsteads are erected close to them. Along major roads and railways, service centres such as Red Willow have grown up to serve the scattered farming populations. Major service centres are much further apart than in longer settled, more intensively farmed areas such as western Europe and China.

land, the use of barbed wire and wind-pumps has allowed farmers to live in isolation. Individual initiative has long been a powerful motive for dispersion, for example the desire of most pioneers to "get away from it all," whether "it" is religious or ethnic persecution, the law or social incompatibility. There exists also the chance of improving one's living standards by raising crop yields and introducing new crops and new methods: projects which might be more difficult to achieve in longer-settled areas.

Much human initiative was released in older countries when serfdom disappeared and when there was still plenty of forest to be cleared and commons to enclose. In England, under the Tudors, many smallholders began to erect their own isolated farms in the centre of the lands newly consolidated following the break-up of the open-field system and its scattered stripholdings. The same happened at about the same time or later in parts of Germany, Sweden and Denmark. The change from communal land ownership to holding in severalty is usually regarded as the main reason for the replacement of the former nucleated village pattern of much of the Cheshire Plain by the present mixed pattern, which embraces many scattered dairy farms as well as villages. Some of the former are almost completely isolated, others are loosely grouped together in small hamlets. These small, scattered settlements make a closer pattern than the dispersed upland settlements of, for example, Wales, because climate, drainage and soils are all superior. Among areas in Britain which have more recently been placed under individual land ownership are a number of intensively farmed areas, e.g. the fruit and hop farms of southern Herefordshire and some of the market gardens in Essex. Here, too, the settlement pattern is mainly dispersed.

The advent of settled, peaceful conditions, and their continuance over a comparatively long period, allows people to disperse more safely over the countryside, especially if communications are improved at the same time and the marketing of surpluses is thereby facilitated. There is, in fact, a growing tendency in many widely separated parts of the world for farmers to scatter over the rural landscape at the same time as more and more rural dwellers are flocking into the large centres of nucleation (i.e. the towns and cities), even though dispersal entails sacrificing the social amenities of a village and paying more for the provision of roads, electricity and water. Thus, in an attempt to raise peasant living standards in the parched, poverty-stricken southern parts of Italy, the Italian Government has shouldered the task of establishing smallholdings which poor families are now working intensively without hired help. In these newly planned areas, irrigation facilities have been extended and the scourge of malaria, which was a main cause of previous neglect, has been eradicated. More-over, it is to be hoped that the need for nucleation on defensive grounds has now gone.

In Egypt, the old "basin" form of irrigation has largely given way to a perennial system, and the peasants (*fellahin*) have now been given the right to own land. Therefore in this country, too, more dispersed farm-steads are being established. In Mexico and many other parts of Latin America, likewise, the break-up of large estates and the promulgation of agrarian reform laws are encouraging dispersion. In Fiji, until recently, the nucleated village was the chief settlement unit, mainly because the land tenure system was based on the patrilineal organisation of labour, on an extended family basis, for all economic activities. This system is slowly crumbling as the demand for cash crops is inducing many ambitious individuals to seek out land for their own independent farms.

THE MEASUREMENT OF DISPERSION

The words "dispersion" and "nucleation," like the words "village" and "hamlet," have no precise connotation, though several statistical methods of measuring the degree of dispersion or concentration have been suggested. B. M. Swainson, for example "Dispersion and Agglomeration of Rural Settlement in Somerset," *Geography*), has computed the per-centage of the population of Somerset living in the following house groupings: 1, 2–5, 6–10, 11–20, 21–50, 51–100, 101–200 and over 200. He is able to say how dominant each group is in each part of the county. In France, it is possible to adopt as a basis for calculation not the number of houses, nor the varying density of settlements, but, more satisfactorily, the number of people inhabiting each unit. The French census distin-guishes for each commune the population of both the *chef-lieu* and the rest of the commune. Demangeon was therefore able to suggest the following co-efficient of dispersion:

$$C = \frac{E \times N}{T},$$

where C is the co-efficient, E is the population of the settlements outside the commune centre, N is the number of settlements excluding the chief one, and T the total commune population. Unfortunately, this formula is not very helpful outside France, and is useless in England.

RURAL SETTLEMENT PATTERNS IN SELECTED AREAS

Malaya and the East Indies

C. Robequain (*op. cit.*) informs us that in Malaya and the East Indies the normal unit of settlement is the loose-knit village which acts as a secure and convenient base for rational cultivation. Absolute dispersal is rare, but the size of rural concentrations varies widely: in Bali and Java one village may contain several hundred dwellings, elsewhere only a few. Families have clustered together from early times, when clan warfare, head-hunting and piracy were rife. They often erected a stout palisade round their villages and shunned the sea-coast. Many built their villages near running water, however, rather than on hill-tops because the desire for water often overcame the need for defence. Agricultural co-operation, made possible by nucleation, is still practised: each family has its plots scattered over the entire communal area, even where shifting cultivation, entailing the removal of the village every few years, is still undertaken. Some villages have expanded so much that they have come to resemble the "agrovilles" of Hungary, but improved security, the spread of communications, the break-up of the large family and the partial adoption of an individual property system are at the same time combining to promote dispersal. Increasing numbers of people are migrating towards roads and railway stations as commercial farming becomes more important. The trade of the towns is dominated by Europeans and Chinese, who live near the town centres, but the more indigenous groups take up semi-rural living quarters with garden spaces attached to their dwellings when they join the urban community.

Rural Wales

Apart from the industrial areas of South Wales and the extreme north-east, Wales is a sparsely populated country in which highland predominates. There is much bare rock and rough moorland, little used agriculturally save for hill sheep-farming and in some areas for raising store cattle, but even these occupations are absent at very high levels. On the coast plains, broad only in the south, and extremely discontinuous in the west, and in the lower, broader river valleys opening out towards England, improved pasture and meadow, together with sporadic fields of fodder crops, support more prosperous stock-raising industries.

Whatever may have been the primeval pattern of settlement in rural Wales, it is now essentially dispersed, and has been so since the Dark Ages. The dominant element is the *tyddin*, the single, isolated farmstead from which a smallholding is worked. Clearly this is the type of pattern one would expect in a well-watered highland region of podsolised soils and restricted accessibility chiefly used for pastoral farming, but the ancient inheritance law known as "gavelkind," by which a father upon his death arranged for the division of his property equally among all his sons, undoubtedly fostered it. To extend their holdings, the children were gradually obliged to ascend higher and higher from the early village in the

Fig. 32.—Harlech, North Wales. Harlech Castle, founded by Edward I in 1285, has substantial curtain walls 40 ft (12 m) high. They stand on sharply rising ground 100 ft (30 m) above the flat, sandy, in parts marshy, Morfa Harlech, a coastal tract on the left of the photograph.

valley or on a lower slope, and take over increasing amounts of the common pasture in order to make a living from the land. As they spread, so did the farm buildings, to form the present dispersed pattern. A few small hamlets grew round the ancient churches established by the Celtic saints, but these had no real nucleating influence.

Under Norman influence, true villages were founded in the broad valleys penetrating westwards from the Midland Plain of England and along the north and south coastlands. The Normans, too, built castles at strategic points in various parts of the country, e.g. at Carmarthen, Pembroke and Tenby in South Wales; Edward I added to their number, especially in the north, where planned "bastide" settlements were laid out, e.g. at Flint, Harlech, Caernarvon and Conway (see Fig. 32).

Primogeniture replaced gavelkind under Henry VIII, and further settlement dispersal became less necessary, but a number of scattered farmsteads were established later by "squatters," chiefly during the land-hungry period of about the mid-nineteenth century. The only empty land by then was roughly at the farming limit (about 1,000 ft (300 m). Many of the less accessible high farms are now being joined together and consolidated into larger, more economic units, partially mechanised. Former homesteads are being allowed to decay or else converted into shelters for sheep and cattle.

Most of the nodal settlements in Wales, developing in some cases into market towns, only began to grow in the eighteenth and nineteenth centuries, e.g. at cross-roads and bridge-points, and round castles, railway stations and nonconformist chapels. Modern tourist centres have emerged, especially along the north coast, and Holyhead and Fishguard have become ferry ports. The quarrying villages and towns in the north-west, coming to life in the early nineteenth century, are now barely holding their own, the cheapness of the modern tiled roof having caused a steep fall in the demand for Welsh slate.

During the present century the pattern of settlement has been modified by Forestry Commission settlements (generally consisting of only two or three houses), and by temporary chalet and caravan settlements (e.g. near Abergele and Prestatyn). The latter have entertainment facilities, shops and other semi-urban amenities, but are almost uninhabited in winter.*

The West Riding of Yorkshire

The settlement pattern in this area is very diverse and again depends upon a number of factors of which perhaps land use and economic resources are the chief.

The fringes of the West Yorkshire conurbation and the smaller conurbation based on Sheffield lie only a few miles from the wholly empty Pennine moor summit area. Between these two zones are dispersed pastoral farmsteads, snuggling in sheltered depressions and valleys up to heights of about 1,000 ft (300 m), solidly built of the local gritstones and sandstones, but now often decayed and abandoned. Here and there are the remnants of half decayed quarry villages. The more subdued landscape of the Coal Measures early favoured a somewhat closer rural settlement pattern, and a number of farm villages, not all in river valleys, remain in this area. The occurrence of workable coal seams and iron ore deposits, and the growth of textile, steel and engineering industries

---

* Most of the material in this section on rural Wales is derived from an essay by E. G. Bowen in *Field Studies in the British Isles* (ed. J. A. Steers), Nelson, 1964.

dependent upon them, promoted the spread of other settlements, including towns and cities. Between these large urban settlements there came to be a tangle of roads and railways and a confused pattern of industrial and mining villages, their eighteenth-century cottages and later drab rows of terrace houses straggling over the landscape so haphazardly that it is hard for a stranger to know where one ends and another begins.

North of the industrial West Riding, rural settlements consist mainly of agricultural valley villages, their inhabitants engaged chiefly in dairy-farming at low levels, sheep farming at higher. A feature here, especially in upper Airedale and Wharfedale, is the large number of stone-built hay-barns or "laithes" on the lower valley slopes, not all of them now in use. In the higher parts of the dales, where agricultural rewards are scanty, settlements are generally no more than single farms. The old lead-mining settlements on the Carboniferous Limestone, generally hamleted, have declined. Near the conurbation, in Airedale and lower Wharfedale,

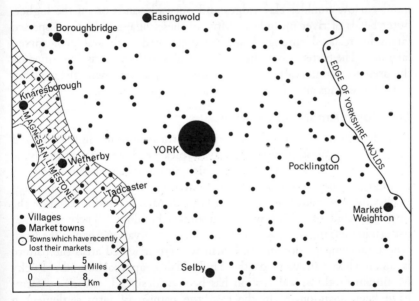

FIG. 33.—Market towns and villages in part of the Vale of York. York, the major route focus of the Vale of York, has become its dominant "central place." Round it is a scatter of villages and, at sparser intervals, small market towns. The latter have decreased in number as transport facilities have multiplied. There are few villages on the thin chalky soils of the Yorkshire Wolds as the enclosure of these uplands for cultivation was begun little more than 150 years ago.

by contrast, a number of villages and small market towns are now expanding in response to the needs of tourists and commuters.

East and north-east of the coalfield, Permian and Triassic rocks succeed each other, but there is much glacial overlay and, in the valleys, spreads of alluvium and gravel. Here, broadly speaking, agricultural opportunities are more promising than further west, and large farm villages, with some secondary dispersion, are a common feature. Approaching Goole, early fen conditions favoured the rise of dry point settlements based on outcrops of drier Bunter and Keuper Sands. Drainage was systematically undertaken in the seventeenth century and some dispersion has resulted. Part of this area and parts of adjacent areas are now worked as a concealed coalfield, and one finds, among the farm villages and scattered homesteads a modern spattering of planned colliery estate villages.

In the western half of the Vale of York there are many pleasantly situated compact villages: large ones of stone on the Magnesian Limestone, generally smaller ones of brick on the vale floor. Many of the latter stand on low boulder clay ridges and outwash sands or on the higher, outer bends of river meanders. Most of these villages, like the dispersed farms intercalated among them, are concerned with arable or mixed farming. The pattern, as in the Pennine Dales to the west, is diversified by the presence, at intervals of about ten miles, of market towns, the majority at river crossings and alongside railway lines (see Fig. 33).

The North American Prairies

Settlement in the Canadian Prairies, North American High Plains and the U.S. Mid-West, is in many ways typical of those parts of the New World first effectively colonised by northern Europeans and now devoted to highly commercialised forms of extensive farming. The pattern is essentially dispersed, as is shown on Fig. 31, page 67, and is based on the single, isolated farmhouse with its attendant buildings. There is a closer pattern in the damp east, where there is more cultivation, than in the west, where ranching predominates, but in western irrigated areas the pattern is again close. In parts of the High Plains, approaching the Rocky Mountain foothills, soil erosion has been widespread, and many farms have been abandoned. In the east, the pattern of farm settlement is loosening out for a different reason. Here, more and more properties are being amalgamated, sometimes by wealthy agricultural companies who run these enlarged units through salaried managers.

The greater part of the prairie region was mathematically surveyed and a gridded land-holding system prepared before settlers moved in. The land was methodically divided into mile-square blocks or sections whose boundaries ran north–south and east–west. Colonists obtained either a quarter section or a multiple of it. Consequently, except where rough topography or a pond intervenes, or where a railway track crosses it diagonally, the typical farm holding is square or rectangular, the farm buildings being set close to one of the bounding straight roads or lanes.

However, the landscape, though superficially uniform over wide areas, is not without its variations. For example, in those parts of the Canadian Prairies which have been taken up by French-Canadian farmers, the holdings are unusual in being long and narrow, thus resembling the "long lots" of the St Lawrence valley whence the farmers sprang. Here, too, in the Prairies, French-Canadian farmsteads are often strung out linearly as in Quebec. Among them gleam silver-spired churches. Other minority groups, notably the Dukhobors and Mennonites, may live in true villages in order to preserve their ethnic or religious identity, but, increasingly, farmers are leaving these villages and contributing to the overall dispersed pattern.

Most of the villages in the North American grasslands are not really villages at all, for they do not generally house either farmers or farm workers. They are rather service centres, located chiefly at cross-roads. They normally embrace a school, church or churches, shops, cafés, a bank, warehouse and garage, arranged on either side of the "main street." Much family business on the farms, and many of the farm household requirements, however, are handled by mail-order firms whose headquarters are in the large commercial cities, notably Chicago. These cities, like the smaller service centres, are laid out in sections separated from each other by a rectilinear mesh of streets.

STUDY QUESTIONS

1. Discuss the influence of climate and vegetation upon buildings in a number of well-separated rural areas.

2. How far do the older buildings of your town or village reflect the local geology?

3. Explain the following terms: (a) wattle and daub; (b) cob; (c) brick nogging; (d) hip-gable; (e) mansard.

4. Contrast the typical farmhouses of Egypt with those of Norway, and account for the differences you mention.

5. Contrast the dwellings of two contrasted groups of nomadic herders with those of two groups of sedentary cultivators.

6. What distinctions would you draw between (a) villages and hamlets, and (b) villages and towns?

7. With the help of an Ordnance Survey map, account for the location and distribution of the villages within a ten- or twenty-mile radius of your home.

8. Referring to specific examples, distinguish between "wet-point" and "dry-point" villages.

9. Analyse the sites of a number of selected villages within the area covered by any particular 1-inch or 1 : 25,000 Ordnance Survey map sheet.

10. Using specific examples, describe and, if possible, explain, the varying forms and functions of English villages.

11. Discuss and illustrate by sketch-maps the various forms which villages may take in any country outside England.

12. Write an essay on the social geography of village England.

13. How does a study of place-names assist the geographer to understand the pattern of rural settlement?

14. Explain the meaning of the term "settlement pattern." Illustrate your answer by reference to any area with which you are familiar.

15. Describe the pattern of urban and rural settlement on (a) a coalfield, and (b) an area of arable farming.

16. With reference to particular areas in Great Britain, point out some of the physical and human factors which affect the pattern of settlement.

17. Compare the settlement pattern in rural Wales with that in the Vale of York.

Part Three

URBAN SETTLEMENTS

Chapter V

The Growth of Towns and Cities

WHAT IS A TOWN?

IN Chapter I some attempt was made to distinguish town and village, and town and city. Here, the question of what constitutes a town or city will be further explored, but there will be no further attempt to justify the use of the term "town" in some contexts, "city" in other.

The town is undoubtedly one of the most striking expressions of contemporary, or indeed of any, civilisation. It completely dominates the region in which it lies and in that sense the world may be envisaged as becoming increasingly a collection of towns and cities and the regions they serve and upon which they depend. Towns are "both places and the sum of the people living in them" (Maurice Barley in *Living in Towns*); therefore, while their study is of the very essence of human geography, they are also the concern of the sociologist, economist, historian, planner, engineer and architect.

Think of the multiplicity and diversity of towns. Included in their number are the industrial nuclei of the Ruhr and West Yorkshire, the country market towns of the English Plain, the ancient hill-top cities of the Mediterranean lands, the modern seaside growths of the West European coast, the mushroom growths of North America, the "agrovilles" of Hungary, the great commercial emporia of all continental margins; and world cities such as London, Paris, Moscow, New York and Tokyo. No wonder Emrys Jones (in *Towns and Cities*) states that a town "seems to be all things to all men": a physical agglomeration of streets and houses, a centre of commerce and administration, a kind of society, even a frame of mind or a way of life. It is without any specific size or population density, is not concerned with any one function to the exclusion of others, has no single shape nor any unique set of characteristics. Every city has its own identity, location and history, but its inhabitants, while sharing the element of "togetherness," often enjoy fewer personal contacts than those who live in a village. Certainly the class structure is more complex, occupations more heterogeneous and human mobility more marked.

If large, a town is more than a mere unit of settlement: it is a synthesis of functionally distinct parts, *e.g.* middle-class and working-class residential areas, a factory zone, commercial and administrative sections, an entertainment quarter, and so on. It provides trading facilities for rural dwellers; it supports an army of craftsmen such as builders, shoemakers and repairers, tailors and dressmakers, garage mechanics and plumbers, as well as men and women providing professional services, such as teachers,

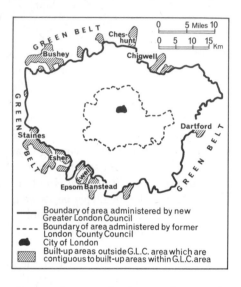

FIG. 34.—London: an "under bounded" city. Most British cities are "underbounded," that is their buildings extend beyond their administrative limits. Even Greater London under its new, enlarged council, is no exception, despite its Green Belt surround.

doctors, lawyers, bankers and accountants. It generally has some factory workers unless its tourist or dormitory function makes large-scale industry undesirable.

Many towns, especially in advanced countries, have now expanded beyond the limits of local administration. Such towns have been called "underbounded" towns, and as geographical expressions of urban settlement, have a larger population than is suggested by statistics based on the "legal" city or town (*i.e.* the area within the boundaries of the municipality). Sydney (Australia) is notoriously underbounded. Its municipal territory covers only 10.6 sq. miles (27 sq. km), but the suburban zone is spread over more than 230 sq. miles (595 sq. km). Many English towns, too, are underbounded, at least along parts of their boundaries. Fig. 34 shows the extent to which even Greater London is underbounded.

"Overbounded" towns, by contrast, have statistical limits which extend beyond their built-up areas. In Japan and the Philippines, and in such American states as Texas and Oklahoma where it is easy to annex land, such boundaries are often so generously drawn as to include not only much rural land but also more than one urban area. Municipal boundaries, of course, are not unalterable, but changes are generally made only after much argument, often leading to acrimony, between the town concerned and neighbouring authorities. Stated populations may suddenly spurt owing to a finally achieved boundary extension and thus a false impression of actual urban growth may be obtained. Tokyo, for example, enlarged its legal area from 33 sq. miles (85 sq. km) to 214 sq. miles (554 km) in 1932, and later 783 sq. miles (2,029 sq. km). These extensions allow it to claim to be the world's most populous city, with more than 11 million people within its lines. (Even so, it is in places underbounded, as are, *inter alia*, New York and the area administered by the Greater London Council.)

LEGAL DEFINITIONS OF A TOWN

For census purposes, and other statistical records, countries have adopted their own methods of defining a town or urban area. Some use an economic criterion, some a criterion based on population numbers, others one based on the form of administration. There is no uniformity, but it is curious to note that hardly any country uses population density or areal size in its definition.

In Israel and Italy, a town is defined, broadly speaking, as a settlement in which a high proportion of the gainfully employed are non-agricultural workers. Denmark, Sweden and Finland, more simply, regard towns as settlements with populations of at least 250; Iceland raises the figure to 300. These numbers, though low, are in the main justifiable since the settlement pattern in these lands is largely dispersed and even small agglomerations have some urban characteristics. Canada, Malaysia and Venezuela take 1,000 people as the minimum population of an urban settlement, Colombia 1,500, Argentina and Portugal 2,000, the U.S.A. and Thailand 2,500, Ghana and India 5,000. In the latter country, the figure 5,000 is coupled with the requirement that such a settlement must have "urban characteristics," *i.e.* more than 75 per cent of the males must be engaged in non-agricultural work; indeed, if this requirement is met, India is ready to admit as a town certain settlements with less than 5,000 people.

In France, the whole population of any commune (or parish, *i.e.* the smallest administrative unit) is included as urban if the commune contains a cluster of more than 2,000. The practice is somewhat similar in Greece and Luxembourg. In Germany, on the other hand, a minor civil division is regarded as urban if it houses at least 2,000 people irrespective of the size of the main cluster. Similar definitions are employed in Spain and Switzerland (where, however, the operative number is 10,000) and in Japan and the Netherlands (where the limiting figure is 20,000).

In most of the central American republics, and also in Brazil and Bolivia, all the administrative centres of even the minor civil divisions are labelled towns. The U.A.R., Turkey, Norway, Tunisia, the U.S.S.R. and the U.K. are among those countries which apply the term "urban" to areas with a particular form of administration. In the U.K., for example, the "urban population" covers all those people who live in county and municipal boroughs, and in urban districts (*i.e.* those who do not reside in rural districts). A quite different method of defining the urban population is used in most African countries where a town is simply a European settlement.

The most sophisticated method of defining settlements according to their urban characteristics is that used, with periodic modifications, in the United States. The U.S. Census Bureau recognises four distinct kinds of units which contribute to its urban population: (*a*) an "urban place" (*i.e.* a place with at least 2,500 inhabitants); (*b*) an "incorporated city" (*i.e.* a town with at least 2,500 people and a separate political identity); (*c*) an "urbanised area," centred on a city of at least 50,000 and including the city's urban fringe or suburban areas, and (*d*) a "standard metropolitan statistical area" (S.M.S.A.)—a group of counties containing at the core at least one city of 50,000 or more people, together with that part of the surrounding area, most of it probably not truly urban, which is socially and economically integrated with it. The surrounding counties are those in which (*a*) non-agricultural workers form no less than 75 per cent of the total employed population of those counties, (*b*) 15 per cent of the workers are employed in the central city county, or (*c*) telephone calls to the central city number at least four times the total number of subscribers in those counties.

In the United States as a whole, therefore, the urbanised area may be viewed as the densely peopled core of the S.M.S.A. In New England, however, different criteria have to be adopted owing to its historically different administrative organisation. Here, broadly, a population density of 100 per square mile is used as an index of metropolitan character, providing the administrative unit concerned is strongly integrated with the central city.

PRE-INDUSTRIAL AND INDUSTRIAL CITIES

According to Gideon Sjoberg, towns may be roughly divided into "pre-industrial" and "industrial" types. The former are still in existence in many countries, especially in those which have not yet fully experienced

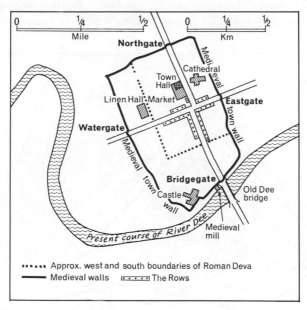

FIG. 35.—Roman and medieval Chester. The Roman settlement at Chester was built about 100 ft O.D. (30 m) on dry ground floored with Triassic sandstone at a time when the River Dee reached the Watergate, where ships could anchor. The medieval walls date from the fourteenth century, but the cathedral—preceded by a Saxon church and monastery—was built mainly in the eleventh; the castle—replacing tenth-century earthworks—in the thirteenth. The Rows with arcaded shops one over the other, are also probably of the thirteenth century and rest upon the debris of Roman buildings. Like nearly all other ancient towns, Chester has now spread well beyond its medieval bounds. A few non-medieval sites have been added to the map to assist orientation.

the kind of Industrial Revolution which transformed society and settlements in Europe in the nineteenth century. It was, however, technological advance which enabled even pre-industrial cities to emerge, for until agricultural techniques had improved sufficiently to allow of the production of food surpluses, even the smallest towns could neither acquire a body of specialised labour divorced from the land nor the kind of administrative and social organisation which would allow food surpluses to be collected, stored and distributed.

Most pre-industrial cities remain small and are set in rural surroundings, but they have often come to be crowded. They normally possess a market-place for traders and workshops for craftsmen, who are often segregated from other people. The leaders of society and other wealthy inhabitants generally reside near the centre, the farmers and poorer people making shift with scattered dwellings on the outskirts. Pre-industrial cities are frequently walled and their narrow streets lead to a central area often

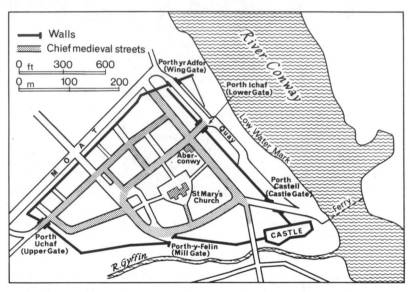

Fig. 36.—Medieval Conway. Conway, a "bastide" town established by Edward I near the mouth of the river Conway, was carefully planned within its harp-shaped medieval walls. The castle and parish church, like the walls, date from the thirteenth century. The church was at first part of a Cistercian abbey. The oldest existing house—Aberconwy—dates from *c*. 1300.

dignified by an imposing place of worship, castle or palace (*see* Figs. 35 and 36). Beyond the walls there may well be *faubourg* within which foreigners may reside, as in medieval Europe.

In industrial towns—sometimes rather misleadingly called "Western" cities since there are now many in the East—large-scale retailing and wholesaling as well as public administration usually employ more people than in the pre-industrial town. The dominant activities, however, are generally factory work and, in the case of coastal settlements, overseas commerce. A town or city hall is often more prominent than a parish church or castle, and many of the élite have forsaken the centre for the expanding suburbs. Such a settlement is a product of power-driven machinery, modern communications and extensive commercial links which tie it, not simply to its own region, but to the larger world beyond.

The simple division of cities into "pre-industrial" and "industrial" groups focuses attention upon only a few broad contrasts. Certain modern, specialised towns, *e.g.* tourist centres and dormitory towns, do not fit into either category. To obtain a clearer notion of the contrasts between towns it is more rewarding to outline their growth in a more conventional historical context and then to examine, in their different regional settings, some of their most marked features as landscape elements.

THE FIRST URBAN REVOLUTION: THE EARLIEST TOWNS

The earliest towns arose during the later part of the Neolithic period, when early farmers, after their first essays in settled agriculture and village life, began to produce, with the aid of the newly invented plough, a surplus of foodstuffs, thus allowing part of society to free itself from work on the land. From about the fourth millenium B.C., in certain fertile riverine plains of the Near East where irrigation water was available—notably Egypt, Mesopotamia and the lower Indus valley—it became possible to

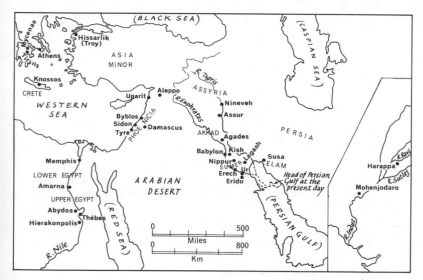

FIG. 37.—Early cities in the Near East. All the towns marked on this map were in existence in 1000 B.C. Nearly all occupy sites on either broad river plains or on trading coasts. Note that the map is interrupted for a distance of about 600 miles between the urban cradles of Mesopotamia and the Indus Valley.

spare some people for non-agricultural work of a kind which benefited from social cohesion, *e.g.* hand-manufacture, trade, and community organisation. Thus arose groups of specialised artisans, of merchants, officials and priests or other rulers. Along with a proportion of the agricultural community, these people gathered themselves together in close-knit societies which came to form the first towns. They were careful to choose favourable geographical locations, generally on river banks where they could take advantage of new forms of transport—the sailing boat and the wheeled vehicle. Examples of these early towns, some dating from the fourth millenium B.C., others from the third, include Eridu, Erech, Lagash, Kish, Ur and Nippur in ancient Sumeria, occupying the Tigris–Euphrates delta, Babylon, further north, and Assur and Nineveh in Assyria, further north again; Memphis and Thebes in the Nile valley; and Harappa and Mohenjodaro in the Indus valley (*see* Fig. 37 and table below).

EARLY STAGES IN URBAN GROWTH

A.D.

1200	French bastides built Towns in medieval Europe beginning to grow spontaneously north of Alps
1000	Venice and other Italian city-states beginning their commercial rise Mayan cities at peak
500	
0	Mayan cities in Middle America arising Alexandria founded
500	Rome and Etruscan cities achieving prominence Greek colonisation under way Persian settlements in West Turkestan acquiring urban status Early Greek cities in flower Rome founded
1000	
1500	Chinese cities, *e.g.* Anyang in middle Hwang-ho valley, coming of age Ugarit and Byblos active on Levant coast, Knossos in Crete
2000	
2500	Babylon founded Mohenjodaro and Harappa flourishing in Indus valley
3000	Thebes and Memphis flourishing in Egypt Earliest Egyptian towns arising
3500	Sumerian cities, *e.g.* Eridu and Lagash, developing

4000
B.C.

Such towns were generally walled for defence, and dignified by temples, pyramids and palaces: tributes to both heavenly and earthly potentates. Besides the trade which developed between these towns and the surrounding farmland which supported them, a number of more distant trade links were fashioned, for the towns needed certain commodities which their own regions might not supply, *e.g.* copper, papermaking materials and timber, which they were able to exchange for the products of their artisans. Since, however, they continued for long to depend for their food supplies upon the productivity of the immediately surrounding land, these towns could not grow into large cities, and seem to have had an upper population limit of about 20,000. It was not until the rise of the Egyptian and Babylonian Empires that their chief cities were able to draw upon wider areas for their essential supplies and thus to expand markedly; on the basis of tribute food it is believed that Babylon was eventually able to house nearly 100,000 people.

From the alluvial plains of the Near East the idea of the city filtered through to Phoenicia, Asia Minor and Crete, as trade in highly localised materials grew. In these areas, during the Bronze Age, a number of new trading centres came into being, *e.g.* Byblos, Ugarit, Tyre and Sidon, Mycenae and Knossos. All were able to benefit from Mediterranean sea-trade, though, like the earliest towns, they were primarily tied to their own restricted areas of agricultural land, which severely limited their growth as population centres. At about the same time, or somewhat later, a few caravan centres, dependent on overland trade, were established in the desert oases of Syria on the margin of the Fertile Crescent (*e.g.* Damascus and Aleppo). Further away, in the Wei-ho valley in northern China, other towns, similar in character to the riverine settlements of the Near East, emerged. From them, the concept of the city was gradually diffused into central and southern China.

THE SPREAD OF TOWNS IN GREEK AND ROMAN TIMES

The cultural and financial capital acquired by the early Near Eastern cities was gradually transmitted into Greece and Italy by traders and colonists who also introduced the germ of the city into north-west Africa and Spain during the second and first millenia B.C. There were similar extensions of urban societies, mostly at a rather later date, into Persia, Central Asia, peninsular India and Ceylon.

The Greek city-state consisted of a city and the rural area from which it obtained its essential supplies. The whole state, in Athens for instance, rarely supported more than 50,000 people, of whom only about a quarter, including slaves and foreign merchants, were fully urbanised. Most of these Greek cities had a hill-top site, and were in close contact with the sea. They were therefore able to import luxuries and other specialised products without difficulty, and it became possible for them to outgrow, to a limited extent, their own narrow rural base. As the population grew, it became common for the go-ahead to establish colonies and secondary trading stations in other parts of the Mediterranean world where they were able to find similar geographical conditions to those of the homeland. Thus, originated Paestum, Neapolis (Naples), Cyrene, Alexandria, and Massilia (Marseilles), mainly in the first millenium B.C. A little earlier, Phoenician traders established an offshoot at Carthage, which itself fathered other towns in North Africa and Spain, and the Etruscans, originally from Asia Minor, founded towns in the northern part of the Italian peninsula.

Thus, by about 500 B.C., examples of urban forms—mostly based on the ancient rectangular grid plan found at Harappa—could be found in a broad belt extending virtually from the Atlantic coast of Iberia to the Pacific coast of China. Iron tools had now come into use, alongside improved ships and land vehicles, and coinage and alphabetical writing were common. All of these developments facilitated ever-widening commercial contacts, and allowed towns to expand beyond the resources of their immediate environment. Even then, however, only a few settlements seem to have exceeded 10,000 people.

Rome had been founded in the eighth century B.C. It was from this political centre, when its power had made it into an imperial city, that urban settlements and the civilisation associated with them were gradually propagated north of the Alps. Rome itself, of course, came to depend increasingly upon more and more distant sources for its supplies of tribute, food and raw materials, which came to it along the excellently engineered roads which were really landward extensions of the Mediterranean shipping routes. Alexandria, founded in the fourth century B.C. by Alexander the Great, became the port through which Nile-valley corn could be funnelled to the imperial capital. This city, the administrative centre of the Roman province of Egypt, became not only the second city of the Empire but, like Rome itself, a great seat of government, education and culture. Other notable cities which grew within the shelter of the Pax Romana (some of them built on the sites of former tribal capitals) included Ostia (the immediate port of Rome), Turin, Arles, Nîmes, Lyons, Strasbourg, Trier, Mainz, Cologne, London, St Albans, Lincoln, York and Byzantium (Istanbul). As strategic bases, administrative centres and commercial emporia, all these towns became the springboards from

which Roman architecture, sculpture, law and language leapt into prominence in western Europe, and came to dominate the lives of non-Italian
people.

The typical Roman town was built, like its Greek forerunners, on a
symmetrically planned grid. At the central cross-roads there was again a
market-place (the forum), and near it stood the principal buildings, including temple, administrative buildings and baths.

In the full flower of Roman civilisation, some functional specialisation
began to manifest itself in certain towns. In Britain, for example, Caerleon
and Chester remained largely fortresses, St Albans and London became
administrative centres, Dover acted as a port, and Bath was established as a
spa. These towns were probably much smaller than those in Italy and
southern France, some of which probably attained a population of 30,000.
Rome at its peak probably reached 250,000.

URBANISM IN THE DARK AGES AND MEDIEVAL PERIOD

The collapse of the Roman Empire in the fifth century A.D., and the
ensuing period of confusion and insecurity caused urban life, no longer
supported by Roman troops and officials, to contract in northern and
western Europe, though it was able to maintain itself to some extent in
southern France and Italy, and to a greater degree in the east where
Byzantium—the New Rome—flourished with the help of sea-power and
the fame and magnitude of its workshop products.

The Dark Ages in Europe set in with the coming of the barbarians,
mainly peasant communities who despised the cultural legacy of Rome
and ignored its towns. The Church, especially in France, just managed to
keep alive the flame of the city, but most urban settlements, after being
sacked and plundered, were largely abandoned. It was not until the
eleventh century that town life, centred upon a market-place, began
markedly to revive as security returned and trade began to flow again
following the more thorough agricultural colonisation of forest and marsh.
Most of the feudal rulers who commanded the new towns, however, controlled only limited territorial domains. Therefore, with few exceptions,
their towns, like those of old, rarely housed more than 10,000 people. By
A.D. 1400 historical aggrandisement and widening trade relations allowed
Paris to reach 250,000 and London 50,000. Other nodes of long-distance
commerce and manufacturing, e.g. Ghent and Bruges, Augsburg, Cologne,
Lübeck, Venice, Genoa, Florence and Milan, also became important cities,
but most urban settlements, largely the outgrowth of focally situated

villages, remained humble market towns acting as central places for the purely local trade generated by restricted rural areas. Their small populations were in many cases reduced still further by the periodic onset of plague.

The typical medieval town was walled for defence and often acted as a refuge, not only for foreign traders and artisans, but also for people from the open country around. Its nucleus was often a monastery, important church, feudal castle or guild-hall, the latter especially prominent in Lombardy and the Low Countries. Other buildings spread outwards from the market-place to the walls, and left room at first for a formless grouping of gardens, courts and winding, irregularly aligned streets. Crowding came as trade and cottage industry developed, until either the walls were rebuilt round a longer perimeter or suburbs grew up beyond them.

There were, however, a number of planned medieval towns, more obviously built to a pre-conceived design. Such were the "bastides" or military towns erected, for example, in Aquitaine by local barons and successive kings to protect their rural populations from attack by other overlords. Similar settlements were established by English rulers in Wales and Scotland to check border raids and to serve as operational bases against the Welsh and Scots. Examples in France include Montauban and Sauveterre; in Wales, Flint, Conway (*see* Fig. 36) and Caernarvon, and in northern England, Carlisle and Berwick. Some of these towns later became mercantile centres, and, like the more amorphous medieval towns, often received charters giving them a large measure of self-government and freedom from feudal dues.

From western Europe, German knights and traders, followed by colonisers, carried the concept of the town east of the river Elbe into Slav territory, which was still being overrun by barbarian invasions long after western Europe had become stable. In these areas—which the Romans never effectively ruled and which possessed very few proper urban settlements of their own—military bases and trading cities were established in the thirteenth and fourteenth centuries. The church and market-square symbolised the religious and commercial motives behind their creation, and their stockades and walls indicated the need for the defence of German values and property among an alien people. They were established, among other places, at Frankfurt-on-Oder, Stettin, Danzig, Königsberg, Breslau, Prague, Warsaw and Posen, many of which, due to the political shrinkage of Germany, now possess Slav names.

In Spain, the Moors founded many towns during the course of their occupation. They include Cordoba and Granada, towns which still possess Moorish architecture (*see* Fig. 38). In northern Spain, less affected

[*Courtesy: Spanish National Tourist Office*

Fig. 38.—The Alhambra, Granada. This photograph shows El Patio de los Leones ("the courtyard of the lions") in the Alhambra, Granada, a model of Moorish architecture situated near the Sierra Nevada in south-eastern Spain. The city and its palace was the scene of the final subjugation of the Moors by the Spaniards in 1492.

by the Arab sway, indigenous fortress towns were established during the Spanish reconquest of the peninsula, especially along the Ebro, Douro and Tagus.

RENAISSANCE AND LATER TOWNS

By 1400, the human habitat in western Europe, central Europe and the central parts of European Russia was covered with compact villages and towns about as far north as 60°N. Not until later were there many effective urban settlements in the lower Danube lowland and the steppes of southern Russia. Between 1500 and 1750, however, many cities in the previously urbanised parts of Europe—under the initial impetus of the Renaissance voyages of discovery and the growing prestige of their rulers —expanded considerably: as capitals and seats of princely courts, or as internationally renowned seaports and centres of internal commerce and domestic handicrafts. Now, far more than previously, a few great cities

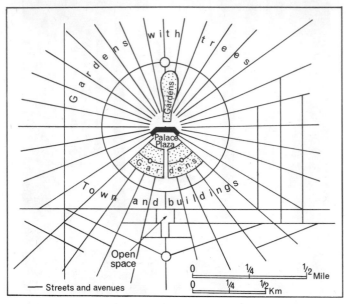

FIG. 39.—Karlsruhe: a Baroque city. Karlsruhe, created in 1715 to enhance the prestige of the Grand Duke of Baden, is a magnificent example of Baroque planning, the ducal palace, fronted and backed by landscaped gardens, being the focal point of thirty-two radial avenues. The town has since expanded to enclose a number of suburbs (not shown on this plan).

began to tower over the rest as a result of the amalgamation under single rulers of large tracts of territory and of the burgeoning of trade. The rise of nation states in Europe was accompanied by the acquisition of new wealth from which stemmed growing princely prestige. One of the consequences was the embellishment of political capitals, both national and provincial. This was the age marked by the grandiloquent splendour of Versailles, Karlsruhe (*see* Fig. 39), Nancy, Potsdam and Mannheim, with their straight, wide avenues, formally designed grounds, and finely built palaces, art galleries and theatres, often erected beyond the limits of the medieval cities which preceded them. It was also the age of expanding ocean ports, *e.g.* Antwerp, Lisbon and Amsterdam, which, through the Atlantic and Asiatic trade, took over the commercial role of the old Mediterranean ports such as Venice and Genoa. Fortified towns became more complex as artillery became stronger and cast iron shot was invented (1480). Town walls were doubled or set with numerous angles to improve their defensive character, and wide moats were often appended. Dignified squares and crescents were laid out in spas and watering-places such as Bath and Carlsbad, which came to be increasingly patronised by the aristocracy during this period.

London, both the capital of a great state and a leading commercial city, grew to 700,000 people by 1700, when it outstripped Paris (*c.* 500,000). Moscow and Vienna, both nodal centres which had become the centralised capitals of powerful Empires, were now entering upon a period of rapid growth, but Berlin's turn did not come until after 1800. Most towns were still small: in England, Bristol and Norwich, the second and third cities, had populations of only 30,000, Exeter and York not 20,000, as late as 1700. The small market town was still the typical urban settlement.

THE SECOND URBAN REVOLUTION: INDUSTRIAL TOWNS

The Industrial Revolution, first convulsing society in England, then erupting in Belgium and the continent, and the Commercial Revolution which accompanied it and made it possible, produced a greater multiplication of towns and a more marked expansion in the size of towns than any events which had gone before. It also gave birth to a new kind of town: that dominated by the industrial function. Manufacturing had long held a place in most towns, but the concentration of this activity in urban settlements, some of which had formerly been mere villages, was as new as the power-driven machines and the factories which housed them.

Many areas indifferently endowed with productive agricultural land and many places unable to benefit from sites on navigable rivers and coastal inlets now assumed importance in urban geography. The need for coal to raise steam in the early factories was the main locating influence on the new industrial towns: in 1901, of thirty-three towns in Britain with more than 100,000 people, twenty were situated on or close to coalfields (*see* Fig. 40). The construction of improved roads, canals and, later, the invention of rail transport and the motor vehicle, allowed such settlements to develop as hubs of communication even when they possessed little, if any, natural nodality. The volume of their manufactures grew with the colonisation of new lands overseas, and the concomitant spurt in world trade produced a rapid expansion of seaports, not only in Europe, but also in the Americas, Asia, Africa and Australasia.

The populations of these industrial and commercial cities grew, not by natural increase,* but by immigration from rural areas, a movement

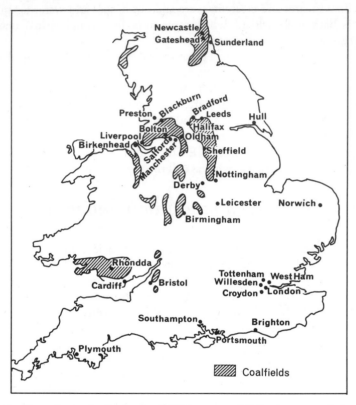

FIG. 40—Large towns in England and Wales, 1900. All the towns marked on this map had populations of more than 100,000 in 1900. Nearly all are industrial towns or commercial ports. Brighton stands out as the major holiday resort. Already the major conurbations of the present day are developing.

facilitated by improved agricultural techniques which reduced the demand for labour on the land. Some cities, *e.g.* London, New York, Tokyo, Calcutta and Shanghai, became "super-cities." London reached a

---

* In the expanding industrial towns, birth-rates were nearly as high as in rural areas, but death-rates were for long very much higher owing to the ease with which disease could spread in congested places where modern sanitation was lacking.

population of nearly a million in 1800, over 2 million in 1850, and nearly 5 million in 1880. In Europe as a whole, between 1800 and 1890, the number of towns with populations exceeding 100,000 increased from 22 to 120. Most of them were primarily concerned with large-scale factory industry or international commerce, though the rapid expansion in the numbers of government employees contributed to the growth of political capitals.

The typical industrial town is not a thing of beauty. It has long been condemned because of the uglification produced by hasty, haphazard growth, and the squalor and repetitive regularity of its working-class streets. Its polluted air and water, and its grimy buildings further disfigure it. A reaction against this kind of town as a living-space set in when the wealthier townspeople began to move away from the immediate neighbourhood of the smoking factories in Victorian times, and especially when the garden city movement gathered strength. Twentieth-century planners are still trying, through urban renewal projects, and with the aid of modern transport and electric power, to change the face of these congested industrial towns, to clean them up, and make them more worthy of their inhabitants.

MODERN TOWNS

The proliferation of towns continues in almost all countries. Areas such as tropical Asia and Africa and the Siberian portions of the Soviet Union, still under-developed, are now experiencing the rapid changes through which western Europe passed a century or more ago. New urban settlements, mushroom-like, are appearing almost overnight. In areas with longer histories of urban expansion many existing towns are becoming multifunctional; others, more highly specialised, are reaching maturity as tourist centres, dormitory and overspill towns, educational centres or petroleum ports. New mining centres and strategic bases are appearing. Labour is becoming more mobile and is migrating not just from country to town but from one town to another. More people are working in the tertiary sector: government, trade and transport, entertainment, professional work. Urban sprawl is becoming endemic in most developed countries, and more and more conurbations are coming into being. The various activities associated with very large cities, *e.g.* administration, manufacturing, commerce, residence, are becoming increasingly segregated, probably for the general good, but urban life is thereby becoming less integrated and is splitting up into a series of compartments.

Most old towns continue to express the legacy of former periods in their layout; they reveal the past in some of their buildings and in some cases in their prime functions. Yet they are constantly changing, both materially and socially. Roads are widened, disused and obsolete buildings demolished and new ones—in the prevailing architectural style, which is far more international in character than ever before—are erected. The civic hall replaces the early parish church as the principal public building. Special shopping precincts are appearing. Smoke pollution is decreasing before the advance of electricity and gas for heating and driving machinery. More open spaces are being provided in urban areas, and standards of housing and office accommodation are improving. But the countryside is being increasingly eroded by the extension of low-density housing, low-rise factories and car-parking facilities beyond existing municipal boundaries.

THE RISE OF TOWNS IN THE NEW WORLD

The earliest towns in the Americas do not pre-date the Christian era, but in the first millenium A.D. there were a number of flourishing cities in Central America among the Maya and kindred people. They included Tikal in Guatemala, Dzibilchaltun in Yucatan and Teotihuacan near the present Mexico City. A little later, c. A.D. 1000, rose the city of Chichen Itza, built by the Toltec successors of the Maya in Yucatan (see Fig. 41). These places were laid out on a grid-iron plan and were noted for their monumental architecture. They lacked the dry, alluvial setting of the earliest cities in the Old World, and were apparently made possible by the ease with which maize surpluses could be accumulated. They were wealthy enough to support a body of priests, noblemen, astronomers and scholars despite their dependence on agricultural areas which lacked both the wheel and the plough and had no domesticated animals. Further south, in the Andes, the Incas—though in many respects a highly cultured people—were only partially urbanised.

It was Europeans, chiefly French and English in North America, Spaniards and Portuguese in South America, who introduced the idea of the city into most parts of the Americas, and also into other temperate areas where they settled, including Australasia. Apart from the small market towns and service centres which grew up in response to the needs of small communities of farmers and fishermen, the main urban settlements in these new lands came to be seaports followed by seats of internal commerce and manufacturing which gained ground as economic resources were tapped, as shipping routes multiplied and railway meshes

[*Courtesy: Mexican Embassy*

FIG. 41.—Ruins of an early Yucatan city. This photograph, taken in Chichen Itza, the capital of the Toltecs near Merida, Yucatan, shows parts of two buildings which combine characteristics of both the Maya and rather later Toltec architectural styles. They both date from about A.D. 1000. On the right is the pyramid of Kukulkan, or El Castillo, formed from nine superimposed platforms with staircases on each side and a temple at the top. On the left is part of the Temple of the Warriors.

were formed. Ports such as Montreal, Boston, New York, Philadelphia, Rio de Janeiro and Buenos Aires, Melbourne and Sydney, were the first cities to achieve prominence. In later years, as the development of the North American interior proceeded, large inland cities began to emerge, especially in the fast-developing U.S.A. They included Chicago, Detroit, Pittsburgh and St Louis. In South America and Australia the largest cities remain tied to the coast except for a few, notably Bogota, in the northern Andes.

Growing governmental responsibilities gave a fillip to the growth of Washington, and, to a slighter extent, to that of Ottawa, and the peopling of the Pacific coastlands of North America stimulated the growth of Los Angeles, San Francisco, Portland, Seattle and Vancouver. Los Angeles had barely 5,000 people in 1860, and only 100,000 in 1900, but by 1932 it reached 1 million and now houses nearly 7 million in its widely sprawling metropolitan area. Altogether, the United States now has 150 cities of over 100,000, and even Brazil, much of which is virtually empty, has more than 30, including the new capital, Brasilia.

THE GROWTH OF TOWNS IN ASIA AND AFRICA

Both Asia and Africa gave birth to some of the earliest towns in the world. Yet, until recent years, the lack of widespread factory industry and of close rail and road networks over large parts of these continents has severely limited the rise of cities except in a few favoured areas. In large countries such as India and China the typical urban settlement was the agricultural market town before western influences made themselves felt. Great cities such as Calcutta, Bombay, Madras, Canton and Shanghai, to which we might add Rangoon, Singapore and Manila, were all either founded or developed as seaports and entrepôts by western traders and officials who required them as collecting and distributing centres for European trade.

India and China remain essentially farming countries with recent localised injections of Western-type manufacturing. Their chief native cities tend to be either present or former political capitals, e.g. Old Delhi, Agra, Hyderabad, Peking and Nanking, or else religious centres, e.g. Benares. Their smaller market towns—expanded in some cases owing perhaps to their command of a railway junction—often resemble European medieval towns in their general character: they are frequently walled and rely upon the exchange of goods between their craftsmen and local farmers to keep them going.

Japan is much more thoroughly urbanised than either China or India, though here westernisation is only a century old. Despite her comparatively restricted area, Japan now possesses seven "million" cities, and another 125 or so with more than 100,000 people, figures almost comparable with those of the much larger U.S.A. Her largest cities are eminent as seats of manufacturing and commerce, but a number of them, especially Kyoto, Nagoya and Tokyo, have their roots in the past. The first became the political capital of the country as early as A.D. 894, the latter two grew as defensive centres round feudal castles. Tokyo is said to have housed over a million people in 1720, and to have then been larger than any other city in the world except Peking, capital of the Chinese Empire. As in Europe, people from rural areas are now migrating in large numbers into Asiatic cities, but as most are unskilled and uneducated they depend largely upon ill-paid casual work and often have to live in squalor, at least at first, in peripheral "shanty towns" or even on the pavements.

The case of Africa is similar to that of Asia, but in this continent there have always been fewer cities. Most of the indigenous people south of the Sahara had no urban tradition. The Yoruba of western Nigeria, however, were at least partially urbanised: walled towns such as Kano (*see*

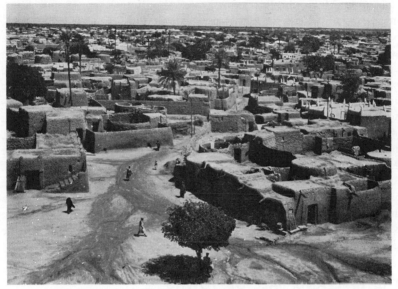

[*A Shell photograph*

Fig. 42.—Kano, Nigeria. Kano, an old, walled town in the dry savannah of northern Nigeria, grew up round a rocky hill overlooking a stream. Its chief buildings are flat-roofed houses built of sun-dried mud, and with few windows. Each has its own compound. The streets are winding and unpaved, as in most pre-industrial towns. East of this old market town is the modern European settlement, with military and administrative quarters and an important airfield.

Fig. 42) and Benin had come into existence as capitals of local native kingdoms in West Africa, and along the east coast, between Mogadishu and Zanzibar, Arab traders had founded several medieval towns which became notorious as slave ports.

Europeans followed the Arabs in establishing strategic bases and ports from which the riches of the interior might be safely plundered. Thus developed such towns as Lagos, Accra and Mombasa. In the mid-seventeenth century Dutch traders selected Cape Town as a supply base for ships plying between Holland and the Far East. Later came a few interior centres of mining and administration, *e.g.* Johannesburg (which has grown into Africa's largest industrial and financial city), Elisabethville (capital of the Katanga mining area), Nairobi (capital of Kenya but originally the headquarters of the Uganda Railway), and Salisbury (capital of Rhodesia, founded as a British South Africa Company post as recently as 1890). Few factory towns have so far been established.

Nearly a quarter of the world's people now live in towns of more than 20,000. In Africa, this fraction is exceeded only in Egypt, South Africa and Senegal, where six of Africa's largest cities are located: Cairo, Alexandria, Johannesburg, Cape Town, Durban and Dakar. The figure, however, is rising as African rulers, with the assistance of planners from Europe and the Americas, are trying to emulate and even improve on the example of white town-builders by erecting cities which will bolster their prestige, often at the expense of their country's rural dwellers. Outside these cities, and outside some of the older Europeanised cities such as Johannesburg, into which country people, especially males, are pouring, unkempt "shanty towns," crowded with temporary workers, are destroying the approach landscape, just as they are in tropical Asia. Again, their replacement by housing estates is too slow. In the more purely African towns—colourful and noisy—services are as few as in many of the shanty towns, and there is much untidiness, but there is far more social cohesion and family life is the norm rather than the exception.

THE RISE AND FALL OF TOWNS

Stress has been laid above on the enlargement of towns as if it were in the nature of urban settlements to expand continually. Each town, however, has its peak period, passed already by some, not yet reached by all. At times, growth may make a sudden spurt, at other times cease altogether or else be replaced by contraction. In 1500, for instance, the world's greatest cities were Constantinople, Paris, Naples, Venice, Milan and Lisbon; Babylon, Memphis, Harappa, all giants of the past, had long been in ruins. By 1800, London had assumed first place, Venice and Naples were in decline, Moscow and Vienna rising. Today, New York and Tokyo at least have surpassed London, and Vienna is less populous than it was. Rome, leading the world in the fourth century A.D., later contracted, but since Italian unification has shot ahead of Milan.

There are, of course, many reasons for the fluctuations in the size of cities. Natural catastrophes such as earthquakes may halt progress at least

THE GROWTH OF TOWNS AND CITIES

for a time, as at Lisbon after 1755, at San Francisco after 1906 and at Tokyo after 1923. Fire gutted much of Chicago in 1871, coastal erosion has removed a number of small towns on the Yorkshire coast, and river and coastal silting allowed Liverpool to replace Chester as the principal port of north-western England. To survive as leading ports, Bristol had to build new docks at Avonmouth, and to improve its commercial and industrial standing, Rotterdam has recently established Europoort (*see* Fig. 81, page 184).

Political changes affect cities as well as countries. Trieste and Hamburg declined when they were cut off from their natural hinterlands by boundary changes; Gdynia grew when, in 1919, Poland was granted a portless corridor to the sea; St Petersburg came into being when Peter the Great, envying Western progress, established his capital there; Bonn, in 1939 known to the outside world simply as the birthplace of Beethoven, has entered upon a new lease of life since it became West Germany's capital; and Ankara has gained at the expense of Istanbul since its selection as the Turkish capital in the 1920s.

The value of a particular site may be enhanced by the finding and exploitation of new sources of minerals, as happened at places on European coalfields in the nineteenth century, and in Near Eastern oilfields in the twentieth. Conversely, minerals may suffer exhaustion or become of diminished value and mining towns may therefore decline, as in western Durham or at places such as Tombstone and Dawson City in the North American West. Site values may also change owing to improvements in trade routes: Kiel was beneficially affected by the opening of the Kiel Canal, Marseilles even more so when the Suez route was inaugurated. Towns on the Great Lakes have expanded since the St Lawrence Seaway was completed, and the growth of traffic on the Rhine has reinvigorated Antwerp.

New towns and cities, as we have seen, have emerged, owing to changing human needs and desires, with the help of rapid and close communications. Such are the many holiday resorts and overspill towns in advanced countries, and industrial and transport towns in more under-developed lands.

URBANISATION

Past centuries have witnessed the birth of thousands of towns and cities, many of which have greatly expanded during the last hundred years. The process continues at an accelerating rate. The present world population explosion is accompanied by an urban explosion as more and more people, in almost every country, flock to the towns (*see* Fig. 43). The word "urbanisation" is used to signify the concentration of an increasing proportion of society into towns and cities and to indicate the processes by which it is brought about.

As a social phenomenon, this proliferation of towns in countries which until recently have been almost wholly rural, and the expansion of

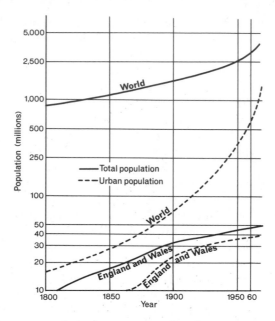

FIG. 43.—The progress of urbanisation. As is evident from this graph, the growth of urbanisation in the world as a whole has been more rapid during the last century and a half than the general growth of population. In England and Wales, the proportion of people living in towns reached 77 per cent in 1900 and 80 per cent in 1931. It declined slightly between 1951 and 1961.

existing towns in both old and new countries is of great significance in the study of settlements. It is clearly associated with the spread of manufacturing, commerce and service industries and with the improvement of rural techniques which call for less field labour. It has been made possible in some countries by the growth of commerce resulting from agricultural specialisation and the production of increased food surpluses, which owing to transport developments, can be more widely distributed, and in other countries it has been effected by rapid industrialisation.

Urbanisation raises many problems: it threatens the extent of the world's agricultural area, it exacerbates the water supply and waste-disposal situation, it produces almost incurable traffic problems, and it creates obvious targets for aerial attack. Yet its pace increases.

Different Degrees of Urbanisation

In 1965 about 30 per cent of the world's population was reckoned as urban; a quarter lived in towns of more than 20,000 people, an increase of 40 per cent in fifteen years; an eighth were housed in towns of over 100,000; and 4 per cent occupied cities of at least 1 million. If the rate of urban increase reached in the decade 1955–65 continues, by 1990 over half the world's people will be living in cities of at least 100,000, and by 2000 a third may be residing in "million" cities. In the older indus-trialised countries such as Britain and Germany, and also in areas of recent colonisation by north Europeans such as Australia, Argentina, California, Canada and the Soviet Far East, there is only a comparatively small demand for farm labour, but a great outcry for industrial workers, and for people skilled in transport, commerce, administration and the pro-fessions. In these lands, the percentage of the population classed as urban lies between 70 per cent and over 80 per cent. The form taken by urbanisation, however, is not the same: in the older countries many small and medium-sized towns, mostly pre-dating modern industrialisation, remain, whereas in the newer advanced countries there has never been a need for numerous market towns, and therefore a larger proportion of the population in these lands inhabit very large cities.

In countries where peasant farming is still important, where agricul-tural capital is lacking, and where there has been little, if any, urban tradition (*e.g.* Uganda, Kenya, Tanzania and the Sudan in Africa, India, Pakistan and China in Asia), the urban percentage, though rising rapidly, is still low: less than 5 per cent in Uganda, barely 20 per cent in India.

In the so-called "backward," "under-developed" or "developing" countries, especially in those where economic progress, in particular industrial advance, is now dynamic, the urban population is growing much more rapidly than the total population. Between 1900 and 1950, the world's population grew by 50 per cent, but the urban population rose by 240 per cent. The increase was particularly marked in the tropical world, where cities now have the advantage of declining mor-tality rates, which allows them to expand by natural increase as well as by rural–urban migration.

What do rural people seek when they migrate into the towns? Besides employment and material progress, they expect better educational pro-vision, more medical care and more amusement, access to electric lighting and freedom from the drudgery and monotony of country life. Unfortunately, they do not always find what they want, for the towns are not able to accommodate all of them. There may be no jobs at all available for some, and only casual employment for others; it may be harder to obtain food, and transport may have to be paid for; there may be no houses or none within their means, and it may be necessary to build their own pitiable shack on the town outskirts; services such as water and electricity may stop where the "shanty" town begins. Disappointment, succeeded by despair, may replace expectation.

In countries which are more advanced economically, the percentage of people living in towns is increasing more slowly, if at all, most of the phenomenal growth having already been experienced. Britain, the first country to undergo rapid and unrestrained urban growth, had 77 per cent of its population living in towns as far back as 1900; by 1930 the figure had become stabilised at about 80 per cent (Fig. 43). Indeed, between 1951 and 1961 the urban percentage fell slightly as some town-dwellers moved into rural districts fringing the towns. The same is true, to a lesser extent, of Germany and the United States. In all three countries, suburbanisation is now largely replacing urbanisation. There is also much inter-urban movement, many people in England, for example, leaving the older industrial parts of northern England and taking up work and residence in the expanding towns of south-east England and the Midlands. Also, while the total urban population is not now growing very markedly, the urban area is still expanding quite rapidly, as housing densities decline. In England and Wales the total urban area doubled between 1900 and 1960, and between 1931 and 1951, while the total population grew by 5 per cent, the numbers of houses increased by over 30 per cent. Fortunately, the total agricultural production, through intensification, is keeping pace with the loss of land. By 2000 it is expected that 16 per cent of the total area of England and Wales will be in urban use. The figure is expected to be similar in the U.S.A., a much larger country. Fortunately for British people, planning controls are more effective in limiting urban sprawl than in the U.S.A. and—partly to limit farmland losses and partly to offset the increasing cost of farmland for building—higher housing densities are now being accepted.

The World's Main Urban Regions

Some parts of the world, as we have seen, are highly urbanised even though individual towns and cities are far apart. Such areas are Australia, New Zealand, the shorelands of Brazil, Chile and Venezuela, most of Canada, and the central and western parts of the U.S.A. and Argentina. In most of these areas, the very large cities are coastal or at least situated on navigable water, and there are relatively few inland towns of any note.

In certain other areas, though the urban proportion of the total population may be no higher, and in some cases even lower, there is a much closer massing of people into more numerous towns and cities. These are the more fully urbanised regions. They include: (*a*) north-western Europe as far north as 60°N, and northern Italy; (*b*) north-eastern U.S.A. and the immediately adjacent part of Canada; (*c*) Japan, excluding northern Honshu and Hokkaido. In all these areas, town and city life is supported by large-scale factory industry, an unusually large volume of internal and external commerce, and the closest networks of communications in the world. Living standards are much higher than the world average, and there is wealth enough to allow large numbers of people to engage in service occupations. The fact that a high degree of urbanisation goes hand in hand with material progress is one of the main reasons why urbanisation is now proceeding so vigorously in the poorer parts of the world.

Chapter VI

Towns and Cities as Landscape Elements

THE DIVERSITY OF TOWNSCAPES

It has already been noted (pp. 10–11) that towns are the most striking features of the human landscape. Something has already been written in Chapter V about the appearance of certain typical urban settlements: the small medieval town, the Renaissance state capital and fortified place, the industrial town and the modern town. Here, we intend to examine further the urban landscape, or "townscape" as it has been appropriately called. We shall find that the principal influences that have acted upon it include changing architectural styles and building materials, site and function, history and culture, but we shall have to take into account the contribution made by conscious and deliberate planning as well as the natural course of growth.

The evidence for the diversity of townscapes is found chiefly in buildings, street patterns and people. Buildings vary in size, shape and height, and thus they determine the "skyscape" (i.e. the horizontal profile of the town), the materials of which they are made, their architectural style and their function. If planned, street patterns most frequently form a rectangular grid though some plans give rise to radial patterns; most patterns—possibly following old field boundaries—are irregular. In old towns, streets are often narrow, in newer ones broad; squares and circles such as were added to many towns in the seventeenth and eighteenth centuries may break up their continuity and so give variety to the townscape. People vary ethnically and linguistically, in their religious and social customs, in their economic status and occupations: they, too, add to the diversity of townscapes.

Contrast the skyscraper city of North America with the agrarian town of the Yoruba in western Nigeria; the nineteenth-century industrial town of northern England with the older country market town; the face of Edinburgh with that of Glasgow; the "civil lines" of a town in British India with the "shanty town" of South Africa; the grid-iron plan of the U.S. town with the indiscriminate formlessness of the Chinese market town. It would seem that these urban settlements have nothing in common. Yet if we isolate the towns of a single region or a particular historical period we find that many similar features do exist, and it is these common features which need special emphasis.

European Towns

Like towns in other parts of the world, European towns vary both regionally and historically, though some aspects of the townscape are more enduring than others. Ewart Johns (in *British Townscapes*) draws our attention to three major zones in Europe, each marked by a particular type of townscape:

1. Southern Europe, where the urban landscape is "boldly exposed, calm and clear-cut," showing both the incisiveness of Greece and the boldness of Rome. This Classical type of townscape, with its straight horizontal line, has persisted throughout historical time in Mediterranean Europe. Garnier and Chabot (in *Urban Geography*) stress the value of the narrow streets, thick walls, high ceilings, paved or tiled rooms, north-facing buildings, roofed balconies and courtyards, with their greenery or their fountains, as devices which enable townspeople to escape from the summer heat.

2. Northern Europe, where the townscape is "protected, vigorous and involved," and where the "line" is predominantly vertical but irregular. Towns often appear organic in origin whether rising from low hill sites or from plains. According to Johns they exemplify the strife between priest, trader and prince, out of which evolved the Romantic style of architecture with its tall, narrow, steep-gabled houses and soaring Gothic churches.

3. Central Europe, where the townscape shows a mingling of southern and northern traditions, the firm line of southern buildings being softened, and the more vigorous and tougher quality of the north made more tender and restful, as, for example, in Switzerland. The richest building style is found in Austria, and owes much to the splendour of the great imperial rulers and the power of the Church. From these elements has evolved the rich, massive, Baroque landscape, found also in Italy and elsewhere during the period following the Renaissance.

In most European countries, whatever their continental location, elements of the Classical and Romantic styles are evident, the Baroque style making a more occasional appearance, especially in churches and palaces. In Britain, for example, at least half the major public buildings display the Classical style of Greece and Rome, but in domestic buildings Romantic aspects are generally more common. Gardens, however, are

FIG. 44.—Elm Hill, Norwich. Enclaves of medieval date, or, as here, of Tudor origin, are still to be found in many historic market towns in western Europe. This typical street is curved, narrow and cobbled. The houses—carefully restored by the corporation—are of colour-washed plaster and timber, their roofs tiled. Both roof and wall lines are irregular.

more often than not formal and geometric, and the terraces of industrial England are as symmetrical, but far less elegant, than the earlier Georgian terraces of well-to-do residential areas. Present day office "slabs" and high-rise flats, though geometrically severe, often show in their irregular layout (*e.g.* in central Coventry and Birmingham) Romantic tendencies. The Romantic elements characteristic of some of the newest suburban areas and of many of the residential neighbourhoods of British New Towns seem to express the desire felt by most people to live half in the country, half in the town.

In detail, one British town differs markedly from another. Many of these contrasts may be ascribed to differences in site, function, architecture and history. Some towns, *e.g.* Chester, York, Alnwick, Norwich (*see* Fig. 44) and Warwick, still possess a medieval core, with narrow meandering streets and unevenly shaped buildings. In Lavenham (Suffolk) most of the buildings pre-date 1500 and attract many artists and tourists in search of old-world charm. Other towns, *e.g.* Bath, Edinburgh (New Town), Brighton, Cheltenham, Buxton (*see* Fig. 45), and Leamington, display many fine examples of upper middle-class residential squares and crescents, broad avenues and parks, which show eighteenth- and early nineteenth-century town planning at its best. The most typical feature of the nineteenth-century industrial town is probably not so much the factories and warehouses in themselves as the juxtaposition of industrial works and

FIG. 45.—The Crescent, Buxton. Modelled upon the Royal Crescent at Bath, and having its counterpart in other inland health resorts, the Crescent in Buxton is situated in the centre of the spa between the Thermal and Natural Baths, and facing St Ann's Well. The Natural Baths occupy the site of a Roman Bath which attracted the town's first visitors. The Crescent was erected in the 1780s by the fifth Duke of Devonshire and is an excellent example of formal, Classical architecture.

long, parallel rows of stereotyped working-class terraced houses, some-times back-to-back.

All these towns, however different in appearance, have certain features in common. Retail shops and business premises are concentrated near the centre, close to the main traffic nodes, and the newer, higher-class resi-dential areas occupy the suburbs, as in most European and North

[*Courtesy: Norwegian National Tourist Office*

FIG. 46.—Bergen, Norway. Bergen, a town of 120,000 people, is Norway's second city and leading fishing port. It retains many fine merchant houses dating from the Hanseatic period, which lasted from the fifteenth to the eighteenth century. Some of these buildings, together with part of the harbour and market, are shown here. They attract numerous visitors, in spite of Bergen's reputation as a rainy place.

American towns. These towns, moreover, are beginning to resemble each other more and more, not only because building materials and structural methods are becoming more uniform the world over, but because of the crowding out of local retailers by multiple stores, each with its distinctive fascia, all alike, except perhaps for scale, in every town.

Modern plans, especially for urban renewal, include in almost all cases, the building of tall office blocks, often with retail businesses on the ground floor. Planning itself, of course, especially on an *ad hoc* basis, is not new. Many towns in France still preserve, if no longer in their buildings, the street plan of a Roman camp. The market-place frequently stands at the crossing of the main Roman roads, and is overlooked by the cathedral or large church, the former focus of city life. In Flanders and the Rhineland, historic guild-halls often usurp the position of the Church in France. The old Hanseatic trading cities, *e.g.* Bergen and Lübeck, tend to be dominated by the houses of the great merchants (*see* Fig. 46). In Hungary, the "agrovilles," such as Szegedin and Debreczin, while possessing the usual commercial nucleus, are largely a mass of farmers' dwellings. They are, in effect, overgrown villages, a response to the need for protection from the Turkish invasions of the sixteenth century. In Spain, the influence of the Moslem occupation is still observable in the narrow, winding streets of many cities and in the architecture of the former town walls and mosques.

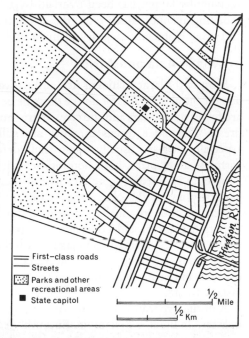

FIG. 47.—Central Albany, New York. This plan of part of the central area of Albany, capital of New York State, shows the grid-iron street pattern, only slightly modified, typical of the New World. In towns such as these the buildings take the form of rectangular blocks.

First—class roads
Streets
Parks and other recreational areas
State capitol

½ Mile
½ Km

Towns in North America

When one turns from Europe to North America, one is immediately struck by the newness of most of the cities. With a few exceptions, *e.g.* Quebec, New Orleans and Boston, few buildings are older than the eighteenth century, and most belong to the present one. Other distinguishing features are the widespread use of the grid-iron plan, which gives rise to straight thoroughfares and rectangular blocks (as is shown in Fig. 47); the "downtown" dominance of the skyscraper; the congestion of the unwavering "Main Street," with its modern shop fronts and ubiquitous neon signs; and the very open character of the spacious, green, residential suburbs, with their brick or clap-board houses and their contrastingly low skylines.

These monotonous characteristics, so different from the variety of the European townscape, are epitomised in the market towns of the agricultural interior, but they are also found in cities such as San Francisco, where the rectilinear plan, insensitively ignoring the contours of the steep peninsular site, has resulted in many precipitous streets. A number of recently constructed freeways, slung and looped through the city, maintain gentler gradients. In the capital, Washington (*see* Fig. 129, p. 288), the original rectangular layout has been overlaid by a functional axis and a series of radiating avenues which recall the disposition of Versailles and Karlsruhe and other eighteenth-century planned towns in Europe.

Towns in Asia and Africa

Most of the largest cities in Asia and Africa have now been Westernised. Their central parts are not unlike those of European cities except that there are fewer motor-cars and the crowds are more colourful in both body and dress. The older towns in what are still predominantly rural areas, especially in Asia, usually retain their defensive walls or ditches, their formless street plans, high housing densities and low skylines. Wealthy people, as in Europe, generally live in their own quarters, but these are generally nearer the centre than in European towns. The artisans and merchants, too, are usually segregated, though there may be a number of dispersed markets and commercial districts. In Africa, the few native towns resemble overgrown villages, with their irregularly spaced huts and compounds, and artisans and shopkeepers are more scattered. Factory districts and central business districts are now developing, especially in Asiatic towns.

A distinctive feature of many Asiatic and African towns is the European quarter. In India, for example, European sections grew up in both "civil" and "military lines" (or cantonments), either outside the existing walls or in some other way removed from the native town, *e.g.* across a railway track. Bungalows, administrative buildings, business premises, clubs, hospitals, and so on, were all laid out in orderly fashion and with generous spacing and well-kept gardens, and formed a marked contrast to the congested, untidy, native city. In Chinese commercial ports, *e.g.* Shanghai, and in other Eastern trading cities such as Singapore, the "bund" was characteristic and has now become the business centre (*see* Fig. 48). It consists of an amalgam of docks, waterfront highway, warehouses, offices and banks, now often in the form of skyscrapers. In Africa, European quarters are again aloof from the native towns. They lie alongside, but separate from, the indigenous settlements with their narrow paths and poorly made, low huts. Dakar, Kano and the north-west African countries furnish good examples.

Another characteristic which distinguishes many Asiatic and African cities, especially those which are growing rapidly, is the "shanty town"

[*Courtesy: Singapore Ministry of Culture*

FIG. 48.—Singapore. This photograph shows part of the waterfront or "bund" at Singapore, with its monumental commercial buildings built in European style and symbolising the international trade relations of this great entrepôt. The port is almost entirely a British creation, and hardly existed before 1819, when Sir Stamford Raffles persuaded the Sultan of Johore to cede it to Britain.

or *bidonville*, an unhappy contrast to the city suburb of the richer continents, and supportable only because most of the countries where it exists have a hot climate. Shanty towns are not confined to Africa and Asia: they are very common in South America, where names such as *favella* (Brazil), *barrio* (Venezuela), *callampa* (Chile) and *villa de miseria* (Argentina) are applied to them. They result from the excessively rapid movement of people from country to town in search of industrial employment. They lack permanent buildings, made roads, piped water, sewers, electricity, and so on. There are no schools and often an absence of shops.

[*Courtesy: Unesco/P. A. Pittet*

FIG. 49.—Porto-Novo, Dahomey. Porto-Novo, capital of Dahomey, like most
urban settlements in Africa, is a mixture of substantial buildings and shanty
dwellings. The closely clustered houses and shacks in the foreground of this
photograph are insanitary as well as unkempt. Their walls are mostly built of
sun-dried mud, their roofs of thatch or corrugated iron. There is an open sewer
on the left, but some attempt has been made at street paving.

Health suffers, and the living accommodation, often built of nothing
better than odd pieces of timber, tar-paper and hessian, easily catches fire.
(*see* Fig. 49). Such temporary settlements are only slowly being replaced
by permanent dwellings, usually in the form of tall blocks of flats, as in
Rio de Janeiro and Hong Kong.

THE CHANGING SKYLINE

From a distance, the appearance of a town is often heralded by its
skyline. American cities grow vertically in their central areas while
their residential areas spread horizontally, generally without a transitional
zone. Pre-industrial cities in all continents lack variety in their low skylines except where a mosque, temple or church breaks the profile, while
most European towns have a varied but graded skyline. The beauty which
a skyline may lend to a city is well shown in Oxford: "city of dreaming

spires." More highly industrialised towns have forests of tall chimneys and electricity cooling towers as their chief landmarks.

Until recently, tall buildings, outrivalling church spires and factory chimneys, were a rarity in Europe, despite the pressure on urban land. But lofty office blocks, often in the form of "slabs", are now replacing lower commercial and administrative premises, and towering blocks of flats are superseding many slum dwellings as urban renewal proceeds. Vast in their dimensions and capable of housing—for work or leisure—hundreds, even thousands, of people, such buildings are reducing urban sprawl but creating almost insuperable traffic problems.

Until a few years ago, Paris limited its new buildings to eight storeys, and London tried to preserve its traditional profile by avoiding the American skyscraper influence. Japan, too, because of the constant threat of earthquakes, restricted the height of its buildings. Now, with the aid of steel, reinforced concrete and other materials, e.g. glass and aluminium, which may be used for "cladding," lofty structures are reaching upwards in all continents. New York retains the worlds' tallest building: the Empire State Building, of 102 storeys, is 1,250 ft (381 m) high. London's Centre Point is of 35 storeys and the G.P.O. telecommunications tower is 620 ft (189 m) high. Paris is building a 50-storey office building, and Tokyo now boasts a 482·ft (147 m) high block. No longer are cathedrals, city halls and palaces necessarily the most striking accents in otherwise undistinguished urban skylines.

It is now technically feasible to construct a "vertical city" two miles high and capable of providing enough space for living, working and recreation to satisfy no less than 250,000 people. Is this a vision of the future city?

THE INFLUENCE OF SITE UPON THE APPEARANCE OF TOWNS

How far is the arrangement of buildings and streets responsible for the townscape? What effect has the physical setting? Certainly we cannot ignore the influence of the natural environment. Compare Scarborough (see Fig. 60, p. 137) and Llandudno and their bold headlands with Blackpool on its flat beach; the incised meander and steep slopes of Durham (see Fig. 57, p. 133) with the milder setting of York; the undistinguished countryside in which Brasilia is being constructed with the magnificent waterfront situation of its predecessor, Rio (see Fig. 50); the linear development of colliery towns in South Wales, penned into their narrow valleys between empty moorlands, with the flatter sites of the newer mining villages of

[*Courtesy: British United Airways*

FIG. 50.—Rio de Janeiro. This panoramic view of Rio, taken from Corcovado Peak (*c.* 2,000 ft (600 m)) shows the spectacular natural setting of the harbour and the control which relief has exerted on the built-up area. In the right centre is the well-known Sugar Loaf Mountain (*c.* 1,200 ft, (366 m)).

Derbyshire and Nottinghamshire; Venice, set on a number of small islands, its streets waterways, with Rome on its seven hills. Was the Italian who wrote: "See Naples and then die" thinking of the beauty of its buildings and the layout of its streets, or of its physical setting, in the shadow of Vesuvius, or both? Certainly the atmosphere or "feel" of a place does not depend solely on its constructional details, nor on its cultural character, but also on the physical environment.

THE EFFECT OF FUNCTION UPON THE APPEARANCE OF TOWNS

Towns vary according to their function as well as the details of their historical growth, culture and site. Manufacturing towns form a distinctive class, but the kind of industry they specialise in brings variety. Textile towns, for example, are commonly distinguished by tall spinning mills and by weaving sheds, usually lower, with their serrated roofs glazed on the north sides. Metallurgical towns are dominated by huge chimneys and blast furnaces, casting a glow on the night sky. Though now giving way to gas- or electrically-fired works, the bottle-kilns of Stoke-on-Trent have given the city its own individuality as a pottery town (*see* Fig. 91, p. 201).

Political capitals reflect the wealth, power, prestige and political organ-isation of the state to which they belong. Typical of such towns are impressive government buildings, museums, theatres, art galleries, large hospitals, massive office blocks, and usually extensive university buildings. They are generally the show-places of their countries, and contrive wherever possible to provide broad vistas, so that their principal edifices are set off to the best advantage.

Port cities, though in detail showing much diversity, normally reveal their main function through their extensive loading and unloading facili-ties, piers, quays and docks, cranes, warehouses and railway sidings, waterfront factories and marine stores. Resort towns, by contrast, are characterised by widespread recreational facilities, numerous hotels and high-class shops, freedom from industrial pollution and consequent cleanliness, and an air of gay abandon.

THE DISTRIBUTION AND SPACING OF TOWNS

Like population itself, the distribution of towns owes much to the effects of relief, climate, mineral resources, road and rail communications, and the pattern of trade. Broadly speaking, cities avoid areas of high relief and cling to the valleys and lowlands, they shun the very cold and arid areas, they are attracted to large mineral deposits (in the nineteenth and early twentieth centuries, especially to coal resources), they seek out navigable rivers, roads and railways, or grow larger and more numerous if sited on roads and railways, and they develop at terminal shipping points.

In well-developed areas, especially in areas whose wealth comes mainly from manufacturing and commerce, towns tend to be numerous, whilst in poorly developed areas they are few. Thus, in most of Europe they are well distributed, especially south of 60° N, but in the southern continents they are mainly confined to coastal localities.

The Central Place Theory

Leaving aside such settlements as mining and industrial towns, tourist resorts, political capitals, seaports and strategic bases, which demand special site requirements or positional needs, we find in a prosperous agricultural area, e.g. the U.S. Middle West, that small market towns normally form a close, fairly even pattern, larger ones a more open one, and regional capitals a very open one. These towns, unlike the more speci-alised ones noted above, are "central places" whose main function is to provide services for people living in the surrounding area. They are places, for example, which farmers and their wives can visit easily for shopping, diversion and professional advice and from which they can conveniently return home the same day. Clearly they form a hierarchy of locations in terms of accessibility, measured both by travel time and transport costs. The larger towns supply virtually all the goods and services of the smaller, but add some of their own, perhaps in the shape of a University, stock exchange, large departmental store, hospital or branch of a national bank.

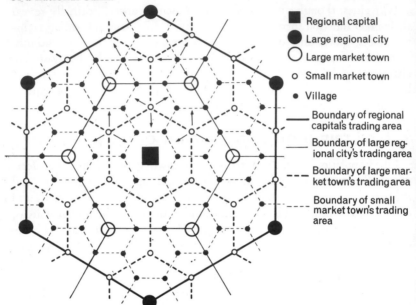

■ Regional capital
● Large regional city
○ Large market town
o Small market town
• Village
—— Boundary of regional capital's trading area
—— Boundary of large regional city's trading area
– – – Boundary of large market town's trading area
- - - Boundary of small market town's trading area

FIG. 51.—Christaller's primary lattice. This diagram shows part of the regular hexagonal lattice which Christaller postulated to demonstrate his theoretical distribution and hierarchy of central places and their spheres of influence. The kind of area in which such a pattern of settlements might be expected to develop would be one in which the terrain, resources, population and purchasing power were evenly distributed, and in which movement was equally easy in all directions.

According to many urban geographers such central places should ideally be spread uniformly over a geographical region. W. Christaller, whose work in 1933 (*Die Zentralen Orte in Suddeutschland*) pioneered many urban studies, postulated a hexagonal lattice as the best means of showing their theoretical distribution (*see* Fig. 51). He believed that such a hierarchical distribution would develop in an area where population and purchasing power are uniformly distributed, where the terrain is homogeneous, the resources evenly spread, and where transport is equally easy in all directions. The service areas of Christaller's settlements would assume a hexagonal shape (because circular shapes would leave gaps or produce overlaps), the better equipped towns, *i.e.* the higher order places, being centred in the largest hexagons. These higher order places would therefore have larger populations and serve more people than lower order places. Each higher order settlement (*e.g.* a town) would serve the equivalent of three settlements of the next lower order (say, a village) and so on. (The number "three," according to Christaller, comprises the village part of the functional structure of the town itself, together with a third share of the six border villages, since each of the latter is divided by three towns.) He felt, therefore, that the progression in the number of settlements serving as central places at various ranking levels would be one, three, nine, twenty-seven, eighty-one, and so on. Thus his highest order city (the chief urban centre in the region) would serve three towns of the second rank, nine of the third, twenty-seven of the fourth, and so on.

Christaller recognised that in reality his model is too rigid and abstract. He was aware that homogeneous areas hardly ever exist in nature; nevertheless, his model fairly well fits southern Germany, to which he himself applied it.

The following factors distort the mathematical simplicity of Christaller's pattern: (*a*) settlements aligned on important routes and acting as transport centres, which tend to form a linear distribution pattern; (*b*) clusters which owe their existence, not to their ability to perform central place functions, but to their development as "non-central places," *e.g.* mining, manufacturing and recreational centres. These towns are located at "points" where special resources are available, *e.g.* minerals, raw materials or power supplies, a sea-beach or a stretch of spectacular scenery.

In sum, the distribution and size of towns in most areas follows no precise pattern. In fact, the distribution appears on a preliminary examination to be entirely random because it is subject to so many different and contradictory factors. Even the most significant of these, distance or accessibility, operates in many ways, *e.g.* distance from market, raw material, power supply and scenic attraction. The pattern is also governed by such matters as the extent to which railways and roads have been laid down and the routes they follow, the purchasing power of the people and the number of motor-cars owned by a community, the standard of material culture, and the stage of economic development attained. It is, however, true that the larger agglomerations are located in the most desirable and accessible places, and that smaller towns tend to be more numerous and therefore closer together than the larger. Spacing is also generally widest in areas of extensive commercial farming, low population density, and little manufacturing.

THE ACTUAL AND OPTIMUM SIZE OF TOWNS

Peter Hall suggests (in *The World Cities*) that in 1960 the largest metropolitan centres in the world, New York-north-eastern New Jersey, and Tokyo-Yokohama, had populations of 14.7 and 13.6 million respectively, though not every statistician would agree with his figures. At the same time, a large number of small towns housed less than 2,000 people.

Clearly, urban settlements differ greatly in size, as measured by their populations. Is there a theoretical maximum size and an optimum size? Griffith Taylor (in *Urban Geography*) and others believe that the ultimate size may be fixed by the increasing difficulty of obtaining enough water to supply unduly large numbers concentrated in a small area, while Lewis Mumford (*op. cit.*) joins those who think that the continued growth of very large cities not only produces more administrative problems than benefits, but also paralyses rather than furthers social relationships, and raises central land values so much that land ceases to be adaptable to new needs. Hence the policies recently adopted by many governments, including the British, to restrict the outward spread and growing populations of their major cities.

Views on the optimum size of a city have altered with the march of history. Plato believed that the most desirable size was 5,000, a figure which would allow everybody to hear the voice of an orator and so participate in active political life and develop varied social relations. Late nineteenth-century garden city enthusiasts in Britain thought that towns of 30,000 to 50,000 would be large enough to supply all necessary human needs, whether medical, educational, social, economic or cultural. The early New Town planners had similar ideas, at least for towns near a metropolis, *e.g.* London or Glasgow, but later planners have raised the figure to about 250,000. It is generally recognised, however, that towns of this size would face far more difficulty in fostering the civic spirit than smaller ones, might cause the *per capita* cost of providing municipal services to rise, and might create undesirable traffic congestion, and an objectionable lengthening of the journey to work.

In Britain, the Department of Education and Science believes that a town of less than 60,000 cannot satisfactorily support a secondary grammar school or technical college. That figure seems also to be crucial for the maintenance of a live theatre, and an adequate range of specialised shops and denominational churches. Such a town, if of open-housing density, would be about three miles across.

PRIMATE CITIES

Most countries have one very large city—the "primate" city—which is also usually the political capital, as well as many much smaller ones ("The Law of the Primate City," by Mark Jefferson, *Geographical Review*). The primate city, having achieved its high rank, tends to extend its influence and importance by attracting the greatest talents and enterprises of the country, and by acquiring the finest theatres, museums, luxury shops, and so on, until it comes to be the clearest expression of a country's culture, and perhaps also of its commerce and its national feeling.

The primate city is characteristically between three and four times the size of the second city, but ratios, as is clear from Fig. 52, vary widely: from seventeen in Uruguay and more than ten in Hungary and Argentina to less than one and a half in Italy, the Netherlands, Yugoslavia, China, India, Syria, Canada, Brazil, Australia and some other countries. On the whole, larger states have the lower ratios and often at least two rival metropolises, *e.g.* Montreal and Toronto in Canada, Sydney and Melbourne in Australia. It is notable that—for a variety of reasons, mainly deliberate selection—the primate city is not the political capital in such countries as the United States, Canada, Brazil, Australia, South Africa, Morocco, India, Pakistan, Turkey and Switzerland. In these states, the capital may still have cultural as well as administrative prestige, and the role of the primate city is thereby weakened.

THE CONCEPT OF A HIERARCHY OF TOWNS

Most urban geographers believe, with Christaller (*see* p. 118), that towns may be grouped into hierarchical classes according to their size and the functions they perform. Others believe there are no distinct grades, but only a continuum. Even those who recognise a distinct series of levels, tend to concentrate on the importance of central place functions as distinct from others, and they also admit that no particular ranking is universally applicable and that the decision as to where to draw the dividing lines is somewhat arbitrary.

The 1851 census of Great Britain recognised, out of 815 existing towns, three main categories: (*a*) the small market town which country people could visit weekly, (*b*) the county town, where the leaders of society could gather more occasionally, and (*c*) the large towns in the metropolitan area round London. The census, however, acknowledged that this simple grading was being disturbed by growing industrialisation, and

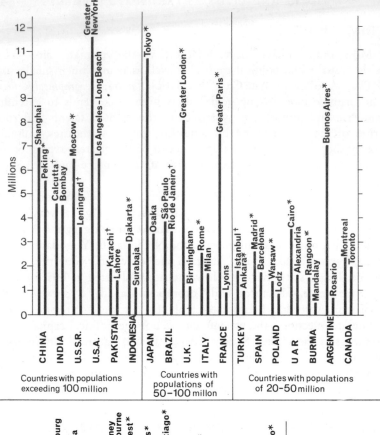

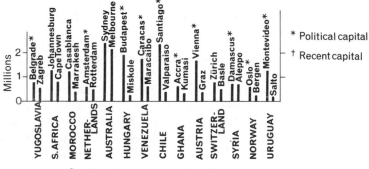

FIG. 52.—Primate cities. All the countries illustrated in these graphs have a dominant or "primate" city, in which much of the country's material and cultural wealth is concentrated. Some countries, however, both small and large, have at least two cities which rival each other for supremacy. One of those is, in nearly all cases, the present or a recent capital.

by the development of watering-places, mining towns and ports. Newer censuses place more emphasis on administrative status, and distinguish rather between county borough, municipal borough and urban district than between market town and county town. Certainly nowadays many county towns, like many state capitals in the U.S.A., are of less demographic consequence than other urban settlements within their own administrative areas.

Methods of Determining Urban Hierarchies

The determination of urban hierarchies, generally limited to between three and six classes, has been based on a varied list of criteria, depending upon the size of the urban field served. Using as his main index the number of telephones per 1,000 inhabitants in the central places of southern Germany, Christaller recognised the existence, not only of market hamlets, but also of small township centres, county seats, district cities, small state capitals, provincial head cities and regional capitals. Other suggested German rankings, based on the fact that structural changes and internal organisations vary with population, are: county towns (average population 2–5,000), small towns (5–20,000), medium-sized towns (20–100,000) and cities (over 100,000).

R. E. Dickinson (*op. cit*), writing about France, distinguishes between: (*a*) *la bourgade* (the market town or canton centre, with perhaps less than 2,000 people); (*b*) *le centre local* (the local centre, averaging 5,000 people), (*c*) *la ville maîtresse* (generally the *chef-lieu* of a department, e.g. Chartres and Perigueux, with 30–50,000 people), and (*d*) *la capitale régionale* (the regional capital, e.g. Toulouse, Bordeaux, Rennes, Nantes, Strasbourg).

F. H. W. Green* and A. E. Smailes,† in England, use different methods of determining a hierarchy, but come to roughly the same conclusions. The former uses the number of bus services to places smaller than the originating centre, the latter the general institutions and functional equipment of a town, e.g. numbers of banks, presence of large stores (especially Woolworth's),‡ the existence of a cinema, newspaper, secondary school, hospital, varied places of worship, employment exchange and head post office. Green adopts the following hierarchy above his "service village": standard or ordinary regional centre, major regional centre (*e.g.* Ipswich, Taunton, York and Exeter), provincial capital (Birmingham, Manchester,

* "Urban Hinterlands in England and Wales" (*Geographical Journal*).
† "The Urban Hierarchy of England and Wales" (*Geography*).
‡ David Thorpe, of Durham University, questions whether it was the town that led Woolworth's to establish a branch in it, or whether the establishment of a Woolworth's store encouraged other retailers to open shops there and so to make it into a fully-fledged town.

Liverpool, Bristol, Leeds, Newcastle, Cardiff, Norwich), and the metropolitan capital (London). Besides "sub-towns," Smailes has small towns, minor cities or major towns (including many industrial centres such as Huddersfield, and several resort towns such as Blackpool), large

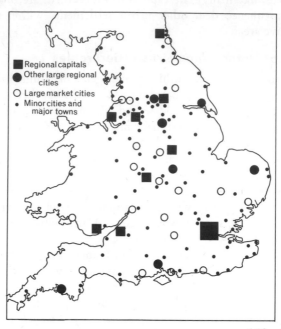

[*After A. E. Smailes*

FIG. 53.—Hierarchy of large towns in England and Wales. This map, based on A. E. Smailes' paper (see p. 123), shows the distribution of the principal towns and cities in England and Wales according to the hierarchical principle. There is a marked concentration of large cities in a broad belt extending from Greater London to central Lancashire.

market cities (*e.g.* Ipswich and Gloucester), provincial cities of great regional importance (Norwich, Southampton, Plymouth, Hull, Sheffield, Bradford and Leicester), regional capitals (Birmingham, Bristol, Cardiff, Leeds, Liverpool, Manchester, Newcastle and Nottingham) and London. The distribution of the top four of these categories is shown in Fig. 53.

Emrys Jones (*op. cit*), following A. W. Ashby and using a simple "shopping index" applied to a farmer and his family, produces the following hierarchy, which, like Christaller's scheme, and many classifications emanating from the United States, introduces the element of distance as well as rank:

Settlement	Distance from farm	Requirements satisfied
Village/Small town	3–8 miles (5–13 km)	Food necessities, sweets, tobacco
Small town	10 miles (16 km)	Household goods, working clothes
Large town	10–30 miles (16–48 km)	Children's clothing
Larger town	15–30 miles (24–48 km)	Better clothing
Provincial centre	50–100 miles (80–160 km)	Display clothing, better furniture
City	100–150 miles (160–240 km)	Expensive jewellery

Emrys Jones agrees, like most British researchers, that London is unique, and completely unrivalled by any other British city. It serves the whole of Britain, not only in government but also in entertainment, various specialist facilities (*e.g.* in hospitals, museums and libraries) and the most luxurious retail commodities.

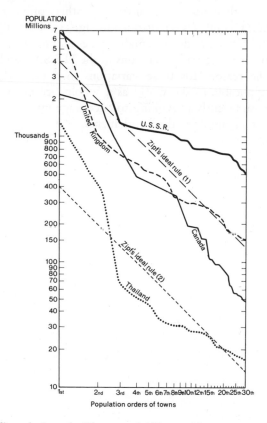

FIG. 54.—Zipf's rank-size rule. These graphs illustrate the extent to which the order of the thirty largest towns in four widely separated countries departs from the rank-size postulated by G. K. Zipf. Both axes of the graph are divided logarithmically.

Zipf's Rank-size Rule

G. K. Zipf's rank-size rule is a useful corrective to those who seek to establish in an excessively rigid form, with pronounced breaks, an arbitrary classification of cities based on their local or regional significance. (G. K. Zipf, *Human Behaviour and the Principle of Least Effort*). He suggests that, broadly speaking, there is a tendency for the populations of cities to descend regularly and smoothly according to their ranking number: thus, the second largest city should have half the population of the first, the third one-third that of the first, the fourth a quarter, and so on, reciprocally. As we have seen, the second city has most frequently only one-third to one-quarter the population of the first, but if we ignore the four or five largest settlements in a country, the others often roughly obey Zipf's empirical formula (as is illustrated in Fig. 54). Certainly they do in the U.S.A. and China, as do the smaller cities and towns of the United Kingdom, but there are wide variations in the U.S.S.R., and some other countries. The reasons for these variations in a rule which is quite remarkably applicable to the world as a whole, are not clear, but the departures are sufficiently provoking to encourage investigation into the relative sizes of a country's urban settlements.

Chapter VII

Town Sites and Situations

As we have already noted more than once, the study of urban settlements is complicated by the large number of variables: varied history and culture, varied building and street arrangements, varied function, and so on. Town sites and situations are equally varied, though again, as with other aspects of urban studies, it is possible to bring some order out of apparent chaos. The examination of town sites and situations, however, is fruitless unless they are considered in relation to function. Obviously, for example, the positional requirements of a holiday resort are quite different from those of an industrial town, a mining centre, or a seaport.

The term "site" should not be confused with "situation." The former refers to the actual ground on which a place is built, and is therefore concerned with local relief features and perhaps also with rivers and springs, with soil and rock, with coastal features, even with microclimates and weather. The latter has to do with wider positional aspects, *e.g.* location with respect to communications, agricultural, industrial and political areas, social and cultural regions, and so on.

Initially, the immediate environment is of commanding importance, but as a town grows, its situation and the use its inhabitants make of it become predominant. New York, for instance, originally sited on an island (Manhattan) at the mouth of a navigable river (the Hudson), from which it has since spread to the mainland, has no particular site advantage, except deep water. It has been the benefits of its situation which have enabled it, through man's intervention, to become one of the world's leading cities: its position at one end of one of the busiest shipping lanes in the world (the North Atlantic crossings), and at the terminus or starting-point of the easiest route through the Appalachians (the Hudson–Mohawk gap), leading to the Great Lakes and the U.S. interior. Fig. 55 supplements these details.

Geneva and Chicago, both sited at the ends of large, navigable lakes, and Oxford and London, built originally on river gravels commanding early fords, should warn us again that it is unwise to place too much lasting value on the site factor, since each of these towns has developed very

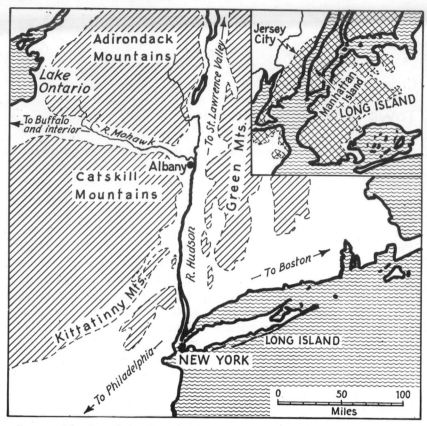

FIG. 55.—The site and situation of New York. New York's original site, Manhattan Island, remains the heart of the city and is dominated by the world's tallest buildings. Numerous bridges, ferries and tunnels link it to Long Island and the mainland, over parts of which the city has spread. Important factors in the growth of New York have been the Hudson–Mohawk Gap through the Appalachians, the development of land routes, and the convergence upon its capacious, deep-water harbour, of shipping lanes from all parts of the world.

differently from its counterpart. Situation has again proved to be more significant in the long run.

Site values clearly change with time. Many settlements, apparently built on unfavourable terrain, may grow into large cities, while others, more favourably sited initially, may remain small or even decline. Bradford, on a small beck a few miles from the River Aire, hemmed into its basin by hills, had neither a favoured site nor any natural nodality, yet it has grown to be the chief commercial centre of the British wool textile industry, and has acquired, as it has grown, the status of a route focus. Shipley, on the other hand, has always been a subsidiary manufacturing town though it is located on the main river and is more of a natural route focus. Chester, for long the principal port in north-west England, declined in favour of Liverpool as the River Dee silted up and ships grew in size. The latter came to be much larger than Chester had ever been because of the industrial development of its hinterland. Glasgow, in contrast to Chester, perhaps because Clydeside people were more enterprising, was able to transform itself from a very minor port into a great commercial one because Clydebank citizens, at the close of the eighteenth century, took it upon themselves to dredge the lower part of the river sufficiently for it to accommodate large ships.

THE EARLY NEEDS OF TOWNS IN RELATION TO SITE FACTORS

Once founded, or grown out of villages, towns rarely change their location even when the original site proves unsatisfactory. This fact not only reminds us that situation is of more permanent significance than site; it also stresses the strength of vested interests in property which, cannot, however, always prevent a town from stagnating or declining.

Many places have the same general location, e.g. a plain, valley or river bank. It is the site details which determine the actual choice of where to establish a community, if choice there is, for chance may play a part. Apart from having easy and immediate access to a food surplus, without which, as we saw in Chapter V, a town cannot come into existence, the sites of early towns were determined by (a) the availability of water (from stream, spring or well), (b) the availability of building materials (commonly timber, clay or stone), and (c) the availability of suitable building land (i.e. land which was both firm and dry.) While all these desiderata are still required, the factor of nearness is no longer as crucial as it was: piped water can now be conveyed to a settlement by aqueduct (even to a desert town like Kalgoorlie, W. Australia); structural materials can be transported long distances by sea, road and rail; soft ground and marshes can be drained or buildings raised on power-driven piles.

The varying functions of towns create other needs. Strategic towns demand sites offering natural defences; mining towns require economically valuable minerals; industrial towns need perhaps local power supplies or raw materials; tourist centres attractive scenery, or a marine beach, a medicinal spring or historical relics; ports require a harbour of some sort.

In order to grow into large towns, all these urban settlements need in addition a satisfactory situation. They must be either natural route foci, or else, through their development, they must secure an advantageous trading position by attracting routes to themselves. Indeed, certain classes of towns, notably large commercial cities (including ports), industrial towns, administrative centres and resort towns, could not come into existence at all until widespread communications had been established.

RIVER SITES

Many of the world's largest cities are situated on rivers, which may be of continuing significance as navigable waterways. In some cases they occupy one bank only, and, even where the river is bridged, may spread much further on one side than on the other. In Roman times, when the Empire was expanding eastwards, Maastricht (Meuse crossing) and Cologne (Rhine colony) were naturally established on the western side of their respective rivers. For similar defensive reasons, later German colonists advancing into Slav territory built their towns on the western side of rivers such as the Oder. Kiev and Stalingrad (Volgograd) were founded on the same bank of their rivers for other reasons: the western banks at these places are the concave ones and are surmounted by high, rocky platforms. London and Paris provide good examples of river cities which are more highly developed on one side (in each case the north, where the heart of each city is located) than on the other. Where a river is wide, twin cities, often with different functions, may develop, *e.g.* Beaucaire and Tarascon on the Rhône, Buda and Pest on the Danube, Minneapolis-St Paul, St Louis and East St Louis on the Mississippi. This is most clearly a tendency where a river serves as a frontier: Detroit and Windsor face each other across the small Detroit River, Strasbourg and Kehl across the Rhine, Rusé and Giurgiu across the lower Danube, Kinshasa and Brazzaville across the Congo, El Paso and Ciudad Juarez across the Rio Grande.

Among the most favoured river sites are the following:

1. *Ford and bridging point.* Many towns (*e.g.* Oxford, Bradford, Cambridge and Bridgwater, in England), betray through their names their origin as towns controlling early fords or bridges. The latter have obviously been the more important, *e.g.* the ford at Westminster dwindled in importance after the first London Bridge had been built. Control of the lowest bridge across a river (as at London and many other

large cities, *e.g.* Newcastle, Glasgow, New York and Hamburg) is usually more significant than control of a higher bridge since roads and railways generally carry more traffic in coastal lowlands than in hillier land. Thus Perth and Stirling have become less notable as bridge points since large new bridges were extended across the estuarine parts of their respective rivers. Bridges, and to a lesser degree fords, obviously confer situational advantages upon the towns which command them, and they therefore facilitate trade, especially where the river is also navigable or accompanied by a main road or railway.

2. *Head of navigation.* There may be more than one head of navigation on a river: that for ocean-going ships and that for river vessels. It may be marked by a natural shallowing or by the occurrence of rapids or waterfalls. Moreover, the head of navigation in one age may not be the same in another. Owing to silting and the growth in the size of ships, York and Cambridge are no longer seaports. The oceanic head is usually the most favoured site for a commercial port, particularly when this coincides with the tidal limit and lowest bridge as, for instance, at Glasgow.

3. *Near waterfalls or rapids.* Like heads of navigation, these features present navigational breaks, necessitating trans-shipment. They may also furnish a source of industrial power, as, for example, at Minneapolis, Lowell (Mass.), Schaffhausen, Tampere. Such obstacles to navigation may be by-passed by road or rail, as at Stanleyville (Kisangani) and near Leopoldville (Kinshasa) on the Congo.

4. *Estuaries and deltas.* Many great seaports are located on estuaries, where there is usually a good depth of water, especially at high tide, more shelter than along simple inleted coasts, and in many cases a longer water-front, particularly where, as at Hull (*see* Fig. 56), another river enters the estuary. Most estuarine ports, seeking to benefit as much as possible from cheap water transport, have been established near or at the head of their estuaries, but problems of silting (as with many funnel-shaped estuaries, *e.g.* the Dee at Chester), constriction (as at Clifton on the Avon near Bristol), or the increased size of modern ships, has led many of them either to decline or to establish outports. Thus Bristol is served by newer docks at Avonmouth, Hamburg by Cuxhaven, Bremen by Bremerhaven, Nantes by St Nazaire, Bordeaux by Pauillac and others (*see* Fig. 80, p. 181). Most of these outports have become passenger terminals because of the time-saving factor.

Deltaic ports are often badly sited owing to the amount of alluvium deposited in their channels, but many have become very large because of the productivity of their valley hinterlands. Some, *e.g.* Alexandria and

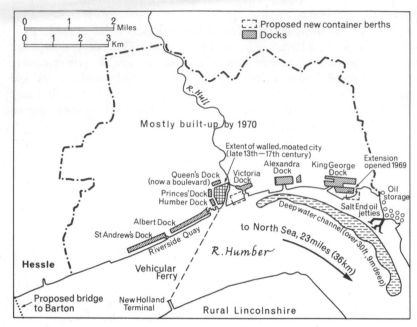

FIG. 56.—The site of Hull, an estuarine port. Hull was established as a trading port as early as the twelfth century and was given its first municipal charter by Edward I in 1299. It soon acquired a defensive moat out of which the old docks were constructed between 1774 and 1830. Its early exports were chiefly wool, followed by cloth. Its rise as a fishing port dates from the sixteenth century. It now claims to be Britain's third port and has a Humber frontage of more than 7 miles (11 km). Its population and trade are still expanding, and should receive a further fillip when the long-awaited Humber Bridge is built.

Karachi, perched on the most western distributaries, suffer less from silting than others due to the eastward movement of lateral currents.

5. *Confluences.* The value of a confluence site lies mainly in the natural routes such a location provides, *e.g.* at Oxford, Lyons, Mainz, Mannheim, Belgrade, Hankow, Allahabad, Ghent and Montreal. Such sites were particularly useful in early days to places built at or near the junction of navigable rivers and in days when water barriers provided defence, though in some cases, *e.g.* at Cairo, at the confluence of the Ohio and Mississippi, large towns could not grow owing to the lack of firm building ground and the liability of the site to inundation.

6. *River loops.* These provide excellent sites for towns, especially loops within incised meanders with difficult land approaches. Again, such sites

provided excellent defensive conditions, as at Durham (*see* Fig. 57), Shrewsbury, Besançon, Toledo and Berne. But these sites have often proved unfavourable for modern commercial development, and cities such as Durham and Berne have had to escape from their confining meanders in order to benefit from modern transport.

7. *Marked river bends.* Some cities, of which Basle, Orleans, Stalingrad (Volgograd), Cincinnati, Kansas City and Nottingham will serve as examples, are located at or near places where the direction of a river markedly changes, and where, therefore, either different lines of route tend to converge, or where traffic leaves a river for land transport. These sites, therefore, may possess also useful situational advantages which stimulate their growth as trading or industrial centres.

8. *Entrance to or exit from river gorges.* Where a river flows through a gorge, lowland routes may have to converge and be reduced to one major

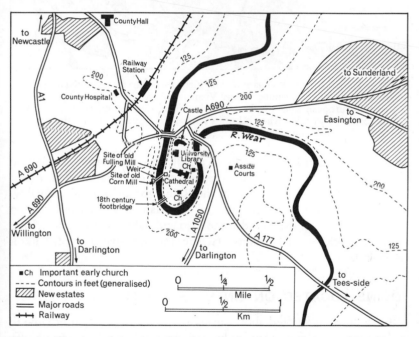

FIG. 57.—The site and situation of Durham. Durham's strategic site— within a deeply incised meander loop of the River Wear—has presented problems of access since the railway and motor-road became the chief means of transport. Consequently this historic city has not grown into a large industrial town like many others on the Northumberland and Durham coalfield, though it remains the county town and an important seat of learning and of ecclesiastical administration.

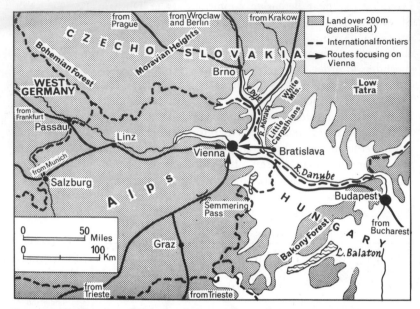

FIG. 58.—The situation of Vienna and Linz. Vienna and Linz are separated by a gorge-like section of the Danube valley. Vienna—where the river finally leaves the central European uplands—has a much more natural nodality. Politically, its importance dwindled when it lost its status as an imperial city on the break-up of the Austro-Hungarian Empire.

route. Moreover, rivers may flow so rapidly through gorge sections as to necessitate portage. Here, therefore, towns may be established, *e.g.* at Bingen and Bonn at either end of the Rhine gorge (and more notably, just beyond the gorge limits, Cologne and Mainz), Vienna and Linz on the Danube (*see* Fig. 58), Dresden and Usti and Laben on the Elbe, Ichang and Wanhsien on the Yangtse (where the man-haulage of junks is necessary).

TOWNS LOCATED ON LINES OF ROUTE

Besides the cities noted above, many of which are sited on or close to navigable rivers, *e.g.* on firm banks, gravel terraces, or flood-plain bluffs, there is a large number of towns on other lines of route, *e.g.* on lake margins, canals, roads and railways. In many of these instances, which we shall examine in turn, the site may again be of much less consequence than the situation. Indeed, the very fact of towns being located on transportation lines indicates the significance attaching to trade routes in their development. It is not surprising that the great French geographer, Vidal de la Blache, went so far as to claim that "les routes on fait les villes."

1. *Lakeside locations.* On lake shores, especially at the entrance to or exit from large lakes, towns have grown because they are among places where land routes give way to water routes or *vice versa.* Illustrative examples are provided by many commercial and industrial cities on the Great Lakes of North America, *e.g.* Toronto, Cleveland and Chicago. Smaller cities such as Lucerne, Lugano, Lausanne, Keswick and Interlaken (the two latter on alluvial flats between paired lakes) are close enough to mountain as well as lake scenery to have become tourist centres.

2. *Ship canal locations.* Many industrial towns have benefited from sites on artificial waterways, whose terminals are generally controlled by commercial ports, *e.g.* Rotterdam, Manchester, Ijmuiden, Colon and Cristobal, Port Said and Port Suez.

3. *Towns on narrow straits.* Narrow straits not only act like large

[Courtesy: National Film Board of Canada

Fig. 59.—Marshalling yards at Winnipeg. Winnipeg is roughly equidistant between eastern and western Canada, and occupies part of a gap between Lake Winnipeg and the U.S.–Canadian frontier. Hence it has come to be important as a meeting-place of both the C.P.R. and C.N.R. main lines across Canada. The marshalling yards shown here—belonging to the C.P.R.—are said to be the largest privately-owned yards in the world. At the close of the Prairie wheat harvest they are thronged with grain-cars.

canals and river gorges in facilitating and concentrating longitudinal movements, they also—if supporting important commercial ports and packet stations—provide useful transverse links between landways. This explains to a considerable extent the development of busy cities such as Istanbul, Copenhagen and Gibraltar, and the growth of ferry ports such as Dover and Calais, Messina and Reggio, Moji and Shimonoseki.

4. *Halts on main roads.* In days of animal transport, many small towns arose round inns, shops and small workshops (*e.g.* farriers' and wheelwrights') at convenient stages, no more than a day's journey apart, on well-used roads. The coming of the motor vehicle, capable of far more mileage, has caused some of these road halts to decline, but some, *e.g.* York, and other towns on ancient Roman roads, such as Verona and Nîmes, have attracted other roads, and they have thus maintained and even extended their commercial influence.

5. *Railway foci.* Railway construction has generally only emphasised the nodality of pre-existing towns, but some urban settlements in both old and new countries owe almost everything to their control of railways. They have indeed, to a considerable extent, become transport towns. Examples are Crewe, Swindon, Moncton (New Brunswick), Oberhausen, Novosibirsk, Winnipeg (*see* Fig. 59), Nagpur and Port Augusta (South Australia).

COASTAL SITES

Reference has already been made to certain towns, chiefly commercial ports, which occupy coastal locations, especially the shores of estuaries, deltas and narrow straits. Other shoreline sites include the following:

1. *The vicinity of coastal headlands.* Many of these sites originally supported military and naval bases, *e.g.* Scarborough (*see* Fig. 60), and Aberystwyth. They may since have grown into small trading ports (or fishing ports), or into tourist centres, if they possess a satisfactory harbour in the lee of the promontory.

2. *Offshore islands.* Offshore islands are often separated from the main land by a strait suitable for sheltered anchorage, *e.g.* at Bombay, Zanzibar, Hong Kong, Mombasa, Venice, Copenhagen and New York. Such sites may therefore nourish settlements which become seaports. On islands such as Singapore, commanding straits other than those between island and mainland, the port may have grown on the more exposed side. At Barrow the mainland has been preferred to the offshore island as an urban site, the channel between them being used for shipbuilding. In British Columbia, Vancouver, on a magnificent mainland inlet, has become the

great commercial port, while Victoria, in the lee of the extensive Vancouver Island, has remained a small port and administrative centre.

3. *Low, shelving beaches.* Broad beaches, especially when built of sand, have often provided sites for seaside resorts, *e.g.* at Blackpool, Southport,

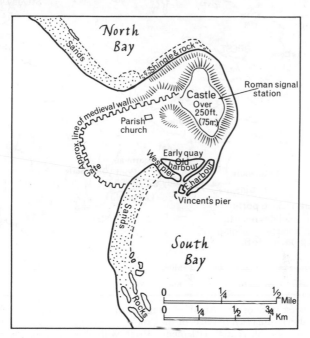

FIG. 60.—Old Scarborough. Scarborough owed its original importance to the defensive look-out site provided by a high limestone promontory projecting into the North Sea. It became in turn the site of an Iron-Age camp, a late Roman signal station and a Norman castle. The double bay, spa and tidal sands encouraged Scarborough's growth as a holiday resort in the nineteenth century. Its well-protected harbour is used by both fishing vessels and pleasure boats. The East Harbour was added in the late eighteenth century, the West Pier in 1820. The Parish Church and walls (now dismantled) were first erected at about the same time as the castle.

Rhyl, Deauville, San Sebastian, Palm Beach and Atlantic City. The offshore waters are usually shallow enough for safe bathing, but rarely deep enough or sufficiently sheltered to encourage the rise of commercial ports.

4. *Fjords and rias.* The former—almost entirely confined to mountainous areas in high latitudes—and the latter—commonly set in upland regions —rarely provide enough room on their shores for the growth of large cities, and their highland backing severely restricts their hinterlands. Rias and fjords do, however, support many fishing ports (*e.g.* Bergen), tourist

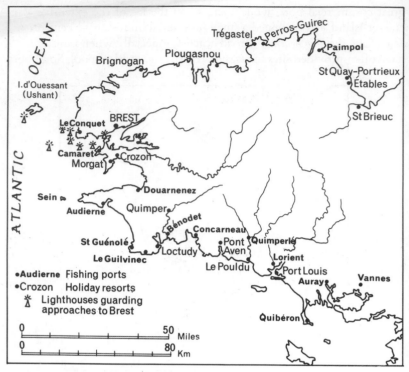

FIG. 61.—Brest and other coastal settlements in western Brittany. Brittany—an upland peninsula rich in inlets of the "ria" type—is well known for the number and variety of its coastal settlements. Brest, with about 135,000 people—is the largest town. It is France's chief naval base and can be approached only through a long, deep, narrow, fortified channel—part of the longest ria in Brittany.

centres (*e.g.* Dartmouth), and—where they are commodious and penetrate well inland—naval bases (*e.g.* Brest, illustrated in Fig. 61). In a few instances, *e.g.* at Oslo and Vancouver, fjords are surrounded by stretches of flattish ground which have permitted the growth of larger settlements. Sydney, on the ria known as Port Jackson, is the best example of a large commercial port built round a ria harbour.

SITES IN HIGHLAND AREAS

Highland areas support few large towns because of their limited productivity and their dearth of road and rail networks. Most of their urban settlements are located on valley roads and railways. Isolated hill-tops, however, have fairly often been chosen as strategic sites, *e.g.* at Delhi,

Edinburgh, Jerusalem, Athens (all notable as defensive capitals), Quebec, Narbonne, Perugia, Stirling, Le Puy and old Kano. Such sites were often strengthened by the erection of walls and castles. To continue to flourish today, hill-top towns have had to grow downwards. They must also occupy accessible situations. Many such towns are located on natural routes, *e.g.* Delhi, Stirling, Edinburgh and Quebec, the first two controlling highland gaps, the second two at handy places on important longitudinal routes.

Other gap towns include Guildford, Lewes and Lincoln, all originally founded as bridge towns at low points on ridgeways, and Belfort, Leeds, Troyes and Vienna. On higher ground stand Kabul, Peshawar and Innsbruck, the last-named on a major valley—that of the Inn—through the Tirol, and north of the Brenner Pass leading southwards to Bolzano in northern Italy.

Piedmont towns—like others occupying positions at the junction of unlike physical and economic regions (*e.g.* land and sea, desert and savanna)—have often acquired commercial significance because they can serve people occupying different kinds of land and producing contrasting products. There are several such towns on either side of the Pennines, *e.g.* Leeds and Rotherham on the east, Bolton and Glossop on the west. Other lines may be distinguished on the east side of the Rockies, where Denver, Cheyenne and Calgary are located, on the north side of the Apennines, where Bologna is prominent, and on the Welsh border, where Shrewsbury is perhaps the most notable. Other examples include Dresden, Colmar, Toulouse and Mendoza. It should be noted that the largest of these commercial towns command ways into or through the adjacent highlands as well as lowland routes.

STUDY QUESTIONS

1. Comment on the various ways in which the word "urban" is defined in different countries.

2. Describe the historical spread of the idea of the town from the Near East into north-western Europe before A.D. 1400.

3. Discuss the assertion that a town is a village which has succeeded.

4. On a map of the world shade the principal urban regions. How has the economy of the areas you have shaded promoted the growth of towns?

5. Why do you think the world as a whole is becoming more urbanised?

6. Contrast the balance between urban and rural populations in India and Australia and try to account for the differences.

7. Review the causes and effects of the "drift to the towns" in *either* tropical Asia *or* Africa.

8. Discuss the rapid growth of towns in the Soviet Union during the last half century.

9. Using specific examples, compare the typical "townscapes" of *four* of the

following kinds of towns: a religious centre, a strategic centre, a textile-manufacturing town, a health resort, a commercial port, a market town.

10. What is a "central place"? What relation does such a settlement bear to other central places of lesser and greater importance?

11. How far is it true to say that the size of a city is a reflection of the economic wealth of the region in which it lies?

12. Account for the pre-eminence of the following cities in their respective countries: London, Paris, Tokyo, Copenhagen, Montevideo, Johannesburg, Mexico City and Shanghai.

13. Find out how far the towns of any selected country follow Zipf's rank-size rule.

14. Point out some comparisons and contrasts in the development of settlements on selected river estuaries in *either* Great Britain *or* North America.

15. Discuss with reference to specific examples the influence motor roads and railways have had upon settlements, especially towns, of varied functions.

16. Critically examine the dictum: "La route a créé la ville."

17. In what respects have large cities a more favourable geographical location than small towns?

18. Relate the distribution of large towns in a selected country or continent to the distribution of important mineral deposits and productive agricultural land.

19. Write an essay on one of the following topics: (*a*) primate cities; (*b*) garden cities; (*c*) the changing urban skyline.

20. Why do you think the first-named city in the following pairs has become much larger than the second: Liverpool and Chester; Chicago and Duluth; Montreal and Quebec; San Francisco and Vancouver; Buenos Aires and Montevideo; Marseilles and Toulon; Copenhagen and Oslo?

21. Make a comparative study of *one* of the following pairs of cities: Manchester and Liverpool; Amsterdam and Rotterdam; Bordeaux and Marseilles; Montreal and Toronto; Philadelphia and Baltimore; Los Angeles and San Francisco; São Paulo and Rio de Janeiro; Cairo and Alexandria; Bombay and Calcutta; Melbourne and Sydney.

22. For any *one* country, give examples of urban settlements which have (*a*) grown rapidly during the past century; (*b*) declined or remained static during the same period. Elucidate the reasons for their varying fortunes.

Chapter VIII

The Classification of Towns

CRITERIA USED IN CLASSIFYING TOWNS

In seeking to elucidate what characteristics towns have in common, urban geographers have suggested various ways in which towns may be classified. We have already attempted (Chapters V, VI and VII) to group towns together on the basis of age, size and geographical location, and have referred also to the use of simple cultural designations, *e.g.* Asiatic, African, European, colonial, pre-industrial and industrial. In many ways the most meaningful basis of classification is that of function, determined in the main by employment structure. The second part of this chapter will be devoted to this subject but it is worth while first to enlarge on classifications based on age.

THE CLASSIFICATION OF TOWNS BY AGE

Groupings based mainly on historical periods, having regard to architecture and layout, were investigated in Chapter V, where we selected for special attention the following classes: the earliest Near Eastern towns, Greek and Roman towns, medieval, Renaissance and Baroque, industrial and modern towns. In the last category there are about a hundred "million" cities, and a large number of new urban forms, *i.e.* suburban towns and conurbations.

J. M. Houston (in *A Social Geography of Europe*) and Griffith Taylor (*op. cit.*) visualise the age of towns in physical terms. Houston selects three stages of growth, which he finds applicable to a large number of European towns:

1. *The nuclear stage*, as commonly represented today by the central area of a large town, perhaps demarcated by at least traces of former confining walls, or—as in Paris and Vienna—by the boulevards or other thoroughfares which have replaced them. Fig. 62 shows the successive walls of Paris.

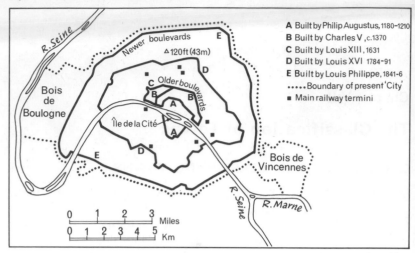

FIG. 62.—The walls of Paris. Like most old cities, Paris was successively defended by walls, the first being erected after the city had spread from its original site on the Île de la Cité to the outer banks of the Seine. As the city grew, the walls were extended by a succession of rulers as shown: A, by Philip Augustus, 1180–1210; B, by Charles V, *c.* 1370; C, by Louis XIII, 1631; D, by Louis XVI, 1784–91; and E, by Louis Philippe, 1841–6. All these defences have now been dismantled, their places taken by broad, often tree-lined avenues and boulevards. The outer railway termini, as in London, were built on the margin of what was in 1840 the built-up area—the present central *arrondissements*. The dotted line represents the boundary of the present city.

2. *The formative stage*, as represented by a nineteenth-century extension following the Industrial Revolution and contemporaneous changes in transport and trade. Such an extension is often marked by the spread of houses and factories beyond the central area and especially along lines of communication.

3. *The modern stage*, marked by the rapid growth of twentieth-century suburbs as motor transport has developed.

Griffith Taylor goes into more detail as a result of an examination of a number of towns, especially in Canada, some of which are only just embarking on their careers as urban settlements, while others are fully established. He recognises the following principal growth stages:

1. *The infantile stage*, represented by towns such as Aklavik and Fort Smith, on the Mackenzie River, where, at the time of writing, there was no separation of domestic and commercial areas, nor of richer and poorer quarters, the buildings being haphazardly distributed. In places like Tuk-

toyaktuk, the Arctic port, there was only one indefinite street: such a settlement might be described as "sub-infantile."

2. *The juvenile stage*, symbolised by Toronto as it was in about 1842, when shops were beginning to amass in the centre, bigger houses to appear on the fringes, and a few scattered factories to arise. Whitby, a small town near Toronto, might be regarded as an "adolescent" town in which the beginnings of industrial and residential zoning can be vaguely discerned.

3. *Maturity*, represented by the Toronto of about 1885, when house-types had become well segregated, the better-class ones on the outer fringes, the poorer ones near the now-developed commercial centre, and where established industrial areas had become apparent along the railways and on the side of Lake Ontario.

4. *Senility*, marked by a cessation of growth, the decay of some districts, and a decline in economic prosperity. This stage has been reached in many of the industrial towns of Lancashire, Yorkshire and Durham.

If, according to Griffith Taylor, a city grows to a very large size, say 500,000, it passes through a number of additional phases, marked, for example, by the submergence of nearby villages and the establishment of a University, by the founding of daily newspapers, and by the administrative annexation of outlying satellites and the formulation of zoning laws. He does not attempt to name these phases of growth.

Mumford's Age Classifications

Lewis Mumford (*op. cit.*), under the stimulus of Patrick Geddes, visualised a town not so much as a physical entity as a social phenomenon. He suggests a twofold classification of settlements:

(*a*) According to their technical equipment, which has been extended and elaborated as human history has advanced, and has been responsible for many social changes.

(*b*) According to their cultural rise and fall.

Adopting the first method, Mumford distinguishes the following phases:

1. *Eotechnic.* A phase characterised by the use of wind, water and wood as sources of power. West European towns were at this stage between the tenth and eighteenth centuries.

2. *Palaeotechnic.* A period in which coal and iron were the main props of the economy, and the blast furnace, canal, steam-driven machine the

main visual evidence. An early form of this aesthetically unpleasing type of city was Dickens' "Coketown," as described in *Hard Times*.

3. *Neotechnic*. A phase beginning to emerge in western Europe in the 1880s, and signalised by the introduction of electric power, the use of the lighter and rarer metals such as aluminium and tungsten, the more complete regeneration of waste, the invention of new means of communication, for example telephone and radio, and the appearance of the internal combustion engine. According to Mumford, the neotechnic city, in its complete form, is an overgrown, shapeless, metropolis, with increasingly tall buildings, central blight, frustrating traffic congestion and urban sprawl.

4. *Biotechnic*. The newest type of city, built by a civilisation dominated more by the biological than by the physical sciences, in which man's knowledge of bacteriology is applied to medicine and sanitation, his knowledge of physiology to nutrition and diet, and his knowledge of psychology to human behaviour. Such cities, partially exemplified in Britain's New Towns, are largely an expression of modern notions about the total environment, and are notable as essays in the blending together of several elements (*e.g.* climate, relief and architecture) into a harmonious, efficient whole.

In likening a town to a living organism, and demonstrating how a single settlement resembles a whole civilisation, Mumford again makes use of Geddes' pioneer work. He sees a town rising through three stages, and then sinking through another three, but he does not exclude the possibility of a town rising again, as, for example, Rome. Here are his six stages:

1. *Eopolis*. The rising village community, normally based on agriculture, mining or fishing.

2. *Polis*. The small market town, with some manufactures, dependent upon and serving a restricted region, and growing out of a suitably placed village.

3. *Metropolis*. The large city, dominating a number of small towns and villages, and developing in a particularly favoured situation. Such a settlement is commonly occupied by a cosmopolitan population, following many specialised occupations, and has a very wide sphere of influence. It begins to suffer from the class struggle, from the increasing difficulty of integrating its diverse cultural elements, and from the growing power of its merchants and bankers.

4. *Megalopolis*. The bloated city, in which material wealth dominates life, standardised products replace original art, size dominates form, and

the evils of bureaucracy intensify, as in second-century Rome, eighteenth-century Paris and early twentieth-century New York.

5. *Tyrannopolis.* The tyrannical city, in which display and expense become the measurements of culture, moral apathy replaces good living and commerce alternates between expansion and depression.

6. *Nekropolis.* The city of the dead, in which war, famine and disease take such a hold that municipal services decline, cultural institutions decay, and towns become shells, like ancient Babylon and Nineveh.

THE CLASSIFICATION OF TOWNS BY FUNCTION

It is common practice to speak of industrial towns, tourist centres, residential towns, mining towns, and so on, and thereby to indicate in summary fashion the function which appears to be dominant. It is, however, not disputed that all towns perform more than one function (*e.g.* manufacturing, transport, residence and education), and that in the largest cities no one function can generally be said to predominate. If we describe, for instance, Sheffield as an industrial city, ought we not also to use the same description for London, for it has a much larger industrial function; and if we call Liverpool a commercial port, can we not also give London that designation? Or should we say London is a political capital and leave it at that? It is obviously impossible to fit very large cities into any satisfactory functional classification.

Not only do all cities perform a number of functions. Their most important one may well change, for all cities are dynamic. Many an early nineteenth-century fishing port in England is now principally concerned with tourist catering. Many an old country market town has come to be noted for its manufacturing. We continue to label Oxford as a university or educational centre, forgetting how vast the motor-car industry has become in recent years.

The earliest towns were amalgams of culture, administration, trade and industry, and all were intimately connected with the surrounding countryside. Most had initially a strong defensive function, and many a notable ecclesiastical function. The significance of defence and religion as differentiating functions has declined in general, but other functions have entered the lists as civilisation has become more complex. Among these are recreational, residential, transport, mining and manufacturing functions, often carried on in specialised towns which may have no fundamental relations with the rural areas in which they are located. They are not among Christaller's "central places."

It is possible, in a very rough and ready manner, to group many towns together in the following ways:

1. *Mining and quarrying towns*—
    (a) Mining towns, *e.g.* Worksop (coal), Butte (copper), Broken Hill, N.S.W. (lead and zinc), Sudbury (nickel), Kalgoorlie (gold).
    (b) Quarrying towns, *e.g.* Bethesda (slate), Shap (granite), Hibbing (iron ore). Such towns are much less common than quarry villages.

[*Courtesy: Philips Electrical Ltd.*

FIG. 63.—Eindhoven. Eindhoven, the largest town in the southern part of the Netherlands, only became an urban settlement about 60 years ago when a village was chosen as the site of what has become the Philips Electrical works. A relatively small part of the huge plant, which covers 2 million square yards and employs 50,000 people, is shown here, partially surrounded by new, but fairly high-density housing.

To this list may perhaps be added oil-drilling and pumping towns such as have recently arisen in Alberta and Saudi Arabia.

2. *Industrial towns.* Some industrial towns, *e.g.* Nottingham, have a wide range of industries. Others are more restricted. Thus there are, for instance, specialised chemical towns, *e.g.* Billingham and Leverkusen; iron and steel towns, *e.g.* Rotherham and Pittsburgh; engineering towns, *e.g.* Düsseldorf, Eindhoven (*see* Fig. 63) and Birmingham; textile towns, *e.g.* Tourcoing and Bradford; pottery towns, *e.g.* Stoke-on-Trent and Meissen.

3. *Transport centres—*

(a) Those concerned with manufacturing ships *e.g.* Sunderland; motor vehicles, *e.g.* Detroit; aircraft, *e.g.* Wichita; and locomotives, *e.g.* Philadelphia.

(b) Those concerned to an unusually large extent with transportation, *e.g.* Crewe and Swindon (rail); all great ports (the sea); Strasbourg (river transport); and Port Said (canal transport).

4. *Commercial towns—*

(a) Agricultural market towns, *e.g.* large towns such as Winnipeg and Kansas City; smaller ones like Evesham and Horsens (Denmark).

(b) Banking and financial centres, *e.g.* Frankfurt and Amsterdam.

(c) Large inland centres with a diversified commercial structure, *e.g.* Manchester and St Louis.

(d) Large commercial ports (*see also* 3 (*b*)).

[*Courtesy: French Government Tourist Office*

FIG. 64.—Carcassonne. The ancient stronghold of Carcassonne, or "la cité", part of which is shown here, is a classic example of a medieval fortress city which is still virtually intact. It occupies the crown of a steep-sided hill above the River Aude, whose valley forms the eastern approach to the gateway leading from the French Mediterranean into Aquitaine. "La cité" is protected not only by its natural site but also by its double rampart of walls and their fifty-four towers. Within, streets and buildings huddle irregularly together. Visible on the left is the medieval Château Comtal, in the centre background the cathedral. In front are gardens and orchards.

5. *Administrative towns and cities—*

(*a*) National capitals, including old ones such as Paris and London, and new ones such as Brasilia and Canberra.

(*b*) Provincial capitals within a federation, *e.g.* Victoria (British Columbia), and Albany (New York).

(*c*) County towns, *e.g.* Wakefield (West Riding) and Beverley (East Riding).

(*d*) Towns forming minor centres of administration, *e.g.* the County and Municipal Boroughs of England.

6. *Strategic centres—*

(*a*) Ancient fortress towns, *e.g.* Edinburgh, Delhi, Peking, and the bastides of south-western France, *e.g.* Carcassonne, (*see* Fig. 64).

(*b*) Naval bases, *e.g.* Brest and Portsmouth.

(*c*) Garrison towns, *e.g.* Aldershot and Catterick.

7. *Cultural towns—*

(*a*) Ecclesiastical centres or places of pilgrimage, *e.g.* Mecca, Benares, Jerusalem, Lourdes and Rome.

[*Courtesy: United States Information Service*

FIG. 65.—Miami, Florida. Miami, the largest holiday resort in the world, is situated on the lagoon coast of Florida. Its climate—as is suggested by its palms, its short shadows, and balconied luxury hotels and flats—is virtually tropical, and it attracts in both winter and summer very large numbers of visitors from the cooler north.

(b) Educational centres, generally with a university, *e.g.* Cambridge, Heidelberg, Bangor, Louvain and Uppsala.

(c) Conference centres, *e.g.* Harrogate, Brighton, Chicago.

8. *Health and recreational centres—*

(a) Spas, *e.g.* Bath, Vichy and Carlsbad.

(b) Seaside resorts, *e.g.* Blackpool, Biarritz, Cannes and Miami (*see* Fig. 65).

(c) Mountain resorts, *e.g.* Davos, St Moritz, Banff, Darjeeling.

(d) Other inland resorts, *e.g.* Tucson and Stratford-on-Avon.

9. *Residential towns—*

(a) Dormitory towns, *e.g.* Ilkley, Harrogate and Wetherby (all serving Leeds), Weybridge, Hornchurch and Guildford (serving London).

(b) Suburban growths, *e.g.* Cheadle (near Manchester), Beverley Hills (Los Angeles).

(c) Overspill towns, *e.g.* Wilmslow (near Manchester), New Towns (*e.g.* those round London).

The Determination of the Predominant Function or Functions

How should the predominant function of a town be determined? Is it to be assumed that the main function is the one that employs the greatest number of people, or should one take most account of how many people work not directly to serve the town itself but to satisfy external needs? Certainly some statistical determinant seems to be required, though any selected figures must to some extent be arbitrary.

In 1943, Chauncy D. Harris (in "A Functional Classification of Cities in the United States," *Geographical Review*), using United States census data for 1930, studied the employment structure of 984 towns with populations of more than 10,000. He selected the following criteria, *inter alia*, as satisfactory for the determination of a town's principal function(s):

1. *Manufacturing cities.* Those having at least 45 per cent of the gainfully employed in manufacturing industry. Nearly 45 per cent of all U.S. towns fell into this category; most were situated in the north-eastern sector of the country.

2. *Retail cities.* Those in which employment in retailing was at least 50 per cent of the total engaged in manufacturing, retailing and wholesaling combined, and in which retail employment was at least 2·2 times wholesale. Half of these cities, as is shown in Fig. 66, proved to be located in the belt between 95 and 100 degrees W. longitude. Three of the largest served oil-producing regions.

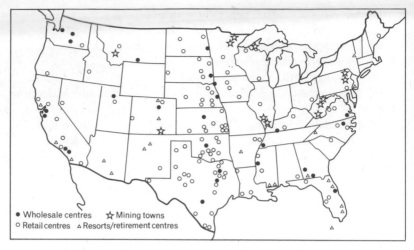

FIG. 66.—The functional classification of some cities in the United States. The cities marked on this map are those which C. D. Harris placed in the categories shown. The proliferation of retail centres in the central, mainly agricultural, part of the U.S.A., and the greater scatter of wholesale centres are very noticeable.

3. *Wholesaling cities*. Those in which employment in wholesaling was at least 20 per cent of the total employed in manufacturing, retailing and wholesaling combined, or in which there was at least 45 per cent as much work in wholesaling as in retailing. These cities included not only small towns engaged in assembly, packing and marketing agricultural commodities but also large regional ones concerned with distribution.

4. *Diversified cities*. Those in which manufacturing, wholesaling and retailing employed less than 60 per cent, 20 per cent and 50 per cent respectively of the employed population. These cities—numbering nearly a quarter of the total—were well-distributed, and included four of the five largest cities in the U.S.A.: New York, Chicago, Boston and Los Angeles. (Philadelphia, the fourth city, was placed in the manufacturing class.)

5. *Transportation centres*. Those in which transportation and communications engaged at least 11 per cent of the working population, at least one-third of those employed in manufacturing, and at least two-thirds of those engaged in commerce. Eighteen railroad centres and fourteen ports were included in this category, but most ports were regarded as wholesaling centres.

6. *Mining towns*. Those in which mining accounted for more than 15 per cent of the gainfully employed. Chauncy Harris found only fourteen such centres in the U.S.A., ten of which were coal-mining towns, three iron-mining ones, but many small settlements could be added.

7. *University and other educational towns*. Those in which at least a quarter of the total population were enrolled in universities and higher colleges. Seventeen small towns, largely seats of state universities in the Middle West, fell into this category.

8. *Resort or retirement towns*. Harris was unable to find any suitable statistical criterion for this group, in which, however, he placed twenty-two towns, some mainly summer resorts, some winter ones. They were well scattered and had a high proportion of workers in domestic and other forms of personal service.

9. *Other towns.* Though undifferentiated statistically, this class included fishing towns, logging camps, farming towns, regional capitals, political capitals, garrison towns, naval bases, professional centres and financial centres. There were no distinctive cathedral and pilgrimage centres, nor fortress towns in the United States.

The Researches of H. J. Nelson and G. Alexandersson

H. J. Nelson, in his study of the occupational structure of 897 American cities in the 1950 census ("A Service Classification of American Cities," *Economic Geography*), continued Harris's work, but introduced more re-fined statistical techniques, based on deviations from the average numbers in various kinds of employment exhibited by individual towns. For example, Nelson found that 27 per cent of all gainfully employed people in his cities work in manufacturing, nearly 20 per cent in retail trade, 11 per cent in professional services (mainly medical, legal and educational), 7 per cent in transport, 6 per cent in personal service, 4½ per cent in public administration, nearly 4 per cent in wholesale trade, just over 3 per cent in finance, insurance and real estate, and 1·6 per cent in mining. If, therefore, in a particular town, 40 per cent of the workers are engaged in manu-facturing, 8 per cent in transport, that town, according to Nelson, might properly be classified as a very important industrial town, and also as a fairly important transport centre. Thus, New Orleans is at once a trans-portation centre, a wholesaling town, and a financial town; and Washing-ton is not only the political capital, but also an important wholesaling centre. Over a third of Nelson's cities prove to be diversified, over 20 per cent outstandingly engaged in manufacturing (*see* Fig. 67).

Alexandersson, in *The Industrial Structure of American Cities*, recognised two groups of urban workers: (*a*) those engaged directly in the service of the town itself, the "non-basic" workers, responsible simply for ensuring the smooth internal working of the town (on average, nearly 40 per cent of the whole, more for large than for small towns); and (*b*) those engaged in "extra-urban" activities, the "basic" workers, or "fundamental population," whose jobs are concerned with satisfying the needs of people outside the town. The latter, according to Alexandersson, determine the real function of the town.

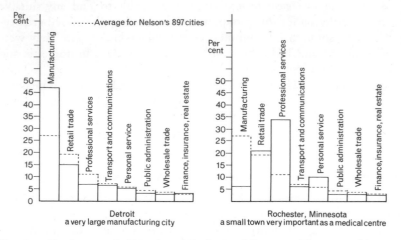

FIG. 67.—Employment in Detroit and Rochester, Minnesota. These two cities vary greatly, not only in population (Detroit has 2 million people, Rochester only 30,000) but also in their employment structure. The former is a great manufacturing and financial centre, the latter the home of the famous Mayo Clinic. The percentages are derived from H. J. Nelson's paper on "A Service Classification of American Cities."

In order, therefore, to determine this prime function, Alexandersson investigated, for 864 urban areas in the U.S.A. in 1950, the minimum percentage of workers in various occupational classes, *e.g.* administration, manufacturing, transport and retailing. These minima, within 5 per cent, he regarded as those required to ensure the satisfactory working of the town as a unit. Any higher percentages would then represent the proportion of workers engaged in extra-urban activity. The higher these proportions were, the more important would be the functions to which they applied. He was thus able to categorise on a functional basis the various towns and cities of the U.S.A. He found, for instance, that about 1·4 per cent of the gainfully employed people in a town are required to provide a satisfactory wholesaling service for the people of the town itself. If in a particular town the percentage greatly exceeds 1·4, then that town can be said to have a significant wholesaling function. For manufacturing he went much further than Harris and Nelson, and was able to list, for example, primary metal towns, furniture and lumber towns, textile towns and chemical towns. Altogether, his functional classes totalled thirty-six. All his settlements had a proportion of their populations occupied in such manufacturing industries as construction, printing and food-processing, and in such service industries as transport, retail trade, education and health, but in no town, however specialised, did he find more than 80 per cent of the gainfully employed engaged in manufacturing, though in a third of the towns 50 per cent were so employed.

Chapter IX

Political and Regional Capitals

NATIONAL CAPITALS AND PRIMATE CITIES

As we saw on p. 121, the great majority of national capitals are primate cities, *i.e.* the largest cities of their states. In a few cases, notably where the capital has been arbitrarily selected, and especially where it is a new city within a federal state, planned to serve as a seat of government from the outset, it may be less dominant. Thus Washington lags behind New York and other great commercial cities in the United States; Ottawa behind Montreal, Toronto and other places; Delhi behind Calcutta and Bombay; Berne behind Zürich. The new capitals Canberra and Brasilia are much smaller than, for example, Sydney and Melbourne, Rio de Janeiro and São Paulo.

Capital cities rise and fall according to the varying political fortunes of the countries to which they belong. Prague, Belgrade and Warsaw, for example, entered upon new careers when Czechoslovakia and Yugoslavia appeared on the map of Europe for the first time after the First World War, and when Poland was resurrected as an independent state. At the same time, Vienna, shorn of a large part of the territory it formerly served, declined when it was reduced to the status of capital of a small republic. Rome, with a population of only about 250,000 when Italy was unified in 1871, and overshadowed by Milan, regained part of its old imperial grandeur when it was selected as capital of the new state, and, with $2\frac{1}{2}$ million people, is now well in front of its rival.

The territorial expansion of a state is indeed mirrored in the greatness of its chief city. Paris, London, Moscow and Berlin all illustrate this statement. Berlin's recent fortunes, however, have been in marked contrast to those of Paris, London and Moscow. As a result of the Second World War it has become almost a unique example of a split city (though Jerusalem provided another example). The eastern part is the seat of the East German Government, while the western sector—islanded in politically alien territory—no longer possesses major administrative status, the present West German Government having chosen the comparatively small town of Bonn as its seat.

SOME CHARACTERISTICS OF POLITICAL CAPITALS

Since the growth of political capitals is linked with that of states, capitals have become symbols of national unity, the chief repositories of a country's culture, and perhaps the keys which open a country's national character. They have generally attracted to themselves not only government institutions, civil service headquarters, foreign embassies and supreme courts, but also national libraries and museums, art galleries, universities, cathedrals, official and other printing and publishing works, luxury industries, a host of theatres and other places of entertainment, numerous hotels and restaurants, and the most highly specialised and largest shops. They usually provide headquarters for the best known industrial corporations, and for banks and insurance companies, and they benefit from the finest medical skills and other talents.

Most of the older capital cities are concerned with more than administrative and service functions. London, for instance, has been called a "super-capital." It is not only the political capital of the United Kingdom but also the central city of the whole of the British Commonwealth. Moreover, in the United Kingdom itself, Edinburgh is no longer a seat of government, and Cardiff is the capital of Wales only by courtesy. Belfast has a Parliament, but Northern Ireland also sends members to Westminster. London is also the greatest commercial port and the principal manufacturing city in the British Isles. Paris is one of the chief river ports in Europe and the leading industrial city in France. Moscow, Berlin, Tokyo, Brussels and Rome are all busy manufacturing centres, for their nodality and their abundant and varied populations act as magnets to industrial undertakings. The newer capitals, e.g. Pretoria, Washington, Ottawa, Canberra and Brasilia, are more exclusively concerned with administrative and professional services.

THE SITUATION OF POLITICAL CAPITALS

Comparatively few political capitals are located in or close to the geographical centres of their states. Madrid (see Fig. 68) is a notable exception, but this city was to a large extent the artificial creation of Philip II in 1560. It was established in the centre of the Meseta with the intention of combating the centrifugal tendencies of the Iberian people, especially the Catalonians. The Spaniards, however, still throng the coastlands, and the interior of the country, a dry, rather unproductive area, remains thinly populated beyond the immediate environs of the capital. Madrid replaced Toledo, another Castilian stronghold, as capital, at a time when Spain gloried in its overseas possessions, a fact which adds to the Quixotism of Philip's choice. Madrid, however, has become the focus of the Spanish rail and road system, it now houses more than 2 million people, and its prestige has stimulated some industrial and commercial development in the Iberian interior.

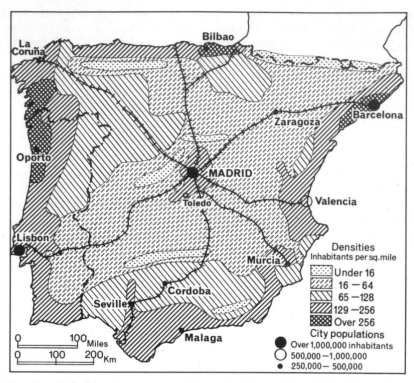

FIG. 68.—Madrid in relation to population densities in Spain. Most of the people in the Iberian peninsula live in coastal areas but the growth of Madrid—as the political capital and principal route focus of Spain—has led to increasing densities in the area immediately tributary to it.

Even though capital cities do not as a rule occupy geographically central locations, they are usually situated in the centre of productive areas, and often in the economic heartlands of their countries. Paris and London, Brussels and Vienna are cases in point. It says much for London's hold on the political and economic life of Britain that during the nineteenth century when the coalfield cities and ports of the Midlands and north rapidly expanded at the expense of the more agriculturally pro-

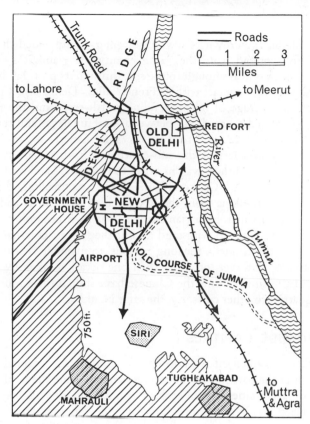

FIG. 69.—The site and situation of Old and New Delhi. The strategic site and situation of Old Delhi—on a low bluff overlooking the Jumna crossing and in a broad gap guarding the entry into the Plain of Hindustan from the north-west—is emphasised by the fact that thirteen cities, including Siri, Mahrauli and Tughlaka-had, arose on or near its present site. The Red Fort was built as a palace by Shah Jahan, a Mogul emperor and founder of the present Old Delhi in 1638. New Delhi, in contrast to the older and cramped walled town, was created by the British as a seat of twentieth-century administration. It has an open layout and its government buildings have a monumental character. Roads and railways link it to other parts of India and also to Pakistan.

ductive but less industrially advanced English Plain, London's position as the national capital was never threatened.

Many of the more peripherally located capitals were originally strong-holds, established for strategic purposes with the intention of guarding their territories against invading armies or navies. Good examples are Edinburgh, Delhi (*see* Fig. 69) and Peking. These are sometimes regarded as "back" capitals since it was chiefly in advance of them, as with London, that their countries developed. Edinburgh, supported by its castle, strongly built on the crown of a volcanic plug, commanded the main gateway into Scotland from the "auld enemy" England, via the east coast plain, and was near enough to the sea, through its port, Leith, to be in comparatively easy contact with its French allies. Delhi, firmly planted near the end of a ridge of hills extending north-east from the Deccan Plateau, commanded a broad gap between the Himalayas and the main part of the plateau, here reinforced by the Thar Desert—a gap through which successive invaders of the sub-continent, having negotiated the Kyber Pass, had to find their way in order to reach the Land of Promise: the fertile, well-watered Ganges Plain. Peking, controlling the main route into northern China from the dry lands of Manchuria and Mongolia, with their former barbarian hordes, was in a position, with the help of the Great Wall, to withstand all but the fiercest external attacks and so to allow the Chinese, for long periods, to maintain their national identity. It was, however, on more than one occasion taken by enemy attack, and from time to time the Chinese have shifted their administrative headquarters to other cities, *e.g.* the safer Nanking.

COMPROMISE CAPITALS

A number of capital cities—known as "compromise" capitals—have been chosen in the past so as to counteract and alleviate the rivalries and jealousies of larger cities, but in each case much thought has been given to their selection. Washington, Ottawa and Canberra are the most notable examples. The first was chosen by the early Atlantic colonists of the United States after they had gained their independence from Britain. It was suitably located roughly half-way between the original northern and southern states, each with their distinctive populations and economies, and was less dominant as a seat of population than Boston, New York and Philadelphia. Now it is a "back" capital since American territory extends as far as the Pacific coast, and it suffers from the charge that it is not only no longer centrally placed within its state, but that its position induces the country's leaders to pay more attention to Atlantic than to Pacific affairs. (Britain and France suffer from much the same accusation: Scotland, Wales and even northern England, though all of course much nearer London than even the Mid-Western states are to Washington, complain that London and its environs too greatly dominate British life and thought. Similarly, Brittany and Aquitaine argue that their interests are neglected in comparison with those of the Paris region.)

Ottawa—chosen by Queen Victoria's advisers—was a small, un-
important lumbering town when it became the capital of the newly
independent Canada in the mid-nineteenth century. Its selection, however, did something to allay the rivalries of Quebec, Montreal, Toronto
and Kingston. It had other advantages: it lay on the border between
French-speaking Lower Canada and English-speaking Upper Canada, it
was accessible to the older settlements, and its population was a reasonable
mixture of most of the ingredients in the contemporary population of
Canada: English, French, Scottish and Irish. Unlike Washington, it

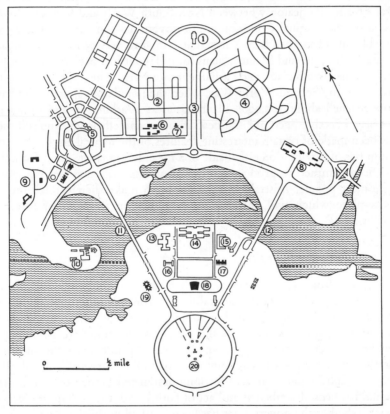

FIG. 70.—The site of Canberra, a new political capital. Key to numbering: 1. Australian War Memorial; 2. Reid residential area; 3. Anzac Parade; 4. Campbell
residential area; 5. Civic centre; 6. Technical college; 7. St. John's Church;
8. Russel offices; 9. University; 10. Hospital; 11. Commonwealth Avenue Bridge;
12. King's Avenue Bridge; 13. National Library site; 14. Parliament House site;
15. High Court site; 16. Treasury building; 17. Administration building;
18. Parliament house; 19. Hotel Canberra; 20. National Centre, Capital Hill.

formed part of an existing political unit (Ontario) and was awarded no specific federal territory of its own; hence the French in Quebec were given grounds for thinking that it is too much influenced by the large English element in Ontario. Like Washington, it was at the time of its inauguration as capital a centrally placed city, but is now marginal to Canada as a whole. Would the Americans and Canadians have a different outlook in national and international affairs if their capital cities were Winnipeg and Chicago, or Vancouver and Los Angeles?

The decision to establish an entirely new federal capital in Australia—to be set, like Washington, D.C., in its own Federal Territory, to avoid exacerbating the jealousy between New South Wales and Victoria—was taken by the original Commonwealth government in 1900. By 1927 a suitable inland site had been selected at Canberra between the two great rivals, Melbourne and Sydney, plans for its layout had been drawn, some building had taken place, and Parliament moved in. The city grew slowly until after the Second World War, when the population spurted and has now reached about 100,000. Planning, as at Washington and Ottawa, has been effective in combining beautification and efficiency, and full use has been made of certain interesting features of the natural environment: a number of low hills on either side of a meandering river, part of which has been dammed to produce a series of ornamental lakes (*see* Fig. 70). Like most people, Australians are anxious to make their capital into a show-place which will enhance their prestige in the eyes of foreign visitors.

FORWARD CAPITALS

Though situated within the area where most of the Australians have chosen to live, Canberra is at least different from the other main cities of the continent, in being located at some remove from the coast. It is a "forward" capital insomuch as the people of Australia are striving to develop the country's interior and be less dependent on the littoral. Brasilia, however, is a much better example of a "forward" capital. Its recent establishment in an area for long designated as the site of a future capital has been described as an "act of faith," and it is perhaps too early to say whether the government has been justified in shifting its administration from the active, magnificently sited Rio de Janeiro, on the well-developed east-coast plain, to this locality in the under-developed interior. If the existence of a capital on the Brazilian Plateau more than 500 miles (800 km) from the sea stimulates the exploitation of the interior, and allows the population in and round Rio and São Paulo to loosen out, then the experiment, costly though it has been for a relatively poor country, will have been worth while. Already the new city is becoming a hub of roads, its population has grown to 400,000, and its daring architectural designs have already attracted wondering and admiring visitors from all over the world.

[*Courtesy: Pakistan High Commission*

FIG. 71.—Islamabad: the Secretariat. Islamabad, a planned capital still in the course of construction, occupies a healthy site a few miles north of Rawalpindi, which will eventually become its main commercial hub. The Secretariat, shown here, designed by an Italian, lies in the shadow of the Margala Hills. The ground in front has been carefully landscaped, but the buildings themselves do not harmonise very well with the environment, though the aim of the chief planner of the city as a whole—the Greek, Doxiades—is to blend traditional Moslem designs with internationally acceptable contemporary styles.

The "forward" policy of Russia found expression during Peter the Great's reign (1682–1725) when the ruler, impressed by sojourns in England and Holland, determined that his motherland should be modernised. To help achieve this aim, he built a "window to the West" on a site with a marshy, unattractive environment at the entrance to the Baltic Sea. Here arose his well-planned capital, St Petersburg, afterwards successively Petrograd and Leningrad. When the inward-looking Communist government seized power in 1917, however, the central administration reverted to Moscow, round which the Russian realm had grown in earlier Tsarist days.

Pakistan provides another interesting example of a change of political capital (*see* Fig. 71). When the new state was set up in 1947, Karachi was perhaps the obvious site as capital because Lahore, the most important inland city, lay too near the troubled frontier with India in the Punjab. There was, however, a lack of government buildings in Karachi, the city was somewhat isolated from the most populous part of West Pakistan, and it was eccentrically located with regard to communications with East Pakistan. Hence a new government site was sought. The choice fell on an area near Rawalpindi, to which the National Assembly moved in 1959. Close by, a new, spacious, linear city is now being built under the direction of Doxiades, a Greek town-planner with an international reputation. It is fittingly called Islamabad, and is designed to accommodate two million people eventually. It will have more than a purely administrative function, for room is being left for both light and heavy industrial areas. Government departments are now moving in. Unlike New Delhi, Lutyen's modern administrative addition to the ancient Indian capital, the buildings in Islamabad are more varied and they are being erected to combine modern functionalism with traditional Moslem designs.

STATE CAPITALS WITHIN A FEDERATION

A federation embraces a number of different administrative units, known, for example, in Canada as provinces; in the U.S.A., Australia, Mexico, Brazil and India as states; in West Germany as *Lander*; in Switzerland as cantons; in the U.S.S.R. as republics. Each of these political units has its own legislature and executive to which the constitution may allocate certain powers which are distinct from those handled by the central government. Thus each state or other administrative division has its own seat of government. In many cases, especially in the United States, there are minor cities, often dominated commercially and industrially by other urban settlements. Thus Olympia, the capital of Washington, is greatly outnumbered in population by Seattle; Salem (Oregon) by Portland; and Tallahassee (Florida) by Jacksonville. Similarly in Canada, Victoria (British Columbia) is overshadowed by Vancouver, and Quebec by Montreal. Such relatively small capitals—especially where remote from other urban concentrations—may assist in safeguarding rural interests, and shield the state's administration from the influence of big business, but they need to be easily accessible from all other places.

Even in North America, some state capitals are quite large, and in many cases these cities, like their more numerous counterparts in Germany, the Soviet Union, and Brazil, and all the state capitals of Australia, are the largest cities in the areas they govern. This primacy is not, however, due to their political status, but to their commercial and industrial interests. Among these capitals are St Paul (Minnesota), Toronto (Ontario), Winnipeg (Manitoba), Boston (Massachusetts), Munich (Bavaria), Düsseldorf (North Rhine–Westphalia), Sydney (New South Wales), Melbourne (Victoria), Kiev (Ukraine) and Tashkent (Uzbek). In such cities administration often seems to be a minor function, and perhaps in consequence the state is the loser.

REGIONAL CAPITALS

Geographers, especially in France, but during this century also in Britain and other parts of the world, have addressed themselves to the task of undertaking regional studies, which involve, in all but the smallest countries, the identification and delineation of areas with some unity of their own which allows them to be distinguished from surrounding areas. The commercial, social and cultural life of such "regions" is often dominated by one main city, a large one where the region is populous and includes other important towns, a smaller one where the region is predominantly rural. Indeed, some regions derive a large part of their individuality from the fact that they consist of the "central place" and its tributary area. Such "city regions" in Britain have been advocated as likely to form better local government units than the present ones, which, unfortunately, divorce town from country.

Many *ad hoc* regions have from time to time been devised by the State, various trade and professional organisations, gas and electricity authorities, etc. Notable among them were the Civil Defence Regions designed during the Second World War to co-ordinate the functions of various British government departments (*see* Fig. 72). Another step in the progress towards regional devolution was taken in 1964 and 1965 when the Government divided England and Wales into nine Economic Planning Regions. These regions contrast somewhat with the more purely geographical entities suggested at various times by geographers, *e.g.* C. B. Fawcett, E. G. R. Taylor and E. W. Gilbert, and their boundaries suffer in that most of them—for convenience in obtaining statistical information—follow county and other local administrative limits. Nevertheless, there is a high degree of correspondence between the extent of many regions, whether planned by the State, by professional geographers, commercial organisations or other bodies, and the same central foci (*i.e.* "regional capitals") keep on recurring. The following list, taken from

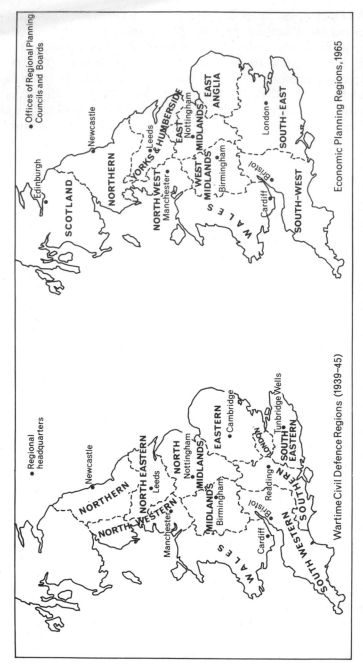

Fig. 72.—Planning Regions in Britain. Civil Defence Regions were devised by the Government during the Second World War, Economic Planning Regions in the mid-1960s. The two should be compared and the towns and cities chosen as their administrative centres noted. In East Anglia the Government has not yet selected a centre from which planning might be directed.

the Government's Economic Planning Regions in England and Wales, gives the most prominent and most widely recognised regional capitals:

Region	Location of Offices of Planning Councils and Boards
Northern	Newcastle
Yorkshire and Humberside	Leeds
East Midlands	Nottingham
East Anglia	—
South-east	London
South-west	Bristol
West Midlands	Birmingham
North-west	Manchester
Wales, including Monmouthshire	Cardiff

None of the above cities, with the exception of London, and the partial exception of Cardiff, is a political capital, but all are very important commercial and industrial nuclei, with a high proportion of workers in the tertiary sector. They have good theatres, universities, newspapers, large departmental stores and specialised shops, specialist medical services, well-known football teams, and above average sports facilities. They contain branches of state administration, most have provincial branches of the Bank of England, active stock exchanges, and many wholesale warehouses. All are route foci and their accessibility allows them to be periodically visited by a large proportion of the people within their regions. They are indeed regional metropolises, but they are not without rivals. Bristol, for instance, may be regarded as only peripheral to the south-west, which encourages the more centrally placed Exeter, also with a university and a distinguished history, and Plymouth, larger than Exeter, to dispute the field. In East Anglia, Cambridge and Norwich compete, and in the north-west, Liverpool—larger than any regional capital except Birmingham—challenges Manchester's supremacy. If England is divided into small regions, we should, moreover, have to admit the claims of such cities as Oxford, Southampton and Carlisle.

In France, the geographer Vidal de la Blache regarded a regional capital as a "natural" capital which has grown not through its selection by the state but because of its superior geographical location and its inhabitants' enterprise. It generally acts as the chief market and cultural centre of its region, and it usually contains some organs of the central government. Obvious examples are Lyons (Rhône Valley), Nancy (Lorraine), Strasbourg (Alsace), Lille (north-east) and Grenoble (Alps). Bordeaux and Toulouse rival each other in Aquitaine, Marseilles and Nice in Provence, Rouen and Le Havre in the lower Seine Basin, Nantes and Rennes in Armorica. As in England, there are places we might call "sub-regional" capitals, *e.g.* Clermont-Ferrand (Auvergne), Limoges (Limousin) and Montpellier (Languedoc).

West Germany's main regional capitals would certainly include Cologne, Nuremberg, Munich, Hanover, Bremen and Hamburg; Italy's Milan, Venice and Naples; and Belgium's Antwerp and Liège. In a large federal state such as the United States, regionalism tends to be less significant economically, socially and politically than the administrative framework of the country based on individual states or their arbitrary grouping (as, for instance, the Pacific and Mountain States, the Mid-West and New England), but one would certainly call such cities as Boston, Chicago, St Louis, Atlanta and New Orleans regional capitals.

Chapter X

Inland Trading Centres

ALL towns have to some extent developed as centres of internal commerce: all have retail outlets, banks and other business offices, and the larger ones also engage in wholesale distribution. Those towns which are specifically referred to as commercial towns usually occupy nodal sites and serve a greater number of people resident in the area surrounding the town itself than, for example, industrial, mining and recreational towns. In other words, they are significant "central places" (see p. 117) to which people from surrounding villages and smaller towns look for the satisfaction of their regular needs.

MARKET TOWNS

Small Market Towns

The small market town is by far the commonest type of urban settlement to be found in rural areas. It is the typical "country town" and is found in all countries, advanced and backward. It provides a place—open or enclosed—and facilities for the exchange of commodities, especially the sale and purchase of agricultural surpluses and the purchase and sale of consumer goods.

In England, before the Industrial Revolution, market towns in well-settled areas were about 5 to 10 miles (8–16 km) apart, i.e. close enough together to allow farmers and their families to visit them on foot or horseback on market day (generally once a week) and return home on the same day. At these small towns they were able to sell their butter and cheese, corn, wool and live animals, and to buy new farm implements, cloth, clothing and footwear, kitchen utensils, salt, the more common spices, preserves and so on. The better-placed market towns, situated at focal points in the more productive and populous areas, were the county towns. Here, more people were concerned not only with administration and commerce, but also with domestic industry. Most market towns supported a few craftsmen, (carpenters, smiths, tanners, saddlers and flour-millers), but in the county towns there were often enough workers in domestic industry to form "guilds," as at Beverley (East Riding), noted for "Beverley Blue" cloth as early as the twelfth century, which had a weavers' and a fullers' guild, and Wakefield (West Riding), which also possessed cloth-workers' guilds.

Yearly or more frequently, fairs were held in the more accessible market towns, and in many cases such events continue to take place, though the economic element now appears to be less important to some patrons than that of entertainment. Fairs were expected to attract people from a much wider area than weekly markets, and in some instances to draw in people from other countries. When Defoe toured England and Wales in the mid-eighteenth century there was still one at Stourbridge, just outside Cambridge. Though this fair was then past its peak, the writer was able to compare it more than favourably with the great continental fairs, still held at Leipzig, Frankfurt-on-Main, Augsburg and Nuremberg. Like Stourbridge, market towns such as Northampton, Winchester, Boston (Lincolnshire) and St Ives (Hunts.) had fairs at least as early as the twelfth century.

Modern Market Towns

The building of railways, which allowed people to travel much farther in a day than had been possible before, led to a decrease in the number of market towns, and a growth in the amount of business done at others. In the Yorkshire Dales, for example, many small markets, including that at Grassington (see Fig. 73), gradually faded, while those at other centres, e.g. Skipton—more nodally situated in a prosperous area than some, and able to serve people in both upper Wharfedale and Airedale—grew (see Fig. 74). Skipton, typical of the modern English market town, supports a large sheep and cattle auction market, recently shifted from the town centre to a roomier site near the railway station. The High Street— overlooked, as in many early market towns by both a medieval church and castle—is now used on market days by a variety of itinerant traders, selling, for example, cloth, hardware, crockery, floor-coverings and cheap jewellery, and on other days is given over to car parking, as is the current practice in market towns. Skipton also possesses four or five banks, several inns, some of which are residential, a number of garages, a bus station, a representative range of shops, including a branch of Wool-worths, another small departmental store and a good book-shop. It publishes a weekly district newspaper, supports a cinema, library, hospital and small museum, and houses the offices of an Urban District Council. It is just large enough (pop. c. 13,000) to have a Grammar School, though a large proportion of its pupils, like its hospital patients, are, of course drawn from a much wider area than the town itself (*see* Fig. 141, p. 317). A fair proportion of Skipton's people are engaged in professional services, including the law, accountancy, medicine and estate agency. There is a large cotton-thread factory and a number of smaller industrial establishments, mostly concerned with textiles, but including also engineering works and tanneries.

FIG. 73.—The main street in Grassington, Yorkshire. Grassington, now a village in upper Wharfedale, with *c.* 1,200 inhabitants, came to life as the Anglian successor to a prehistoric village on the moors above. Part of the site of the medieval market is shown just off the main street on the right of the photograph. Today Grassington no longer has a market. The square where it was held now serves as a car park for tourists and for shoppers from the higher parts of the dale.

Not all English market towns provide as wide a range of services as Skipton, but most—even those with populations of only about 2,000— have at least a primary school, three or four banks, several cafés and hotels, a few branches of multiple firms selling such articles as footwear and pharmaceuticals, and at least one church and chapel. They often suffer from acute congestion, especially on market days, because their streets, dating in most cases from the Middle Ages, are often too narrow for the easy movement of modern traffic. Many towns, like Skipton, have

acquired some factory industry; many—because of their historic buildings
and rural setting—attract tourists, and some—especially those near
densely populated areas—have developed dormitory functions and include commuters in their populations. All are intimately connected with
their surrounding agricultural areas.

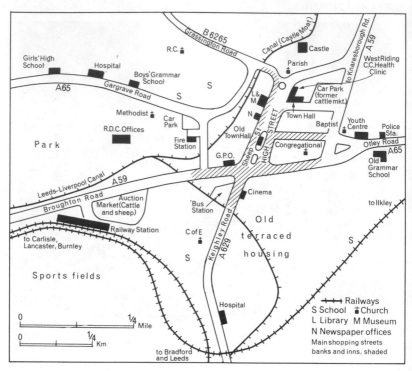

FIG. 74.—Some urban features of Skipton. Skipton is an old market town well placed
to tap the trade of upper Airedale, part of Wharfedale, and the villages and small
towns to the south-west, such as Barnoldswick. The features marked on this
map are typical of the English market town of 10 to 20,000 people which acts
administratively as the centre of both its own urban district and a wider rural
district. The key to this Fig. is on the site of a new housing estate.

If an English market town has fairly well-developed urban facilities
and its economy is not unduly bolstered up by industry, administration
and the housing of commuters and retired people from outside, it usually
serves about twice as many people in its rural hinterland as those inhabiting the town itself, though in some cases it may serve four times as many.
In France, where a greater proportion of the people live in country towns
than in England, the smallest market towns (*les bourgades*) have popula-

tions of about 2,000 and cater for about three to four times that number, the larger ones (*les centres locales*) serving proportionately more. In the United States, small country towns are usually further apart than in England and France: those of about 3,000 people may be 25 miles (40 km)

[Courtesy: Netherlands National Tourist Office

FIG. 75.—Alkmaar, Netherlands. Alkmaar, in North Holland, holds a cheese market every Friday from April to September. It attracts many tourists who enjoy watching the loading and transport of the sledges from canal barge to the market-place and from the market-place to the fifteenth-century weigh-house. The work is done by white-clad men whose differently coloured straw hats signalise the four sections of the guild to which the porters have belonged for the past 300 years.

apart, the somewhat larger ones 30–40 miles (48–64 km) apart. One reason for this is, of course, the lower average population density, another the more extensive use of agricultural land, a third the much greater size of the country which accustoms the people to travelling greater distances, a fourth the larger fraction of the population possessing motor cars.

Certain market towns, like some larger commercial centres, specialise in one article. Good examples are provided by fishing ports such as Stavanger and others in Norway. In the Netherlands, largely maintained as a tourist attraction, is the Friday cheese market at Alkmaar (*see* Fig. 75). Cheeses sold here are collected from factories over a wide area and handled by traditionally dressed porters belonging to long-established guilds. The cheeses are weighed at the ancient weigh-house fronting the market square. Similar, but of more recent origin, is the flower auction market conducted weekly at Aalsmeer.

It should be noted that while markets are commonly held in towns, they are not precluded from areas with no permanent settlement. In the North African desert and savanna lands, for instance, temporary markets or *suqs* are held weekly at traditional places near wells and springs. Here, exotic foodstuffs and articles of dress are offered for sale by itinerant, tent-dwelling, professional merchants. There are also quarters for the buying and selling of local products, and places, too, for cobblers, harness-makers, blacksmiths and barber-surgeons. Such al fresco markets perform for a widely scattered nomadic population the same kind of services as market towns set permanently in the midst of settled farming communities.

COMMERCIAL CITIES

The Situation of Large Commercial Cities

Most of the world's largest cities, not excluding political capitals and great seaports, have attained their stature largely because of the volume of internal trade they are able to transact thanks to their very favourable geographical locations. Nearly all of them possess more natural nodality than neighbouring towns. Many, *e.g.* Paris, Cairo, St Louis and Chungking, are more or less centrally placed within a productive agricultural region; others, *e.g.* Pittsburgh, Manchester, Birmingham and Düsseldorf, are centred in important industrial regions. A large number occupy key sites, for instance at or near the confluence of major rivers, like Wuhan, Khartoum, Lyons, Mainz and St Louis, or near the entrance to broad highland corridors, like Leeds, commanding the approach to the Aire Gap and also in touch with both industrial and agricultural Yorkshire; Vienna (Fig. 58, p. 134) commanding both the Danubian corridor and the Moravian Gate, and also in the area where Alpine Austria gives way to Lowland Austria; and Toulouse, where the Aquitaine Basin narrows into a passageway between the Pyrenees and the Central Massif of France.

The Varied Character of Large Commercial Cities

Most of these large commercial cities, though generally having a long history of trade, expanded rapidly in the nineteenth century when the Commercial and Transport Revolutions in Europe and North America followed in the wake of the Industrial Revolution. As their importance as

[*Courtesy: South Africa House*

FIG. 76.—Johannesburg: a large commercial city. This modern industrial and commercial centre, is the largest "European" city in Africa apart from Casablanca. Its tall office-blocks are perhaps more typical of large American cities than of western European ones. The white mounds in the background—gold-mine spoil heaps—are a reminder that Johannesburg began its career, as recently as 1886, as a mining town. Today, it is not only the business centre of the Rand, but the main road and rail focus and commercial hub of all South Africa.

traffic nodes was increasingly confirmed, they attracted manufacturing industries which benefited from their transport facilities, the supplies of labour and the consumers' market they could provide, and the capital which accrued from their commercial transactions. Hence, besides developing further as merchanting centres and regional capitals, they also extended their industrial functions, especially if they found themselves on or near coalfields, the main source of motive power in the nineteenth century. Some, instead of diversifying themselves commercially and industrially, found it more profitable to intensify their interest in a particular direction. Thus in England, while Leeds became the undoubted regional capital of at least West Yorkshire, and acquired a wide range of factory industries and trading activities, Bradford remained truer to the long-established wool industry and became its commercial headquarters. Manchester, though sometimes called "Cottonopolis," diversified its occupational structure more than Bradford and became a regional capital without relaxing its hold on the cotton trade. Leicester, while retaining a subsidiary interest in leather, concentrated on hosiery, Nottingham became important not only for hosiery and other textiles but also for bicycle engineering, tobacco and chemicals. Johannesburg's prosperity was founded on gold (*see* Fig. 76), that of Winnipeg on wheat, Kansas City's on livestock, that of Caracas on petroleum, and that of Lyons on silk.

Commercial cities are undoubtedly the most diversified of all cities. All of them possess, near their centres, numerous shopping streets, wholesale warehouses, and a large number of banks* and other business premises (often nowadays housed in soaring architectural blocks, of which the ground floor may be let to retailers, especially the directors of multiple stores). Many of their inhabitants work in transport undertakings as well as in factory and workshop industry. Most of them possess either universities or other higher seats of learning, *e.g.* colleges of technology and commerce, and schools of languages. Culture is further represented by at least one theatre, several cinemas, well-stocked municipal libraries, art galleries and museums, and by the publication of at least one daily newspaper. Administration is commonly centred in a monumental town or city hall, from which it may have expanded into neighbouring buildings, some purpose-built, others in premises diverted from other uses.

* A number of large commercial cities (for example, New York, London, Paris, Amsterdam, Zürich and Frankfurt-on-Main), have acquired particular significance as financial centres.

Chapter XI

Ports

THE RISE OF PORTS

IT is significant that among the world's largest cities a number of ports have always been included. Athens had its Piraeus, Rome its Ostia. Alexandria was the second city in the early Roman Empire, and Byzantium (Istanbul) took over the role of Rome itself in the fifth century. In 1400, Paris and Milan, both inland emporia, were among the world's leading cities, but so were the seaports of Florence, Genoa, London, Venice and Bruges: all entrepôts through which commodities from distant lands were forwarded to European markets. Even Paris was at least a river-port. In 1500, following the early Renaissance discoveries, Lisbon entered the list of great seafaring cities and was shortly joined by other Atlantic ports: Antwerp, Amsterdam and Bristol. Beyond Europe, many very large cities arose as bustling commercial ports in the later part of the nineteenth century. Among them were New York, Philadelphia, Montreal, Rio de Janeiro, Buenos Aires, Shanghai, Canton, Bombay, Calcutta, Tokyo-Yokohama, Sydney, Melbourne, Cape Town and Durban. Today, at least half the world's "million" cities are seaports.

In early times, landways were few and generally poor, and the unit of transport—human porter, pack or draught animal—was small and slow-moving. This was true right up to the advent of the railway and the motor vehicle. At sea, piracy was rife and it was cheaper to find natural shelter than to construct elaborate artificial harbour works. Hence most ports were sited as far from the open sea as was consistent with the maintenance of water-borne trade. Estuary heads were especially favoured as sites, but in their absence other inlets or the leeside of coastal islands were called into service.

Nowadays, it is less essential for ports to be located away from the open sea, for metalled motor roads and steel railway tracks provide excellent landways. Moreover, to function efficiently, many kinds of ports, e.g. fishing ports, ferry ports and naval bases, may need to be very close to open water. Also, ships have grown much bigger, and the only water deep enough for their accommodation may be near the mouths rather than at the heads of coastal indentations. Silting may have contributed to the seaward migration of large ports, and technology is now advanced enough and man himself experienced enough to construct large artificial harbours on the open coast. Yet ports far from the sea persist in many cases, partly through inertia, partly due to extensive dredging operations, and partly because, at least for the transport of heavy, bulky commodities, water transport remains cheaper than overland transport. Especially numerous, even today, are commercial ports located well up large navigable rivers. London, Hamburg, Antwerp, Rouen, Bordeaux, Calcutta, Shanghai, Tientsin, Montreal, Philadelphia and New Orleans are prominent examples. From a number of these ports it is possible, through transshipment on to smaller vessels, to transport cargoes further inland without losing the advantage of water carriage.

THE VARIETY OF PORTS

Commercial ports have always been the largest coastal cities. The busiest are foci of oceanic routes which permit the easy and economic assemblage of goods from a variety of overseas sources. They also allow —through a network of river, canal, rail and road communications—the concentration of domestic merchandise for shipment to many foreign destinations. Such great ports include, *inter alia*, Rotterdam, Antwerp, New York, London, Yokohama, Singapore and Calcutta.

Ports of smaller significance as world cities include: (*a*) inland ports such as Düsseldorf and Strasbourg, which are inaccessible to ocean-going ships; (*b*) packet-stations commanding short sea crossings; (*c*) ports of call on long-distance routes; and (*d*) a variety of specialised ports equipped to handle chiefly fish or mineral products, or so strategically placed as to be able to act as naval bases.

THE REQUIREMENTS OF COMMERCIAL SEAPORTS

In order to function as an active trading centre, a port, like an inland commercial centre, requires both a favourable site and a favourable situation. The chief site factor is the nature of the harbour, the leading situation factor is the extent and character of the hinterland (i.e. the area served by the port). Other factors to be taken into account include the kind of land available for erecting port buildings and other urban structures; the extent to which the port is equipped to handle cargoes; the number of roads and railways focusing upon the port, and the presence or absence of navigable rivers and canals; and the number and frequency of shipping lines and other marine routes converging upon it.

Thus a port can only grow into a major commercial centre, handling a large volume and variety of sea-borne trade, if its harbour is suitably commodious and deep, satisfactorily sheltered and well equipped, if its hinterland is well developed and prosperous and threaded by numerous surface communications; and if it is the terminus of shipping routes from diverse parts of the world.

THE HARBOURS OF COMMERCIAL PORTS

Mention was made in Chapter VII of several typical harbours, ranging from those located on estuaries and deltas, on rias, fjords and islands, to those at the end of canals or other artificial waterways. To this list may be added harbours in the lee of rocky headlands, *e.g.* Cape Town (*see* Fig. 77); those formed by the breaching of volcanic craters, *e.g.* Lyttelton (*see* Fig. 78), the port of Christchurch, New Zealand; those produced by the submergence of fault blocks, *e.g.* Port Nicholson, the bay on which

[*Courtesy: South Africa House*

FIG. 77.—Cape Town, South Africa. This aerial view of Cape Town shows the port's artificial harbour on Table Bay, and the town's buildings sandwiched on gently rising ground between the sea and the flat-topped, eroded Table Mountain, ascending sharply to 3,500 ft (1,060 m). Founded by the Dutch in 1652, Cape Town still acts largely as a half-way house between western Europe on the one hand and southern Asia and Australia on the other.

[*Courtesy: High Commissioner for New Zealand*

FIG. 78.—Port Lyttelton, New Zealand. Port Lyttelton, the port for Christchurch, 7 miles (11 km) to the west, is located on the north-western edge of the volcanic Banks Peninsula. The harbour, shown here, has been formed out of a submerged volcanic crater, whose steep, curving slopes overlook the geometrically laid-out town. Oil installations are prominent on reclaimed land near the harbour which is now being extended seawards (extreme right).

Wellington stands; and those on bays protected by spits or marine bars, *e.g.* Galveston, Durban and Lagos. Though many harbours are initially chosen for their natural advantages, most, if not quite all, have been improved or extended artificially by the provision of breakwaters and piers, wharves and docks, and so on. A few—mostly on broad embayments or on unindented coasts—are entirely artificial.

Some harbours are particularly well favoured because, while themselves deep, sheltered and commodious, they lack nearby rivals. Such are the coastal openings at San Francisco and Rio de Janeiro. Western Europe is fortunate in having many deep-water estuaries, *e.g.* the Mersey, Severn, Humber, Thames, Clyde, Forth and Tay in Britain; the Seine, Loire and Garonne in France; the Weser and Elbe in Western Germany and the Scheldt in the Low Countries. Hull and Immingham, on either bank of the Humber, benefit from the way in which the deep-water channel swings from one side of the estuary to the other opposite these two ports. Hull has the additional advantage of the extra water frontage provided by the banks of the River Hull where it joins the Humber, as shown in Fig. 56.

While most estuarine ports are helped by tidal rise, which not only permits large ships to enter them, but may also scour them out, as at Liverpool, on its unusual bottle-necked estuary, not all are as well placed as Southampton and Cherbourg, which benefit from two double high tides each day. Though tides are on the whole helpful, they make the loading and unloading of ships difficult, and necessitate the construction of docks fitted with lock gates so that vessels within them may be protected from a quickly changing water level.

Icing presents a hazard to the efficient operation of certain ports in high latitudes, *e.g.* Churchill (on Hudson Bay), normally icebound for nine months, and Montreal (four months). Ports on the Baltic margins, and others such as Arkhangelsk (White Sea) and Vladivostok, are normally kept open, though with difficulty, by the use of icebreakers.

PORT INSTALLATIONS

A harbour is effective only when it is properly equipped with quays, cranes, warehouses, transit sheds, shipping offices, custom-houses, road and rail facilities, wet and dry docks, tugs and perhaps lighters. Quays or wharves alongside the waterway are often supplemented by others built at right-angles to it, as at New York (*see* Fig. 79), San Francisco, Vancouver, Sydney and other large ports. Rotterdam and Amsterdam, Manchester and other cities have extensive open docks which extend the accommodation available for shipping. At ports such as London, Rouen, Hamburg, Antwerp and New York, lighters are used to effect the quick transit of cargoes direct to warehouses, railway termini, sugar refineries, flour mills, and so on, or to consuming centres further upriver.

Ports lacking suitable harbours may have to arrange for the transshipment of cargoes from ocean-going ships standing out in deep water offshore into smaller vessels, *e.g.* open boats or lighters, which lengthens the time taken to handle merchandise. Ports dependent on this kind of operation include Accra, Mozambique, Arica and Tocopilla. The trade of these ports is being increasingly taken over by newer ones which provide more adequate facilities, *e.g.* Takoradi and Tema, Lourenço Marques and Beira, and Antofagasta.

A number of ports, even those possessing excellent harbours and adequate hinterland links, lack good building land. Especially is this true of places from which high ground rises abruptly landwards, as at Marseilles, Genoa, Bergen, Seattle, Vancouver, San Francisco and Victoria (Hong Kong). Other problems exist at such ports as New York, whose different quarters can be linked together only by numerous river crossings; at

[*Courtesy: United States Information Services*

FIG. 79.—Port facilities in New York. New York has nearly 600 miles (960 km) of water frontage, and is by far the greatest port in the Americas. The photograph shows two large liners passing each other on the lower Hudson River, whose banks are lined with wharves. The skyscrapers of Manhattan loom up in the background.

Venice, which is almost inaccessible to motor traffic on account of its multiple-island site, and at Hull which lacks the advantage of a Humber bridge, though plans for building one are now being made.

PORTS AND OUTPORTS

As we saw in Chapter VII, many large commercial ports, especially those located well up river estuaries, are supplemented by outports. Most of these have deep-water accommodation and many developed because their parents—owing in most cases to excessive silting and to the growth in the average size of ships—are now less able to perform all their functions satisfactorily. Even where waterways have been improved by dredging operations, outports are not always absent because their use may save pilotage dues and also allow passengers, mail, and high-value freight to shorten their water-borne journeys and so save time. From such outports, traffic may proceed inland by rail or motor vehicle or it may be taken upriver or to other coastal localities by smaller ship.

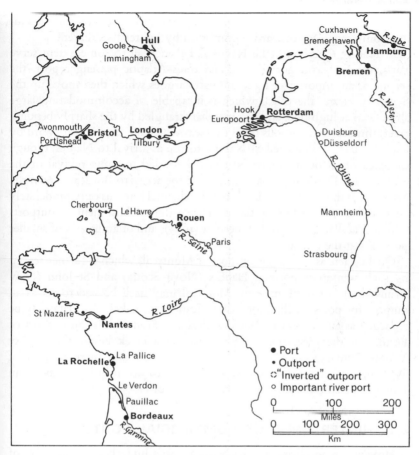

Fig. 80.—Ports and outports in Western Europe. Western Europe is richer in outports than any other part of the world. Goole is an "inverted" outport and Europoort (Europoort) is the new outport of Rotterdam. A few important river ports have been added to this map.

Western Europe is particularly rich in outports (*see* Fig. 80). In Britain, two of the best examples are Avonmouth and Portishead, both established in the 1870s as extensions of Bristol, though remaining under the same port authority. Congestion in the Pool of London and on the riverbanks below the Tower led to the opening of Tilbury docks in 1886 as a special passenger terminal, and in a sense all the ports in south-eastern England, not excluding Southampton, act as outports of London. Familiar examples of ports and outports in Germany are Hamburg and Cuxhaven on the

Elbe, the latter serving mainly as a trans-Atlantic passenger port, and Bremen and Bremerhaven, the latter another passenger port but also handling some cargo for onward transmission by lighter to Bremen.

In France, Cherbourg, Le Havre and Rouen all to some extent serve Paris, the first as a port of call and trans-Atlantic passenger port, the second as an importer of light and part cargoes which then move up the Seine by barge, the third, which is incapable of accommodating large ships even at high tide, and is somewhat strangled by the sharply bending river, imports many goods from overseas which are then sent forward by barge to Paris. Silting led St Nazaire to rise as a rival to Nantes, though the excavation of an improved channel has led to some revival of the earlier port. Dredging has also improved the access to Bordeaux, 60 miles (96 km) up the Gironde estuary, but the channel remains only moderately deep and is not easily negotiated. Hence the establishment of outports both at Pauillac (1894) and at Verdon (1933), and of a number of smaller ports along the estuary.*

Quebec acts as a summer outport of Montreal, which is further served by such winter outports as Halifax (Nova Scotia) and St John (New Brunswick). In some measure Montreal may itself be said to act as an outport for ports on the North American Great Lakes. La Plata may be regarded as an outport of Buenos Aires and Fremantle as an outport of Perth, but the great port of Shanghai, on a creek beside the mighty Yangtse estuary, can no more be looked upon as a mere outport of Wuhan, further up-river but still accessible to ocean-going traffic, than Hull can be considered simply as an outport of Goole.

THE HINTERLANDS OF COMMERCIAL PORTS

However magnificent the harbour, a port's hinterland is generally of more lasting significance. This fact is well illustrated by the large number of roomy, sheltered inlets in mountainous countries such as Norway and Yugoslavia which fail to attract more than a few trading ships, and, conversely, by the large volume of trade transacted by many deltaic ports which possess very inconvenient sites but have good access to highly productive hinterlands.

The kind and variety of commodities a port handles, the total tonnage and value of those commodities, and the port's balance of trade (*i.e.* the value of its imports compared with its exports) are all mainly dependent upon the size and economic character of its hinterland. For certain kinds

---

* Further details about European outports may be read in N. J. G. Pounds, "Port and Outport in North-west Europe," *Geographical Journal*, Vol. 109, 1947.

of merchandise the hinterland may be international, for others national, regional or local. Thus a well-developed port may be said to possess not one, but several hinterlands. Vancouver, for instance, exports timber and wood products from the immediate area, and wheat from the Prairies. For tea and silk its import hinterland extends as far as Eastern Canada. Liverpool serves Lancashire as an importer of raw cotton and an exporter of manufactured cotton, Yorkshire as an importer of wool and an exporter of wool textiles, and the Midlands as an importer of metals and an exporter of motor vehicles and other engineered products. For the trade of Lancashire it competes with Manchester, for that of Yorkshire with Hull, for that of the Midlands with London and Southampton. Thus hinterlands are never clear-cut and are often competitive.

Were Antwerp and Rotterdam simply the chief ports of Belgium and the Netherlands respectively, they would transact very much less trade than in fact they do, for they also serve the Ruhr industrial area in Western Germany, and have thereby come to be counted among the world's largest ports. Similarly, Beira taps the trade of Rhodesia and Malawi, Lourenço Marques that of the Rand: if these two ports were outlets simply for Portuguese Mozambique their trade would be quite small.

THE TRADE OF COMMERCIAL PORTS

Most large ports are liner ports, *i.e.* they deal mainly with traffic (cargo and passenger) carried in ships running on fixed routes at scheduled times. Such vessels carry "general" cargo which either is packed in some way or else consists of an actual article such as a motor-car. Tramp ships, which have no fixed schedules and are specially chartered, carry cargoes in bulk, *e.g.* coal, metal ores, sugar and grain. They use the facilities of both small, specialised ports, and also those of large liner ports. Tankers, especially oil tankers, now dominate the world's shipping patterns. They include the largest ships afloat: ships which can berth only at a few places with deep-water anchorage, *e.g.* Milford Haven and the modern, seaward extension of Rotterdam, known as Europoort (*see* Fig. 81).

Many of the world's major ports act as entrepôts, *i.e.* they import cargoes for resale through trans-shipment following inspection, testing and grading, for which they provide special facilities. Among them are London, especially important for tea and wool, Amsterdam (tobacco, spices and other "colonial" products), Singapore (rubber), Hong Kong (products destined for China or originating in that country) and Copenhagen, the great port of Scandinavia.

Coastal transport is a function of many ports, especially those in countries with long coastlines, *e.g.* Britain and Denmark, and in those with poor land communications, *e.g.* Norway, Chile, Alaska and Greece. Many of the smaller commercial ports in these countries are almost wholly concerned with coastal shipping.

The trade of commercial ports is always in a state of flux: its volume varies with changing physical, economic and political conditions. Harbours, as we have seen, may suffer silting, which may cause ports to decline unless dredging operations and other costly engineering projects,

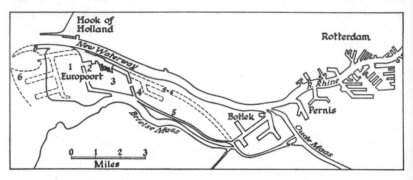

FIG. 81.—Rotterdam and Europoort. Already Rotterdam is the world's leading port. Its pre-eminence will grow still further as its outport approaches completion. Both Pernis and Botlek are oil ports; further oil storage and refining facilities are being provided in Europoort (3 on the map). Other operations include: 1. projected blast furnaces and steel works; 2. storage depot for bulk goods; 4. large ship-repair yards; 5. link with inland waterways; 6. possible new oil-port facilities for giant tankers.

perhaps including the construction of outports, are undertaken. Thus Chester and the Cinque Ports of south-east England declined, while Glasgow and Newcastle, thanks to the deepening of the Clyde and Tyne, grew in strength. In the fourteenth century, Boston in Lincolnshire, now an insignificant coastal port, had a greater trade than Hull; and York, Doncaster, Cambridge and Norwich were seaports. In Europe, Bruges was the chief outlet of Flanders, then at the peak of its prosperity, but the silting up of the Zwin allowed Antwerp to overtake it.

In North America, the trade of the north-east Atlantic ports swelled as people spread into the interior of the United States and as Pennsylvania and the Mid-West, following the example of Europe, became industrialised. New York stole a march on its rivals when the Erie Canal— the easiest route across the Appalachians—was opened in 1825. On the Pacific coast, San Francisco benefited from the impetus provided by the discovery of gold nearby in 1849, and received a further stimulus when the first trans-continental railway (the Union Pacific) was completed twenty years later. The opening of the Panama Canal in 1914 led to a quickening of its trade with Europe, but probably the chief factor in the port's development was the agricultural and industrial development of its Californian hinterland. Like San Francisco, Vancouver benefited from the opening of the Panama Canal, and henceforth was to rival Montreal as a port. A few years earlier, the Suez Canal produced a resuscitation of such Mediterranean ports as Venice, Genoa and Marseilles.

Danzig, Gdynia, Odessa and Trieste are among ports which have been markedly affected by political events. Danzig (Gdansk)—the natural port of the Vistula Basin, the heart of Poland—was designated a Free City by the League of Nations in 1919, as it was a German-speaking enclave within the territory of the newly independent Poland. To secure a port of its own, Poland established Gdynia as a rival. Now both ports are under Polish control and, along with the recently acquired Stettin (Szczecin), they act as partners rather than as keen competitors. Odessa lost its chief function and entered a period of decline after the 1917 Revolution when Russia ceased to export large quantities of wheat. Trieste, the great port of the Austro-Hungarian Empire, suffered a severe loss of trade when it passed under Italian rule after the First World War and was denied most of its former extensive hinterland. It became even more peripheral to Italy in 1954, and now possesses a very restricted hinterland.

NEW PORTS

Though there is a growing tendency for the larger ports, attracting as they do both liner and tanker traffic, to expand at the expense of smaller ports in their vicinity, new ports continue to appear, especially in economically backward countries, which are now expanding their international trade, and in countries which have recently changed their political alignment. The establishment of these new ports also necessitates, of course, the construction of new roads and railways, without which they could not build up their trade. Examples from two areas will suffice.

The Kingdom of Jordan, denied by Israel the use of the old Palestinian ports of Haifa and Jaffa, is now developing the port of Aqaba for its sole use. Israel, as part of its programme for developing the Negev, is trying meanwhile to boost the import of petroleum and the more general Eastern trade of Eilat. However, she is not neglecting the further economic expansion of her Mediterranean zone where the new, completely artificial port of Ashdod is being built to relieve the strain on

Haifa during the citrus season and to supplant the less satisfactory road-steads of Jaffa and Tel Aviv, where there is less room for new port installations.

In West Africa, Ghana, Togo and Dahomey have all striven to extend and improve their overseas outlets since independence, partly because of planned economic expansion, partly because of the surf-beaten approach to the shore which renders such ports as Accra unsatisfactory. Takoradi, in Ghana, was opened more than twenty years ago as a deep-water harbour accessible to large ships, and its facilities were extended in the early 1950s. At about the same time developments were initiated on a site at Tema, a little fishing village close to Accra. By 1964, its total trade had surpassed that of Takoradi (D. Hilling, "Tema—the Geography of a New Port," *Geography* (*see* Fig. 82)). Meanwhile, there are plans to create deep-water ports at Cotonou (Dahomey) to serve both Niger and Dahomey, and at Lomé and Kpémé (Togo).

[*Courtesy: Cadbury Bros.*

Fig. 82.—Tema: a new port in Ghana. The port of Tema, opened in 1961, and, more recently, extended, was built so as to provide for eastern Ghana similar shipping facilities as Takoradi was already providing for western Ghana. Its trade is at present dominated by the export of cocoa and the import of petroleum and cement, but it may become more diversified as its hinterland—embracing bauxite mines and the Volta River project—develops. The photograph shows some of the quays, transit sheds and warehouses, and, in the background, some indication of the growing new town.

THE INDUSTRIES OF LARGE PORTS

Large ports attract manufacturing industry not only on account of their intimate trade relations with other countries but also because of their reservoir of labour, the considerable market they themselves provide and their numerous hinterland connections. As shipping centres, large ports are clearly well fitted to undertake ship-building and ship-repair work, ship-breaking and the manufacture of marine engines and other fitments needed by ships, but of course not all do so. Among desiderata are not only a broad, deep, sheltered waterway, but also a surplus of inexpensive land not required for docks, warehouses, customs sheds, and so on.

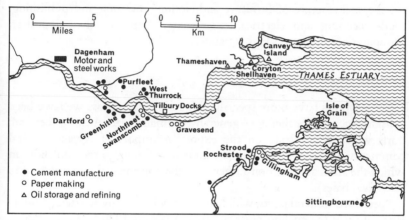

FIG. 83.—Some heavy industries on the Thames below London. This map should be contrasted with Fig. 109. Here, below Woolwich and Albert Docks, most of the industries require heavy or bulky raw materials for the carriage of which ships are most suitable. Hence the waterside location of most of the works.

Many port industries are concerned with the conversion of bulky imported commodities into more valuable products for sale either direct to the consumer or to other manufacturers. Hence the importance at many ports of industries such as oil-refining, the treatment of metal ores, the manufacture of heavy chemicals and fertilisers, sugar-refining, oilseed crushing, flour-milling, leather tanning and paper-making. If a country has to import heavy commodities such as iron ore and has to bring in coal as well, or is fortunate enough to possess a coastal coalfield, it is obviously advantageous for a port to be selected as the site of a steel works. Hence the construction of steel mills at places such as Margam and Newport (South Wales), Sparrows Point (Baltimore), Velsen (near Ijmuiden, Netherlands), Dunkirk, Port Kembla and Newcastle (New South Wales), and Yawata (Japan). The need for machinery for steel-making and other industries, and the demand for port installations such as conveyors and cranes may stimulate a variety of derivative engineering industries.

The distribution of industries in the London area illustrates the effect of cheap water transport. Heavy industries and those concerned with bulky commodities, *e.g.* saw-milling, paper-milling, cement-making, oil-refining, sugar-refining, flour-milling and steel-making, together with electricity and gas works dependent on coal shipments, are located on the banks of the Thames estuary below the City. In central London and on the northern and western fringes of the capital, the emphasis is on lighter industries which can more easily bear the cost of road and rail haulage, *e.g.* the manufacture of furniture and clothing, printing and publishing, food-processing and electrical engineering. Some of these industrial groupings are shown on Figs. 83 and 109.

SPECIALISED PORTS

Certain ports have more specialised functions than those we have been considering, and are therefore generally of smaller size. Among them are ports which concentrate on the export or import of certain mineral commodities, those which are best known as fishing ports, and those in which the strategic function rather than the commercial one holds sway (*i.e.* naval bases).

Specialised mineral ports, which are usually backed by restricted hinterlands, include the coaling ports of South Wales and Durham, *e.g.* Barry, Blyth and Seaham, all nowadays adversely affected by competition from petroleum-oil exporting ports such as Maracaibo, Abadan, Mersa el Brega (Libya), Willemstad (Curaçao), Houston and Tuxpan, and importing ports such as Milford Haven, Fawley and Lavera (near Marseilles). They include ports shipping iron ore, *e.g.* Narvik, Bilbao and Sept Iles (Quebec); copper, *e.g.* Lobito Bay; lead and zinc, *e.g.* Port Pirie; nitrates, *e.g.* Iquique and Tocopilla; china clay, *e.g.* Fowey and Par (*see* Fig. 84). A few ports specialise in the export of vegetable commodities, *e.g.* Churchill and Bunbury ship wheat, Santos coffee, and many small Swedish ports, (*e.g.* Sundsvall), export timber.

Neither the import and export of minerals, nor the landing and exporting of fish is necessarily confined to specialised ports. For example, Algiers exports large amounts of iron ore and Baltimore imports large quantities; both Rotterdam and Le Havre are major importers of petroleum, but none of these is highly specialised. Hull is one of the two principal fishing ports in Britain, Boston one of the main ones in the U.S.A., but the trade

[*Courtesy: English China Clays Group*

FIG. 84.—Par: a china-clay port. The small, specialised port of Par, whose harbour has been constructed on the west side of a small tidal bay, is only about six miles east of the St. Austell kaolin quarries. It imports coal and exports china clay and china stone for the English China Clay Company. The white deposit on the buildings and quayside is blown clay.

of these ports is by no means confined to fish. More specialised fishing ports include Fleetwood, Stornoway and Newlyn, Concarneau and Fécamp, Gloucester (New England) (*see* Fig. 85), Biloxi (Mississippi), Scheveningen, Stavanger and Tromsö—all adjacent to productive fishing grounds and all possessing harbours which are large enough and deep enough to accommodate the rather small vessels required by the fishing industry.

Naval bases usually occupy easily defended sites, they possess harbours which are commodious enough not only to accommodate many ships but to give them room to manoeuvre, and they are established in those situations which will not only enable them to defend the coast or well-used shipping route from enemy attack but also allow them speedily to seek out the enemy while it is still on the high seas. They do not require a productive hinterland. Examples include Portsmouth, Brest, Toulon, San Diego, Norfolk, Key West, Pearl Harbor, Valletta, Gibraltar, Taranto and Yokosuka (on Tokyo Bay). Most of them have ship-repair

[*Courtesy: United States Information Service*

FIG. 85.—Fishing vessels at Gloucester, Massachusetts. Gloucester has been a significant fishing port since 1660. Two-thirds of its present population (about 25,000) depend directly or indirectly upon fishing for their livelihood. Lining the harbour are fish quays and warehouses.

yards, some also ship-building facilities, and a number also have room for merchant shipping.

PACKET STATIONS AND PORTS OF CALL

Packet stations or ferry ports are more restricted by physical geography than any other class of port. They are most common in certain well-populated countries, where they allow passengers, mail and perishable or fragile cargoes to be carried expeditiously and regularly over short sea-crossings. Their harbours need be neither very deep nor very large; many are artificial. They are served by good rail connections, often providing speedy links between the capital city and the coast. Examples are numerous in south-eastern England (*see* Fig. 86), in particular Dover, commanding the shortest sea-crossing to France (Calais) and Belgium (Ostend), Newhaven (with sailings to Dieppe), Folkestone (for Boulogne)

FIG. 86.—The main British ferry ports. Many passengers and goods move across
the narrow seas between Britain and Ireland, and Britain and the Continent.
Hence this country is notable for the number of its specialised ferry ports or
packet stations. The regular connections between, for example, Southampton
and French ports (*e.g.* Cherbourg and St Malo), and those between Hull and
Rotterdam, Newcastle and Bergen, Liverpool and Dublin, are not shown since
Southampton, Hull, Newcastle and Liverpool are all primarily large commercial
ports.

and Harwich (for the Hook of Holland, Ostend and Esbjerg). South-
ampton also has a ferry function, with connections to Le Havre, St Malo
and Cherbourg, and from Weymouth tourists are conveyed to the
Channel Islands. Most of these services now include car-ferry facilities.
In Scotland, Stranraer operates services to Larne (for Belfast), and in
Wales ships travel from Holyhead to Dun Laoghaire (for Dublin) and
from Fishguard to Rosslare. Train ferries operate between several of the
Danish islands, and the country has ferry connections with Germany and
Sweden. It should be noted that the construction of bridges and tunnels

(*e.g.* between Jutland and Fyen in Denmark and between Honshu and Shikoku in Japan) is reducing the need for certain ferry ports. It is interesting to speculate about the changes which may come to Dover and Calais if the projected Channel Tunnel becomes a reality.

Ports of call, which usually possess other functions as well, are located at convenient places on long-distance shipping routes so that vessels may unload part cargoes and disembark a proportion of their passengers, and take on fresh fruit and vegetables, fuel, water, and perhaps other cargo and passengers. They include, on the route from England to Bombay via the Cape, Funchal, Las Palmas, Cape Town and Durban, and on the route to Calcutta, Colombo. The Suez route is punctuated by Gibraltar, Valletta and Port Said. *En route* from San Francisco to Wellington are Honolulu and Suva. Some ports of call, *e.g.* Plymouth, resemble out-ports in that they enable passengers and mail to make speedier journeys to their destinations, in particular London, than would be possible if the whole journey were accomplished by sea.

INLAND PORTS

Most inland ports are inaccessible to ocean-going ships, but have the advantage of water transport for merchandise carried in bulk. Obvious examples include such riverine cities as Düsseldorf and Duisburg, the busy Ruhr ports, Mannheim and Strasbourg further up the Rhine, Paris, Chungking, Stanleyville (Kisangani), St Louis and Asuncion. Lake ports include Baku and Krasnovodsk on the Caspian, Kisumu on Lake Victoria and Guaqui on Lake Titicaca.

A number of inland ports, paradoxically, are within reach of oceanic liners. They are most numerous on the North American Great Lakes and include Toronto and Chicago. A thousand miles up the Amazon is Manaos, actually on the Rio Negro, and over 400 miles up the Yangtse is Hankow, the port section of Wuhan.

AIRPORTS

Airports are entirely a product of the present century, and have not yet, in general, given birth to fully urban settlements. Since they require a considerable amount of space, and increasingly long runways as well as almost level ground, their siting is not easy. The largest are those equipped to serve major cities, from which, however, they may have to be as much as 20 or more miles (30 km) distant. Ultimately, unless prevented by planning controls, cities may be expected to grow towards them, despite the problems of noise which become more acute as the number of supersonic jet aircraft increases.

A few, generally smaller, airports, *e.g.* in Australia, have been built to overcome the isolation of thinly peopled areas with poor ground transport facilities. Others, *e.g.* Gander in Newfoundland, Goose Bay in Labrador and Sondre Stromfjord in Greenland, act as ports of call or emergency stations on long distance routes.*

* Much of the material in this chapter is based on F. W. Morgan, *Ports and Harbours*, Hutchinson, 1952.

Chapter XII

Mining and Industrial Towns

IN a sense, mining and industrial settlements are as old as towns them-selves, for as early as the Bronze Age civilised people required the products of copper and tin mines, and ornamental articles of gold and silver were not unknown. Moreover, all the ancient towns had their craftsmen, *e.g.* potters, weavers, smiths and leather-workers. As fully-fledged towns, however, mining settlements are fairly recent phenomena, many of them dating only from the Industrial Revolution, when coal and iron began to be worked on a big scale, and what we generally regard as industrial towns (*i.e.* those in which a majority of the gainfully employed are engaged in manufacturing) date from the same period.

Most mining settlements are small, and in general remain no more than "camps" or villages unless they acquire some manufacturing industry, and attain some commercial significance. Industrial settlements—which are on the whole much larger, though they include many industrial villages—often number miners among their workers, especially when they are situated on coalfields. They often, too, become important commercial centres. Thus mining and industrial towns are not necessarily mutually exclusive.

MINING TOWNS

The Situation of Mining Towns

In their distribution, mining towns show less regard to general environ-mental conditions than any other class of town. Many, in fact, are situated in areas which would be entirely unattractive and unrewarding to settled populations but for their mineral wealth, consequently they are often isolated from other settlements, though in order to dispose of their products and to obtain supplies, they are rarely without rail and road communications with the outside world. In the harsher and less accessible areas they arise only where the mineral or minerals upon which they depend occur in large quantities, or where the deposits are of high grade and value, or where they lie near enough to the surface to allow of cheap working. In more kindly environments, with higher population densities and more close-knit communications, e.g. on the coalfields of Britain and the iron fields of Lorraine, the minerals may be of lower grade and of lower value, they may be more deep-seated, and they may occur as less extensive bodies.

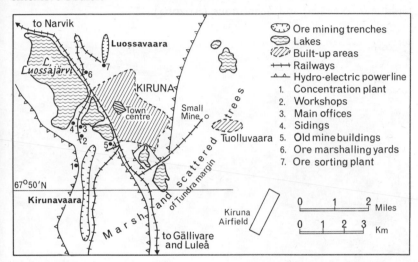

FIG. 87.—Kiruna, Sweden: a modern mining town. Kiruna—in area said to be the largest town in the world—has a population of less than 30,000. It is situated 100 miles north of the Arctic Circle on the southern margin of the Swedish tundra: an area occupied by marshes, lakes and stunted trees. The main iron deposits—formerly obtained by terrace-cutting, now by deep-working—are of high-grade magnetite (60 to 70 per cent metal content). They are chiefly railed to Narvik, Norway (open all the year), but some are sent in summer to Luleå, Sweden (closed by ice November–May), for export to Germany, Great Britain, Belgium, etc. Some ore is railed south to steel plants in central Sweden.

Among mining towns in regions of difficulty, or even privation, are the following: Kiruna and Gällivare in Sweden (see Fig. 87), and Schefferville in Quebec (iron-mining centres on the tundra margin), Kalgoorlie and Marble Bar (gold-mining towns in the desert of western Australia), Cerro de Pasco and Oruro (base-metal mining towns in the high Andes), and Mackenzie City (a bauxite-mining settlement in the steaming forests of Guyana).

The Rise and Fall of Mining Towns

Many mining towns grow very rapidly, especially at first when their wealth is most accessible, and particularly when the magnet of a precious metal, notably gold, lures fortune-hunters to their sites. While, however, they may quickly "mushroom," they may decline with comparable speed, and indeed become "ghost towns." In some cases, the interval between "boom and bust" may be less than 50 years, as was the case with Dawson City in the Klondike valley on the Alaskan border, scene of a gold rush in 1898, and with many other towns in North America such as Goldfield (Nevada) and Tombstone (Arizona).

[*Courtesy: Australian News and Information Bureau*

FIG. 88.—Broken Hill, New South Wales. The setting of Broken Hill, like that of most mining towns, is far from attractive. On the left of this photograph is the virtually exhausted central part of the Broken Hill ridge, severely gashed by miners excavating for lead, zinc and silver. In the centre mid-ground is an old residue dump. On the right is a small, outlying part of the town. The main part lies off the photograph to the left.

To survive, such towns must attract some new activity—which may be difficult in a harsh environment—to gradually replace the primary occupation as the output of the mines declines. This secondary activity is usually, at first, concerned with metal processing, *e.g.* concentration and smelting, but may later develop into refining and engineering. These "transformation industries" include, for example in Magnitogorsk, and at a number of places in the Jurassic ironstone belts of eastern England and Lorraine, the manufacture not only of pig-iron but of steel. In the

Katanga mining area of central Africa they include not only the smelting of copper but also its electrolytic refining. In the case of Johannesburg, which was born as recently as 1886 but had over a million people 80 years later, the discovery of the Rand gold reef caused its population to make its initial spurt. It has since become a great city because it has attracted a very wide range of industries, most of which have no connection with mining, and has become the chief centre of internal commerce in South Africa (*see* Fig. 76, p. 173).

Broken Hill, in New South Wales, though much less diverse in its occupational structure than Johannesburg, and much smaller (pop. *c.* 30,000), has lived through a similar experience (*see* Fig. 88). Its ores—of lead, silver and zinc—were discovered about the same time as the Rand gold, and what was hitherto a ranch grew in consequence into a mining town, an old drovers' trail becoming its main street. Though still one of the world's major mining centres, and surrounded, like Johannesburg, with spoil heaps, it is not only engaged in mining and in the concentration of lead and zinc, but it has come to act as the regional focus of an extensive pastoral area supporting over 2 million sheep and 20,000 head of cattle. It possesses a few dairies and some of its people, thanks to a water pipeline from Lake Menindee, have found employment as market-gardeners.

Employment in Mining Towns

Mining towns, as distinct from mining camps and villages, rarely support more than 15 per cent of their working population by what is regarded as their dominant activity, except for those dependent on coal-mining where the percentage, as in parts of south Yorkshire and the Ruhr, may exceed 60. These colliery towns are usually more stable than other mining settlements, partly because seams of coal often yield their riches for much longer periods than other mineral deposits, and partly because they can more easily attract other industries since coal, like petroleum, is a source of power as well as a raw material. Viewed purely as mining settlements, however, they do, in the long run, like other towns dependent on mining, lack permanence. West Durham and South Wales, the exposed part of the Ruhr coalfield and the western part of the northern coalfield of France are all punctuated not only with derelict mines, the result of exhaustion or pit rationalisation, but also with half-deserted settlements, most of which, however, are villages which failed to develop industrial functions.

Like other mining towns, colliery towns provide a hard and dangerous life for men and offer little to women, who must, therefore, either remain without paid work, enter domestic service, travel daily to another town (*e.g.* from Barnsley by special bus to textile factories in Huddersfield) or emigrate with their families to other areas which provide more varied employment opportunities. Thus, unless mining settlements succeed in attracting other enterprises, and so evolve into industrial and commercial centres, they must remain the least permanent of towns.

INDUSTRIAL TOWNS

The Growth of Industrial Towns

The earliest industries were concerned with the working up of local agricultural commodities, *e.g.* grain, leather and wool, or other local products, *e.g.* timber and clay, with a view to satisfying neighbourhood, often simply family, needs. A step forward was made, and a definite industrial function initiated when some of these craft-made articles were produced in sufficient quantities for a wider market to be tapped as a result of developing trade. It was, however, the advent of powered machines, and especially the application of the steam engine to production that brought about the true industrial town, freed from its former excessive dependence upon its surrounding rural area. The hand-processing of commodities, even in advanced countries, still continues, *e.g.* in the tailoring industry, but industrial towns owe their chief charac-teristics to the powered machine, and to the spread of railways, canals and metalled roads, the advent of the motor vehicle and power-driven ship, and the extension of world-wide commerce.

The Distribution of Industrial Towns

The Industrial Revolution had its beginnings in eighteenth-century Britain, whence it spread into Belgium and through the European main-land, across the Atlantic into North America, and later into other con-tinents. Most of the world's industrial towns are located in Europe, the U.S.S.R., the United States and Japan. In other countries, large-scale manufacturing is most often an attribute of populous commercial ports and of political capitals, though most continents provide a few other examples. Among these are São Paulo in Brazil (*see* Fig. 89), which not only processes locally grown coffee, and cotton, but also has factories turning out electrical goods, iron and steel products, chemicals and rubber tyres; Johannesburg in South Africa, with gold refineries, large engineer-ing and cement works, and soap and food factories; Novosibirsk, in south-central Siberia, with both steel and flour mills, oil refineries, textile, clothing and furniture factories, chemical plants, and motor-engineering works turning out tractors and other vehicles; Tashkent in Soviet Central

[Courtesy: B.O.A.C.

FIG. 89.—São Paulo, Brazil. São Paulo, now overtaking Rio de Janeiro in population (4 million), is the greatest manufacturing city in South America as well as a leading seat of internal commerce. Its central area—part of which is shown here—is an amalgam of several architectural styles. While the city park and its palms are reminiscent of Portugal, the concentration, height and shape of the newer buildings recall North America.

Asia, noted for its cotton textiles and agricultural machinery, its sawmills, leather and tobacco factories, and its food-processing works; Shenyang, the great engineering city in Manchuria; and Kanpur (Cawnpore) in India, which has a diversified industrial pattern.

Most of the older industrial cities, especially those in Europe and north-eastern U.S.A., grew up on coalfields, and gathered round themselves factories which used coal as a form of power and in some cases iron and steel works which burnt coal or coke as a direct fuel. Many of these towns grew very rapidly and merged to form conurbations, e.g. those in the west Midlands, south-east Lancashire, west Yorkshire, Le Nord (north-eastern France), the Ruhr and west Pennsylvania. Other, generally more recent industrial centres, have developed near hydro-electric power plants, e.g. São Paulo, Grenoble (French Alps) and Jinja (Uganda), or on

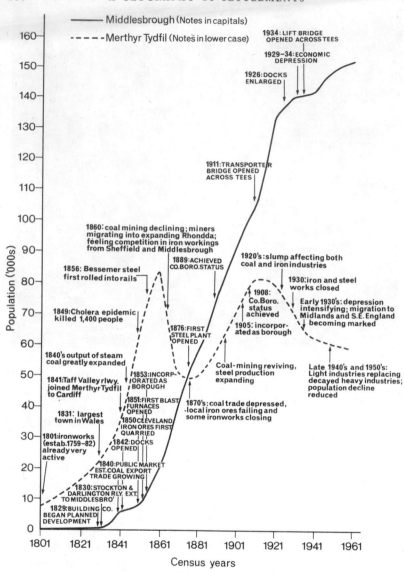

Population ('000s)

—— Middlesbrough (Notes in capitals)
- - - - Merthyr Tydfil (Notes in lower case)

1934: LIFT BRIDGE OPENED ACROSS TEES

1929-34: ECONOMIC DEPRESSION

1926: DOCKS ENLARGED

1911: TRANSPORTER BRIDGE OPENED ACROSS TEES

1860: coal mining declining; miners migrating into expanding Rhondda; feeling competition in iron workings from Sheffield and Middlesbrough

1889: ACHIEVED CO.BORO.STATUS

1920's: slump affecting both coal and iron industries

1856: Bessemer steel first rolled into rails

1930: iron and steel works closed

1908: Co.Boro. status achieved

Early 1930's: depression intensifying; migration to Midlands and S.E. England becoming marked

1849: Cholera epidemic killed 1,400 people

1876: FIRST STEEL PLANT OPENED

1905: incorpor-ated as borough

1840's output of steam coal greatly expanded

Coal-mining reviving, steel production expanding

Late 1940's and 1950's: Light industries replacing decayed heavy industries; population decline reduced

1841: Taff Valley rlwy. joined Merthyr Tydfil to Cardiff

1853: INCORP-ORATED AS BOROUGH

1870's: coal trade depressed, local iron ores failing and some ironworks closing

1851: FIRST BLAST FURNACES OPENED

1831: largest town in Wales

1850 CLEVELAND IRON ORES FIRST QUARRIED

1801: ironworks (estab.1759-82) already very active

1842: DOCKS OPENED

1840: PUBLIC MARKET EST. COAL EXPORT TRADE GROWING

1830: STOCKTON & DARLINGTON RLY. EXT. TO MIDDLESBRO'

1829: BUILDING CO. BEGAN PLANNED DEVELOPMENT

1801   1821   1841   1861   1881   1901   1921   1941   1961

Census years

FIG. 90.—Population changes in Middlesbrough and Merthyr Tydfil. This graph illustrates the contrasting fortunes of two towns heavily dependent on the manufacture of iron and steel. Prior to the world depression of 1929–34, Middlesbrough was one of the most rapidly growing towns in Britain. It remains an important steel-making town. Merthyr Tydfil—already a town in 1801—grew with equal vigour until 1861. Its population has since fluctuated but has been in decline since 1911. It no longer manufactures iron and steel.

[*Courtesy: Josiah Wedgwood and Sons Ltd*

FIG. 91.—Early pottery works in Stoke-on-Trent. This scene—showing bottle kilns at the factory at Etruria, Stoke-on-Trent, where Wedgwood pottery was made from 1769 to 1939—is becoming much less typical of the "Potteries." The Wedgwood Company, in its new works at Barlaston, just beyond the city boundaries, now uses electric ovens. Many of its competitors have also abandoned coal in favour of electricity or gas for firing their wares. The face of Stoke is becoming much cleaner, but less distinctive.

certain oilfields, *e.g.* round Baku and along the Gulf Coast of the United States.

Iron, like coal a very bulky commodity, has often been a magnet attracting industrial development, *e.g.* at Sheffield, Merthyr Tydfil, Ebbw Vale, Valenciennes, Essen, Jamshedpur and Pittsburgh (near all of which coal seams were also present), and at Thionville, Middlesbrough and Magnitogorsk. The last two illustrate the rapidity with which industrial settlements, like mining towns, may grow. In 1831, Middlesbrough had a population of only 150, but, largely owing to the opening up of the Cleveland iron beds from 1850 onwards, it spurted to 55,000 in 1881 and to 138,000 in 1931 (*see* Fig. 90). The expansion of Magnitogorsk, based initially on the iron ores of Magnitnaya Gora (Magnet Mountain) and on Kuznetsk coal, was even more remarkable. Its site was virgin in 1926 but by 1939 the town already had a population of 146,000, which had swelled to 310,000 twenty years later.

A few industrial towns have become important as much from the force of human initiative as from the availability of power supplies and raw materials, though in each case their geographical situations, especially as regards communications and access to markets, have been favourable. Thus Detroit became the main seat of the motor-engineering industry in the U.S.A. thanks to the organisational ability of Henry Ford; and Oxford, long regarded simply as a university city, adopted an industrial career when the future Lord Nuffield, building on his experience as a bicycle repairer, set up his Morris works in the suburb of Cowley. Josiah Wedgwood introduced the porcelain industry into north Staffordshire at a time when only coarse earthenware was being produced in the neighbourhood (*see* Fig. 91); and a niece of MacIntosh, the Scottish rubber pioneer, persuaded her husband to start a rubber factory in Clermont-Ferrand where they lived.

The Varied Character of Industrial Towns

Some industrial towns have a diversified industrial structure and generally benefit from low unemployment rates. Others, less stable and more prone to economic recession, have remained loyal to one dominant industry, to which have usually been added a few ancillaries. Thus among industrial centres there are important route foci and large commercial cities like Manchester, Leeds and Nottingham in England; Chicago, St Louis and Atlanta in the U.S.A.; Toulouse and Lyons in France; Cologne in Germany, which are able to support a wide variety of industrial activities, and other, generally smaller settlements, such as Consett (iron and steel), Dewsbury (wool textiles), Widnes (chemicals), Stoke-on-Trent (pottery), Clydebank (ships), Luton (motor engineering), Kirkcaldy (linoleum), to quote a few British examples, which are sustained in the main by one major industry. Wool towns such as Huddersfield often also possess engineering works (originally devoted to textile engineering only) and chemical works (initially producing little more than textile dyes and associated chemicals). Pottery towns such as Stoke have similarly linked industries, *e.g.* the manufacture of colours, glazes, brushes and items of machinery used in the chief manufacturing industry.

Many small towns developing, for instance, within the interstices of the growing conurbations of East Lancashire and West Yorkshire, had as their nucleus a single textile factory, just as numerous mining towns owed their origin to the exploitation of one mineral vein or the sinking of one coal pit. On a larger scale, more notable towns have been created, in some cases in a previously rural environment, by the demand for workers to serve a single, very large industrial plant. Eindhoven, in the Netherlands, furnishes a good example (Fig. 63). Here, the Philips electrical works employ three quarters of the workers. At Leverkusen, in Germany, two-thirds of the gainfully employed work in the Bayer chemical plant, and at Billingham-on-Tees, in England, the I.C.I. corporation is the only large industrial employer.

Clearly, there are many different kinds of industrial towns, some containing long-established commercial or cultural nuclei round which factories have been built within the last two centuries or less, some, in both advanced and developing countries, almost entirely new. Many industrial towns are very large, others quite small. The older ones are often dirty, run-down and in desperate need of urban renewal, many of the younger ones are clean and pleasant. Some have varied industries and also other significant functions, but some are precariously dependent on a single factory. Nearly all have congested communications and have to compete for markets with their counterparts in other continents. Their inhabitants increasingly suffer stresses and strains due to the growing competitiveness of industrial production.

Chapter XIII

Towns with Miscellaneous Functions

FORTRESS TOWNS AND OTHER MILITARY CENTRES

MANY historic towns, as we have seen (Chapter V), were established for defensive reasons. Among them were numerous Roman towns, *e.g.* Chester (Fig. 35, p. 83), Lincoln and York, the medieval "bastides" of south-west France, Wales and Scotland, the settlements established by German knights and traders in Eastern Europe and the fortresses at Quebec and Pittsburgh in North America. Most medieval towns had at least walled defences and some had also castles round which merchants and craftsmen gathered. Favoured sites were the crowns of steep-sided hills, as at Athens, Perugia, Angoulême, Nuremburg and Edinburgh; the cores of incised meanders, as at Durham (Fig. 57, p. 133), Besançon and Toledo (*see* Fig. 92); riverine islands, as at Paris and Berlin; the "safe" margin of rivers, as at Maastricht and Frankfurt-on-Oder; confluence forks, as at Pittsburgh; and coastal headlands, as at Scarborough (Fig. 60, p. 137) and Aberystwyth. Situations commanding gaps through which marching armies might pass, as at Carcassonne, Belfort, Cracow, Lewes and Delhi, (Fig. 69, p. 157), were often chosen.

In most of these historic strategic centres defence is no longer a dominant function, and surviving fortress towns now depend mainly upon trade, and perhaps also upon administration, manufacturing and receipts from tourists, to maintain and possibly strengthen their position in the urban hierarchy. Their forts and castles, where they have not decayed or been dismantled, are commonly used today either for quartering local troops or as historical museums. They no longer have any real military significance.

Existing military bases do not generally take the form of complete urban settlements. Most consist of barrack blocks and married quarters and are diversified, at best, by a few shops and social buildings, as at Tidworth on Salisbury Plain or Catterick Camp in Yorkshire. They usually lie alongside military training areas.

Naval bases, discussed briefly in the last chapter, are a special type of

[*Courtesy: Spanish National Tourist Office*

FIG. 92.—Toledo, Spain: a defensive centre. Like Durham, Toledo owes its defensive character to its position within the loop of an entrenched meander. The Tagus is crossed here by two bridges, one of which (the Puente de Alcantara) is shown on this photograph. It dates from the thirteenth century and is closed to motor traffic. The gate tower leading from it into the city was built in 1484. In the highest part of Toledo, dominating the photograph, is the ruined Alcazar, the fortress-palace erected by Charles V on the site of a Roman fort. It is now an army records centre.

strategic centre. Among examples in Europe are Portsmouth, Devonport, Brest (*see* Fig. 61, p. 138), Toulon and Cuxhaven, and in North America, Norfolk, San Diego and Esquimalt. To their naval functions have often been added others, *e.g.* merchant shipping and fishing.

RELIGIOUS CENTRES AND HOLY CITIES

As with strategic towns, so with religious ones: the descriptive adjective by which they are often best known is in most cases no longer adequate to express their principal function. Jerusalem, for example, an ancient fortress town as well as the historic centre of Judaism and an important seat of the Moslem faith, is probably today more of an administrative, commercial and educational town than a strategic base or holy city. Rome, the headquarters of the Roman Catholic Church, Benares, sacred to the

Hindus (*see* Fig. 93), Amritsar, the hub of the Sikh religion, and the more recently established Salt Lake City, the leading city of the Mormon faith, are all notable pilgrimage centres, but their permanent populations today are more concerned with administration, trade and industry than with the

[*Courtesy: Air India*

FIG. 93.—Benares, India: a holy city. Benares (Varanasi), the Holy City of the Hindus, is always crowded with pilgrims, who visit the many temples overlooking the Ganges and purify themselves in the waters of the sacred river. Platforms bordering the *ghats* (steps) leading down to the river are shaded by huge parasols, an indication of the intense summer heat of India.

practice of religious rites and the propagation of sacred beliefs. Mecca, the birthplace of Mohammedanism, remains a more purely religious city, but an even better example was, until recently, provided by Lhasa in Tibet, the transcendental monastic city.

The reputations of many religious centres, *e.g.* Canterbury and Citeaux, derive from the planting of early churches or abbeys on their sites. Others,

[*Courtesy: French National Tourist Office*

FIG. 94.—Lourdes, France: a pilgrimage centre. Lourdes became the most famous place of pilgrimage in the Roman Catholic world after the child Bernadette's vision of the Virgin Mary in the grotto shown here. Near the grotto are springs and pools for the immersion of the sick and diseased who hope for miraculous cures. The beautiful setting of Lourdes near the Pyrenees doubtless attracts many non-Catholic tourists as well as believers. The candles shown on the photograph still burn day and night in front of the Virgin's statue, but the iron railings and the discarded crutches (on the left of the photograph) have been recently removed.

like Lourdes (*see* Fig. 94), have acquired sanctity because of the visions observed there and the supposed miraculous value of their holy waters, or like Kandy, because of their religious relics (in that case a tooth of Buddha), or like Bethlehem, because of a holy birth. Canterbury, besides being the seat of the first English church, gained added importance as a place of pilgrimage when Thomas Becket, canonised in 1172, was buried there.

Religious towns—especially when set in attractive surroundings—receive many visitors either as pilgrims or as more profane sightseers. Some, especially perhaps Mecca, Lourdes, Benares and Rome, draw in people from all parts of the world, but even the least significant of cathedral cities derive some benefit from tourists. They must, therefore, provide varied kinds of tourist accommodation, good shops, restaurants, and so on. Some of their inhabitants obtain an income from the manufacture or sale of articles of devotion, *e.g.* statuettes, sacred books, candles and rosaries, others by acting as guides, information officers and religious teachers.

UNIVERSITY TOWNS AND OTHER EDUCATIONAL CENTRES

Secular culture, like defence and religion, is not nowadays among the dominant urban functions. Therefore, although many towns and cities undoubtedly gain prestige by being the homes of universities and colleges, one would hesitate before referring to a majority of them as educational or cultural towns, even when they have more than the usual complement of well-stocked book shops, libraries and museums. How far are we justified, for instance, in labelling such political capitals as Paris, Moscow and London as educational centres, or such large provincial cities as Manchester and Toulouse as University towns? All these important cities certainly have large universities, with thousands of students, and also many other people who busy themselves, at least partly, by serving them, as teachers, clerical and cleaning staffs, caterers, shop-keepers, and transport workers, but far more men and women in these cities are engaged in general commercial and industrial occupations than in educational work. Paris, Moscow, London, Manchester and Toulouse, therefore, in common with

[*Courtesy: German Embassy*]

Fig. 95.—Heidelberg, Germany: a university town. Situated in a narrow gorge cut by the Neckar near its entrance to the Rhine rift valley, Heidelberg has a beautiful setting which attracts many tourists. Best known for its university (founded in 1386), a small part of which is illustrated here, the city, like Oxford, has recently become industrialised. Its population now exceeds 100,000.

many other seats of learning, are cities with universities rather than university cities.

The oldest universities date back to the twelfth and thirteenth centuries in Europe. Bologna and Paris are of twelfth-century origin, Oxford and Cambridge, Naples, Toulouse and Salamanca date from the thirteenth, Pisa and Florence, Valladolid, Prague, Vienna, Cracow and Heidelberg (see Fig. 95) from the fourteenth. Among the newest universities are those established in England in the 1960s. Some of these—like those in Bradford and Salford—have grown from technical colleges, others—like those in such historic towns as York, Canterbury, Colchester, Lancaster and Norwich—have begun ab initio in very different, less industrialised, surroundings.

Argument is rife about whether universities are best located in small, dignified towns, where students may work without too much distraction in a peaceful, historic milieu, or whether they are more advantageously located in bustling multi-functional cities where students may be stimulated by an active, competitive environment. Possibly the most satisfactory situation is a "campus" on the fringe of a busy city (on the American pattern), or a precinct within it, as at Oxford. In such surroundings, students and teachers have their own scholastic environment not far removed from the bustle of contemporary urban life, and where "town and gown" are able to make frequent and regular contacts which should enrich both.

It has been observed that many towns which house universities are also concerned with commercial and industrial functions. Even such old university cities as Oxford, Uppsala and Heidelberg, for instance, are now being swamped by the growth of modern industry. Present-day Oxford has been wittily referred to by Emeritus Professor E. W. Gilbert as the Latin Quarter of Cowley. The city is also the main regional focus of the Upper Thames Basin. Cambridge, also with some claim to be regarded as a regional capital, is smaller and nowadays more obviously dominated by its university. Its main industries, too, are more appropriate to those of an old market and traditional university centre: they include the manufacture of jam and the production of electronic apparatus and precision instruments.

Perhaps the purest examples of educational towns in Britain today are St Andrews and Bangor. Germany has Marburg and Tübingen. In the United States, many towns were specifically founded as university seats: they are, in fact, universities with towns rather than the reverse. Among them are Ann Arbor (Michigan), Bloomington (Indiana) and Urbana (Illinois). Each has a high proportion of its workers in tertiary occupations, especially in domestic, clerical and professional service. The stagnation which deadens such towns during vacations is now being overcome by the introduction of light industries which provide more continuous employment for their citizens.

RESIDENTIAL AND DORMITORY TOWNS

The terms "residential" and "dormitory" as applied to towns indicates that they house far more adults than are gainfully employed there. The "surplus" inhabitants of a "dormitory" town commute to a neighbouring settlement (usually a large, multi-functional city). Those of a residential town generally include a considerable number of migrants who have retired from active employment elsewhere. The existence of a commuting population implies the availability of several good motor roads and rapid, frequent connections by rail and/or bus with the nearby city. The large numbers of retired people living in the residential town suggests that it can provide a more peaceful and pleasant environment than that to which they were accustomed when working. Both commuters and aged people value this kind of town because it represents a means of escape from the dirt, noise and confusion of the more commercial and industrialised city, and so provides both physical and mental refreshment.

Apart from purely suburban centres, such as Evanston, a suburb of Chicago, Hendon, a suburb of London, or Roundhay, in Leeds, there are, round all large cities in advanced countries, a number of pleasant country towns set in a rural environment which may be called residential towns. They include, in England, such places as Ilkley and Harrogate, chiefly serving Leeds; Grassington, serving Bradford; and Rugeley serving the Black Country. Near Manchester are former villages such as Cheadle Hulme, Wilmslow, Bramhall and Prestbury; near Liverpool various towns in the Wirral; and, outside London, Guildford, Dorking, Woking, Reigate and many other such settlements.

Many holiday resorts function in part as dormitory towns, and most attract also a number of retired or chronically sick people. Good examples of resorts providing dormitory facilities are Brighton and Southend (for people working in London), Southport (for Liverpool), Weston-super-Mare (for Bristol), Whitley Bay and Tynemouth (for Newcastle and Gateshead). Bournemouth is an excellent example of a town, enjoying a mild, sunny climate, which has attracted a high proportion of old and ailing people. Other residential towns of a similar kind are to be found in Florida and California and on the French Riviera.

The New Towns of Great Britain, discussed at some length in Chapter

XVIII, were designed essentially as "overspill" towns intended to provide more satisfactory housing for people previously living in large cities whose further physical growth was deemed undesirable. Since, however, they were planned as "complete" towns, with a sufficiently wide range of employment opportunities to make commuting unnecessary, and since most of their inhabitants are young or of early middle age, such "overspill" settlements cannot properly be regarded as residential or dormitory towns.

RESORT TOWNS

The Growth of Tourist and Recreational Centres

Though the thermal waters of such places as Bath and, probably, Buxton, in England, were used for bathing by the Romans, pleasure resorts as such, attracting large numbers of tourists from wide areas, are essentially modern, and have greatly multiplied in number and population during the last hundred years. The virtues of various mineral springs were extolled by medical opinion in the seventeenth and eighteenth centuries, and it was this period which saw the rise of modern spas, *e.g.* Bath, Harrogate, Cheltenham, Vichy, Carlsbad and Wiesbaden, in many European countries. Sea-bathing and even the drinking of sea-water were also recommended, especially by Dr Wittie at Scarborough (also a spa), and Dr Russell at Brighton, and marine cures became fashionable in their turn. To these inland and coastal health resorts and watering places, to many of which, like Bath, Tunbridge Wells, Cheltenham, Brighton and Weymouth, royalty extended its beneficial patronage, were later added, again at first largely on the strength of medical advice (for example, that of Dr Gruner, in Switzerland), a number of mountain resorts, especially in the Alps. Most of these health centres later converted themselves into almost purely recreational centres: places where the body and mind may certainly be refreshed by a change of routine and air, and by a relaxation from the stresses of ordinary work and household chores, but where taking the waters or hastening a recovery from sickness is no longer the prime reason for their existence.

Up to a century ago, only the well-to-do and leisured could afford to take a holiday away from home. Hence most resorts were small and in the main provided only genteel accommodation; they posed as centres of fashion and privilege as well as therapeutic centres. Today, at least in advanced countries, most of the poorer people can also afford an annual holiday and a change of environment, and it is unusual now for resorts to be as exclusive as they were though a few still cater mainly for the higher social classes. The great majority of recreational towns now provide a wide variety both of accommodation and entertainment, and appeal to the broadest possible range of taste and affluence.

Instrumental in promoting the rapid growth of tourist centres during the past century have been the expansion of rail and road transport, the introduction of the motor-coach and family car, the grant to industrial workers of holidays with pay, the widespread desire—now that the opportunities are available—to seek temporary escape from industrial smoke and dirt and from occupational and traffic frustrations, and the chance to participate in such sports as mountain and water-skiing, sailing, sea-bathing, underwater swimming, mountaineering and trail-riding, which are not usually available at home. Radio, television, the press and extended education, have all contributed to a mounting public interest not only in historic buildings, museums, art galleries and zoos, which have given many old country towns a significant stake in the tourist trade, but also to an increasing awareness of the geography of foreign countries. Hence many resorts nowadays, especially in Europe and North America, depend for at least part of their income upon visits made by people from other countries. The limits of holiday travel are continually expanding as living standards rise and the popularity of sea and air transport becomes more marked. Many British tourists, for example, are no longer content to visit Blackpool, Brighton and the Lake District (except perhaps for a day or weekend); they now proceed to Spain, Italy, France and Belgium. The richer and more adventurous are prepared to go as far as the Holy Land, North Africa, the Black Sea coast and the West Indies in search of the sun and new experiences.

Attributes of Resort Towns

Whether they are spas, mountain resorts, or seaside places, recreational towns have certain attributes in common. All depend for their existence upon their ability to offer a different environment from that to which most of their patrons are accustomed. Manufacturing industries never dominate and are often altogether absent. A large proportion of the working population finds employment in tertiary occupations, espècially catering. The number of elderly, retired people is often high, particularly where resorts are located in the warmer parts of the countries concerned, e.g. in Devon, Florida and the French Riviera. Commuters are often numerous if the resort is not too far from a large centre of population, e.g. Atlantic City near Philadelphia and Southport near Liverpool. Hence recreational towns are generally also residential towns. Skilful propaganda and vigorous publicity, combined with a variety of man-made

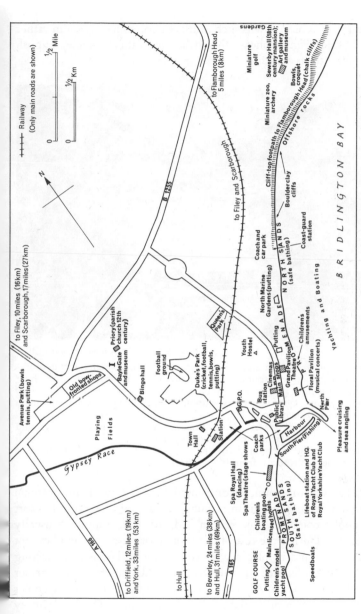

Fig. 96.—Bridlington: amenities of a seaside resort. Like most seaside resorts, Bridlington, on the Yorkshire coast, provides a mixture of natural and man-made amenities to attract holiday-makers. There are both outdoor and indoor attractions, and the old historic town contrasts well with the newer parts near the sea. Gypsey Race is an interesting example of a chalk stream: like some of the "bournes" of southern England, it flows readily in winter but is absorbed by the chalk in dry summers. Like other resort towns without significant manufacturing industries, Bridlington suffers from widespread unemployment in winter.

attractions, *e.g.* bathing-pools, piers, fun-fairs, sports grounds, parks, gift shops, and musical concerts, may lure as many visitors as natural scenery, and are made much of in towns such as Blackpool which are set in rather tame countryside. Fig. 96 shows the attractions a much smaller English resort may offer to its visitors.

[*Courtesy: Swiss National Tourist Office*]

FIG. 97.—Davos, Switzerland: a mountain resort. Davos, a mile-high resort in south-eastern Switzerland, was founded as a health resort for sufferers from lung disorders, but it now also attracts the physically strong who take advantage of its winter ski-slopes, golf course, swimming pools, skating rink and mountain cable-cars to enjoy their sport. The town stands close to a small lake on the *adret* (sunny) side of a wide glacial valley. Peaks such as those in the background (Tinzenhorn and Piz Michel) give it some shelter from cold winds. The small mountain hut in the foreground is, typically, of wood, its roof-covering held down by stones to protect it from high winds.

A marked seasonal rhythm, accompanied by casual work and seasonal unemployment is another distinguishing feature of the typical resort town. In cooler countries, *e.g.* Britain and Norway, summer is usually the busy season. During the rest of the year resorts are moribund except in mountain areas and in places with large enough hotels and meeting places to attract conferences, *e.g.* Harrogate and Brighton. In warmer areas, *e.g.* Florida, southern Arizona, Jamaica and the Canaries, the cooler part of the year is often preferred for holiday-making. The opportunity for people to escape from summer heat by seeking out local highlands is not neglected. Thus from Sydney many people make expeditions into the Blue Mountains, from New York into the Catskills, and from the Indo Gangetic Plain into Simla and Darjeeling. Such mountain resorts as Davos (*see* Fig. 97), Zermatt and St Moritz in Switzerland, and Banff and Jasper in the Canadian Rockies, which provide winter-sports facilities as well as summer recreations, are organised to handle one influx of visitors from December to March, and another from June to September.

Favourable resort sites include those provided by broad bathing beaches and shallow water (as, for example, at Atlantic City, Miami and San Sebastian), attractive lakeside hollows in spectacular mountain country (*e.g.* at Lugano and Interlaken), and an interlacing of canals and bridges (*e.g.* at Venice, Bruges and Amsterdam).

Many settlements which can hardly be classed as pleasure resorts have their transient tourist populations. Among them are political capitals, which attract visitors because of their national monuments, magnificent museums, art galleries and theatres, and old, historic towns with ancient castles, cathedrals, abbeys and art collections. University towns such as Oxford and Cambridge entice by the architectural merit of their college buildings.

Climate, or the expected weather, is often a potent factor, especially to people whose homes lie in cool, cloudy areas such as England. Easy access to large centres of population often promotes growth. The larger English resorts, *e.g.* Southend, Brighton and Blackpool, are all well served by roads and railways and are in close touch with large conurbations. They can draw in short-stay, as well as period, visitors, and therefore have the advantage over less conveniently located resorts such as those in Cornwall and the Scottish Highlands.

The holiday trade in Britain continues to boom in the big, expanding resorts, many of which are now suffering from an excess of motor traffic. The once leisurely promenades and quiet residential avenues are jammed in the season with private cars, motor cycles and coaches, and life is becoming as hectic as in the commercial and industrial cities from which people flee in search of relaxation. Hence growing numbers of people are seeking out the smaller, quieter, less sophisticated towns which present a more marked contrast to their domestic environments. Tiny, almost forgotten fishing ports, small, unspoilt market towns and peaceful country retreats are now, through their refurbished inns, country clubs and farm cottages, beginning to appeal to discriminating tourists. Will such places develop as the large, popular resorts have done? It is certainly significant that in 1851, Bournemouth had a population of only 700, Southend, 1,100 and Blackpool, 2,500. The first and third now have 150,000 people, the second 170,000!

STUDY QUESTIONS

1. Comment on the ways in which towns may be classified according to their age.

2. Indicate the factors which have influenced the growth of: (a) a mining settlement in Australia or Canada, (b) an administrative city in Asia or South America, (c) an industrial city in western Europe outside the British Isles, (d) a large seaport in Africa.

3. Examine the problems involved in classifying cities: (a) on a functional basis, (b) according to their sites.

4. Explain the following terms and illustrate them by specific examples: (a) dormitory town, (b) ghost town, (c) entrepôt port, (d) packet station, (e) holy city.

5. Select (a) any two large cities, (b) any two small towns, all of which differ greatly in their principal functions. Elucidate these contrasts.

6. Outline the methods you would use to differentiate the following: a commercial town and an industrial town; a fishing port and a seaside resort; a housing estate and a dormitory town.

7. Select *four* coastal settlements with different functions in *either* Great Britain *or* on the mainland of Europe. Discuss the reasons for their diverse characters.

8. Discuss, with reference to specific examples, how considerations of (a) defence, (b) rivers, (c) compromise, have affected the establishment of capital cities.

9. How does the occupational structure of people living in capital cities differ from that of people living in industrial towns and holiday resorts?

10. Describe the locations, and compare the relative importance in their respective countries of *three* of the following capital cities: Madrid, Delhi, Brasilia, Washington, Paris.

11. Compare London and Paris as route centres.

12. What do you think will be the outcome of establishing the new capitals of Brazil and Pakistan far away from their earlier capitals?

13. Examine the main functions, other than administrative, of three of the provincial capitals of Canada.

14. Which towns would you choose as the most suitable "regional capitals" of the following areas in Great Britain: Wales, south-west England, East Anglia, Cumbria? Justify your choice.

15. Attempt an explanation of the situation of market towns within a radius of about 20 or 30 miles (30–50 km) from your home.

16. Try to explain why so many of the world's largest cities are seaports.

17. Describe the physical requirements of a good harbour, and the ways in which man can improve on what nature provides. Is a good natural harbour essential for the growth of a great port?

18. Name four new ports in the Old World, and give reasons for their establishment.

19. Discuss with the aid of specific examples the industries that tend to grow up in ports.

20. What factors have influenced the location of the major industrial cities of Great Britain, excluding those situated on the coast?

21. Review the factors which have favoured the growth of industrial towns in *either* western Europe, *or* north-eastern U.S.A.

22. Referring to actual examples, comment on the natural factors which favour the growth of holiday resorts.

Chapter XIV

Million Cities and Conurbations

MILLION CITIES

O NE of the most striking and significant phenomena of our time is the proliferation of "million" or "millionaire" cities, that is cities with a population of at least a million. Probably the earliest of these were in China. London reached that figure by about 1800, Paris followed (1850), and then New York (1860), but even as recently as 1920 there were only about twenty "million" cities in the entire world, and probably no more than fifty in 1940.

It is impossible to say what the exact number is today; urban populations are constantly expanding, statistics are not always reliable and relate to different years, and there are varying definitions of a "city." In most cases, the administrative or legal city is smaller than the physical city or true urban agglomeration. Even if we exclude from our list of million cities, however, such polynuclear concentrations as Leeds–Bradford, Manchester–Salford, Merseyside and the Ruhr, it is incontrovertible that there are now more than a hundred million cities in the world. Their combined population is probably about 300 million and they therefore accommodate about 8 per cent of all mankind. Fig. 98 shows their distribution.

Population statistics vary considerably according to their source. Thus, the 1966 edition of the United Nations *Demographic Yearbook* (used by A. B. Mountjoy as source material for his article, "Million Cities: Urbanization and the Developing Countries," *Geography*) gives, *inter alia*, the following populations for some of the largest urban agglomerations:

City	'000s	City	'000s
New York	11,291 (1963)	Calcutta	4,580 (1964)
London	8,187 (1964)	Peking	5,420 (1958)
Moscow	6,443 (1965)	Mexico City	3,118 (1963)
Paris	7,369 (1962)	Bombay	4,538 (1964)
Buenos Aires	7,000 (1960)	São Paulo	3,825 (1960)
Shanghai	6,900 (1957)	Rio de Janeiro	3,323 (1960)

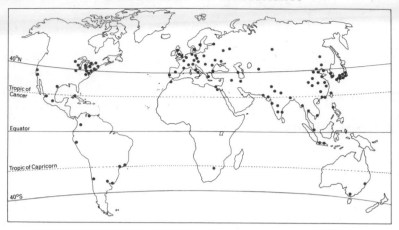

FIG. 98.—The world's million cities. Over 100 "million" cities are marked on this map. Temperate and tropical Asia compare well with Europe, but Latin America has almost three times as many million cities as Africa. Barely 10 per cent of the total are located in the southern hemisphere.

Corresponding figures based on work done by the International Urban Research Unit, an American research group which took as its basis the Standard Metropolitan Area concept used by the U.S. Census, and then sought equivalents in other countries,* are as follows:

City	'ooos	City	'ooos
New York–North-eastern New Jersey	14,759 (1960)	Buenos Aires	6,763 (1960)
		Calcutta	6,243 (1961)
London	11,547 (1961)	Peking	5,420 (1958)
Moscow	7,884 (1959)	Mexico City	4,816 (1960)
Paris	7,810 (1962)	Bombay	4,698 (1961)
Shanghai	6,900 (1957)	Rio de Janeiro	4,692 (1960)
		São Paulo	4,369 (1960)

If we adhere to the statistics laid down in the *Demographic Yearbook*, which, somewhat illogically, excludes, for example, the Ruhr from its list of million cities but includes both the Manchester and Leeds conurbations, we find two cities (New York and Tokyo) of more than 10 million, and another eleven (London, Paris, Buenos Aires, Shanghai, Los Angeles, Moscow, Chicago, Peking, Calcutta, Philadelphia and Bombay, in that order) with more than 4 million.

* Peter Hall, in *The World Cities, op. cit.*, uses the findings of this Research Unit as his statistical framework.

World Distribution of Million Cities

The continental distribution of million cities is roughly as follows:

	Early 1950s	Early 1960s
Europe	23 (including 2 from U.S.S.R.)	30 (including 6 from U.S.S.R.)
U.S.S.R.	2	8
Asia	30	46 (including 2 from U.S.S.R.)
North America	17	21
South America	7	8
Africa	3	4
Australasia	2	2

Individual countries with large numbers, besides the U.S.S.R., are the U.S.A. (16), China (14), India (8) and Japan (7). Two of these countries are very highly industrialised and may be labelled "developed," the other two are simply "developing," their rural populations still reaching 75 per cent of the total.

During the past forty years or so, more and more million cities have arisen in tropical latitudes (*see* Fig. 98). In fact, the number has grown from three to at least twenty. This increase is not entirely due to greater industrialisation. Indeed, the developing countries in which these huge cities have been mushrooming are still overwhelmingly rural in their complexion. Many of these new million cities, especially those in Asia, lack proper sanitation and piped water supplies, they suffer from gross overcrowding and from the appendages of "shanty towns," and hardly resemble at all the commercial cities established in such countries as India by pre-war colonial powers. The populations of such cities as Chungking and Karachi swelled as a result of the in-movement of wartime refugees, but in the main these new million cities have grown to their present uncomfortable dimensions because of increasing rural unemployment and underemployment. Migrants from the countryside have crowded in, and continue to do so, in the hope of finding work and a place in the sun, a hope which is rarely justified and seldom realised. In too many cases, as Professor D. J. Dwyer points out ("The City in the Developing World and the Example of Southeast Asia," *Geography*), there is a "danger of the cities becoming infected with rural ideals and aspirations rather than the rural migrants themselves becoming urbanized."

Ninety per cent of the world's million cities are located in the northern hemisphere. Over a third are political capitals: the most genuine of all metropolises. Nearly a third are great commercial ports, accessible by ship as well as land. Most of the rest, *e.g.* Chicago, Detroit, St Louis, Pittsburgh, Birmingham (England), Johannesburg, Kharkov, Shenyang,

Kanpur and Lahore, are multi-functional cities especially noted for the volume of their industrial production and the value of their internal commerce. Some, *e.g.* Leningrad, Rio de Janeiro, Karachi, Milan, Munich and Kiev, are former capitals which retain much of their prestige, while others, *e.g.* São Paulo, Hyderabad, Toronto, Guadalajara, Sydney and Melbourne, are capitals within large federations. All million cities are places of high accessibility, most are located on navigable rivers or lakes, and nearly all, except a few ports, are set in areas of marked industrial or agricultural productivity. Some, for example Buenos Aires, Santiago, Copenhagen, Sydney and Melbourne, contain what appears to be an undue proportion (one-fifth to one-quarter) of the populations of their respective countries. Montevideo—an extreme case of this sort—houses more than 40 per cent of the people of Uruguay.

The Future of Million Cities

Not only are million cities growing in number, they are also growing in size. They are consuming more and more agricultural land, and their population growth rates are higher than for the world as a whole. The prospect in some countries is alarming, and there seems to be a need for the widespread adoption of effective "Green Belt" and "New Town" policies modelled on those adopted by post-war Britain for the purpose of halting the further expansion of its largest cities. It is estimated that if Calcutta and Bombay, for example, are allowed to grow only as fast as India's total population is expected to, their populations will exceed 10 million in less than fifty years. If Los Angeles expands as much in the period 1960–2000 as it did between 1900 and 1960, it will contain 80 million people!

In most European countries, growth rates have generally begun to slacken. While such cities as Caracas, Teheran, Seoul and Karachi have increased their populations from between seven and eight times, and Delhi, Kowloon and Lima between five and six times in the last thirty years, Stockholm, Rome and Madrid have merely doubled their numbers, Copenhagen, Milan and Hamburg have grown by only a half, and Vienna, Brussels and London have remained virtually static, though their built-up areas now spread more widely.

Advantages and Disadvantages of Million Cities

As places of work and residence, million cities have both advantages and drawbacks. They normally offer a wide variety of employment opportunities in commerce, administration, transport and manufacturing, and their citizens are able if they wish, to change from one job to another without the upheaval of moving house. Employers benefit from the diversity of financial, legal, technical and advertising facilities available, and residents find accessible a generous range of shops, including highly specialised retailers' and departmental stores. Places of entertainment (*e.g.* theatres and clubs) and cultural opportunities (*e.g.* concert halls, art galleries and museums) are numerous. There is usually a choice of several good schools, and well-equipped, well-staffed hospitals.

On the other hand, million cities often lack something of the community spirit which permeates smaller urban settlements. Their populations are less stable and many of their citizens have their roots elsewhere. Traffic congestion has become endemic and parking problems are overwhelming. The journey between residence and workplace is often uncomfortably long and—during the rush-hours—frustrating, and in some cases detrimental to mental health. Large-scale air and water pollution may endanger bodily health. Increasingly, the countryside is being drained of its younger and more active people because of the magnetism exerted by very large cities. The housing of these rural immigrants is a never-ending task which the administrative staffs of all million cities have to face, and, as we saw on page 219, the task is often too formidable to be completed satisfactorily. Poorer migrants may be compelled to eke out their lives in shanty towns, another hazard to the maintenance of health standards, and a slur on any self-respecting community.

CONURBATIONS

Conurbations as Urban Forms

Patrick Geddes, a leading proponent of regionalism and regional planning, was probably the first writer to use the term "conurbation," which has now fully entered the English language. In his book *Cities in Evolution*, first published in 1915, he considered various names, *e.g.* constellations and conglomerations, city regions and town aggregates, for what were then new forms of population groupings, before settling on "conurbations." Professor C. B. Fawcett, writing in 1932 ("Distribution of the Urban Population in Great Britain," *Geographical Journal*) provided the following definition: "an area occupied by a continuous series of dwellings, factories and other buildings, harbours and docks, urban parks and playing fields, etc., which are not separated from one another by rural land, though in many cases in this country such an urban area includes enclaves of rural land which is still in agricultural occupation."

The existence of such urban agglomerations in Britain was first officially recognised by the Central Statistical Office in the 1951 Census, when a conurbation was defined as: "an area of urban development where a number of separate towns have grown into each other and become linked by such factors as common industrial or business interest, or a common centre of shopping or entertainment."

Nearly all conurbations, except those based on a more or less linear knitting-together of neighbouring coastal resorts, (*e.g.* in this country, Christchurch–Bournemouth–Poole, and Lytham St Annes–Blackpool–Cleveleys–Fleetwood, and, on the Mediterranean coast, the most closely settled part of the French Riviera), are based on intensive commerce and manufacturing, and on a very close mesh of communication facilities. They often occupy, especially in Europe, either extended port zones or coalfields and their margins. Most are without a plan and without definite form. They are often begrimed with smoke and dirt, they rarely possess through roads, their central areas are often in need of urban renewal, and their outer parts usually exhibit undesirable sprawl. Most lack a comprehensive governing body which encompasses within its administration the whole of the built-up area, and overall planning authorities have seldom been established.

It is common to distinguish, as Professor A. E. Smailes has done (in *The Geography of Towns*), between polynuclear (or polycentric) and uninuclear (or monocentric) conurbations. This distinction may be unreal, for the uninuclear type, though growing by accretion (*i.e.* by growth round a single nucleus, as in London) generally involves the engorgement of other expanding towns (*e.g.* Harrow and Croydon), while in conurbations of the polynuclear type, which are produced by the coalescence of a number of neighbouring but separate nuclei, one city is often much more dominant than the rest, *e.g.* Birmingham, in the West Midlands conurbation, and Glasgow, in the Clydeside conurbation. The uninuclear type, where it exists at all, is more characteristic of new countries, especially Australia, the polynuclear type, of older countries, especially those in Europe.

The million cities just discussed may be regarded as essentially uninuclear conurbations,* though some writers would add to the list of million cities such polynuclear agglomerations as the Ruhr and the West Yorkshire conurbations.

Conurbations are not always regarded as necessarily supporting a very large number of people, though their average densities must be high for them to qualify. Most of the world's "major" conurbations, however, have populations of well over 1 million. Indeed, New York and Tokyo, regarded as conurbations, may run as high as 16 or 20 million. Such

* The addition of the word "Greater" to such cities as London and Paris suggests their status as conurbations rather than as cities in the stricter sense.

writers as T. W. Freeman (in *The Conurbations of Great Britain*) recognise "minor" as well as major conurbations, and include in this category small agglomerations whose total population may not exceed 50,000. This usage of the term conurbation is exceptional, but there seems to be no reason why the term should not be applied to urban agglomerations with, say, 500,000 people, especially when these are of the polycentric variety, *e.g.* Sheffield–Rotherham and adjacent built-up areas outside their borough boundaries, Greater Bristol, Tees-side and perhaps the Potteries.

The Major British Conurbations

In his quest for urban growths "of confused and labyrinthine squalor," Geddes (*op. cit.*) named the following examples in Britain: Greater London ("this octopus . . . polypus rather, a vast irregular growth"), Lancaston (extending from Manchester to Liverpool), West Riding (the wool-manufacturing area), South Riding (centred on Sheffield), Midlandton (centred on Birmingham), Southwaleston (like the previous four, closely associated with a coalfield), Tyne–Wear–Tees, and Clyde–Forth (extending from Glasgow and Ayr to Falkirk, Grangemouth and Stirling, and approaching Edinburgh–Leith).

All these conurbations certainly existed, at least in embryo, in Geddes' time, and to some extent in the mid-nineteenth century when the Industrial Revolution was already a hundred years old. If, however, we restrict the term "major conurbation" to the larger and more continuously built-up areas, we can reduce Geddes' eight conurbations to the seven which Fawcett (*op. cit.*) identified in 1932 and whose choice, within modified boundaries, the 1951 Census confirmed. They are as follows (*see* Fig. 99):

	Approx. area (sq. miles)	Approx. population 1951 (000s)	Approx. population 1961 (000s)	Approx. density 1961 (per sq. mile)
Greater London	721	8,346	8,172	11,300
South-east Lancashire	379	2,421	2,427	6,400
West Midlands	268	2,236	2,344	8,750
West Yorkshire	484	1,692	1,703	3,500
Merseyside	150	1,382	1,386	9,250
Tyneside	90	835	852	9,500
Clydeside	324	1,759	1,802	5,550

A number of important facts arise from this table: (*a*) Greater London is by far the most populous of all British conurbations; (*b*) population densities are high, but much less so in West Yorkshire than in the other conurbations; (*c*) British conurbations are not now notably increasing in population, and London—owing probably to the adoption of a Green

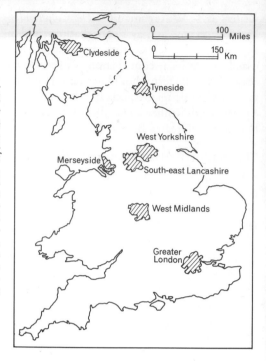

FIG. 99.—The major conurbations of Britain. All these conurbations, defined within census boundaries, are associated with manufacturing and commerce, and five of them include major ports. All except Merseyside and Greater London include coal-mining areas. Between the Mersey and Humber the map is misleading: there is, in fact, a tract of high, unpopulated moorland between the conurbations of south-east Lancashire and west Yorkshire.

Belt policy combined with the widespread demolition of houses in the inner parts and an extended commuter range—is actually decreasing. (In fact, apart from the West Midlands, which has attracted more new industries, there has been no appreciable growth in any British conurbation since 1921.) Further, it should be noted that 37 per cent (41 per cent in 1951) of all the inhabitants of England live in one of its six major conurbations, whose combined area is very little more than that of Norfolk.

The Major Conurbations of England

As a realistic conurbation, *Greater London* (*see* Fig. 100) has now exceeded the limits of the agglomeration as defined by the Central Statistical Office, and probably houses, in all, some 12 million people. Its more recent residential areas and industrial districts now extend about 15 miles (24 km) from the centre, *i.e.* as far as Reigate in the south, Hatfield in the north, and Romford in the east. In common with most conurbations with one marked central nucleus, its population is decreasing in the inner zone (the County), and even in the outer ring, but is continuing to expand, through breaks in the Green Belt, beyond the area governed by the Greater London Council.

The *South-east Lancashire* conurbation, like that of West Yorkshire, was formed by the fusion of a number of towns whose suburbs virtually interlock with their neighbours'. It extends into Cheshire, where almost 20 per cent of the total population lives. It is dominated by a large central city, Manchester, and is therefore often referred to as the Manchester

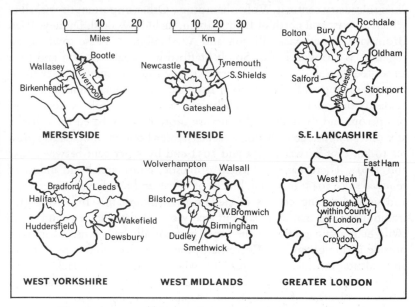

FIG. 100.—The major conurbations of England. These maps show the main administrative divisions included by the Central Statistical Office in the conurbations thus defined in the 1951 and 1961 Census Reports. Only the county boroughs are named on these maps.

conurbation. Other nuclei, notably such industrial towns as Bolton, Bury Rochdale, Oldham, Ashton and Stockport, and the mainly residential Altrincham, form a girdle of satellites about 5 to 10 miles (8–16 km) from Manchester and its Siamese twin, Salford. All, save Altrincham, climb up the valleys of Rossendale Forest and the Pennines. Each is jealous of its administrative and social independence, and has its own shopping centre and central business area. Opportunities for employment in the staple industries of coal-mining and the cotton industry—whose expansion brought the conurbation into being—are now declining, but attempts are being made, with varying success, to attract replacement industries. Slums and sub-standard nineteenth-century houses are slowly being cleared, and their occupants are being rehoused mainly in tall flats on cleared land or in separate dwellings on peripheral estates. Modern urban sprawl is most marked on the south side of Manchester, where there is cleaner air, more open spaces, and altogether a less dispiriting environment.

Birmingham dominates the *West Midlands*, or Black Country, conurbation even more than Manchester takes precedence over the smaller towns of South-east Lancashire; it houses nearly half the total population. The chief subsidiary centre is Wolverhampton. Other important towns, all of which lie west and north of Birmingham, include Walsall, Dudley, West Bromwich, Smethwick, Bilston and Wednesbury. These towns grew together as the working of South Staffordshire coal and iron and their associated iron and steel industries expanded in the nineteenth century. As coal-mining and iron-smelting declined, other metal-using industries came to the rescue. Economically, the area as a whole is now more prosperous and the industrial structure more broadly based than that of any other English conurbation except Greater London. Population grew by 16 per cent between 1931 and 1951 and by 5 per cent between 1951 and 1961. There has been much domestic, commercial and industrial renewal since 1945: many tall blocks of offices and flats have been erected, and new shopping centres created, *e.g.* Birmingham's Bull Ring (the traditional retail market area), but many out-of-date factories and much twilight housing remain in the inner parts of all the towns. Moreover, outside Birmingham and Wolverhampton, there are too few recreational and cultural facilities. The area as a whole suffers from a lack of open spaces: there is less "green" land between its several nuclei than in the South-east Lancashire conurbation. Again, too many local government bodies are responsible for administration, and there is a lack of the overall planning schemes which such a close-knit conurbation requires. Birmingham, however, has been more successful in its boundary extensions than most large cities and now has an area twice as large as Manchester and Liverpool and three times the size of Glasgow.

Like South-east Lancashire and the West Midlands, the *West Yorkshire* conurbation is a congeries of industrial towns situated on or close to a coalfield, but its chief city, Leeds—the regional capital—though accounting for more than a quarter of the total population, is less dominant than either Manchester or Birmingham, and has a distinct rival in Bradford, the merchanting centre of the woollen and worsted industries. The main towns—Huddersfield, Halifax, Dewsbury and Wakefield, as well as Leeds and Bradford—have a roughly peripheral distribution in the Aire and Calder valleys. All provide employment in the wool textile trades, most also in engineering and some in chemical industries. The more central parts of the conurbation are partially filled in with small industrial towns and villages. A few of the latter remain agricultural and the overall population density is much below that of the other English conurbations, and has shown no marked growth since 1901. As in Lancashire, but to a less extent, there is a need for modern "growth industries," *e.g.* electronics, motor engineering and plastics, for more urban renewal (despite much recent redevelopment), and for more regional planning. There is, however, less fusion of industrial towns and no pressing overspill problem. Alone among British conurbations, West Yorkshire has no demand for satellite New Towns, though residential areas are spreading north of Leeds and Bradford.

The *Merseyside* and *Tyneside* conurbations are port conurbations. The former, completely dominated by Liverpool, takes in Birkenhead and the residential areas of the Wirral, while the latter, less completely over-shadowed by Newcastle, extends across the Tyne to Gateshead, and sea-wards down both sides of the estuary as a linear, double-beaded agglomer-ation. Both conurbations have depended largely on overseas commerce for their growth, and both have shipbuilding, engineering, chemical and food-processing industries, though considerable mining communities are found only on Tyneside. Population reaches the same high densities on both Merseyside and Tyneside, and both areas have modern trading estates, overspill schemes, plans and achievements concerning urban renewal, but still much sub-standard housing, especially near the dock-side and industrial areas. Again, there are too many local councils to allow planning proposals to be easily co-ordinated.

The Ruhr and Other Conurbations

Most advanced countries have their conurbations, resulting either from the expansion of a major city (*e.g.* Paris, Berlin, Chicago and Tokyo) or from the fusion of a number of distinct towns and cities (as in the Pitts-burgh district, the Lille–Roubaix–Tourcoing triangle in north-eastern France, along the French Riviera, in Donbass and Upper Silesia, and along the western side of Lake Erie between Detroit and Cleveland).

Among the most notable, and well-contrasted examples of conurbations in the world are Los Angeles–Long Beach and the Ruhr. The former consists of a contiguous, sprawling city as extensive as the West Yorkshire conurbation. Its population numbered only about 100,000 in 1900 (when West Yorkshire already had well over 1,600,000), but it increased to nearly 3 million by 1961. The whole urbanised area now supports almost 10 million people, 85 per cent of whom live in houses built since 1920, two-thirds of which are detached.

The Ruhr conurbation (*see* Fig. 101) is quite different. The nuclei of its existing towns were established at an early date on the margin of a Hercynian massif (compare South-east Lancashire and West Yorkshire). The growth of the Ruhr as one of the world's major industrial areas stems from the working of one of Europe's richest coalfields, the growth of

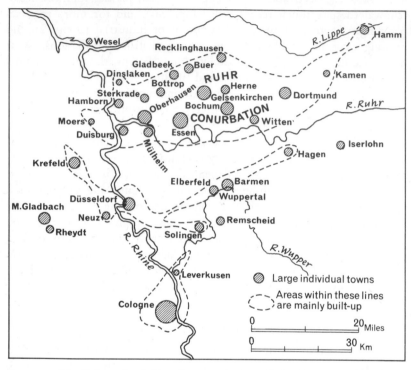

FIG. 101.—The Ruhr and neighbouring conurbations. What is commonly referred to as "the Ruhr" includes a major conurbation, chiefly north of the Ruhr River, and now extending well to the east of Dortmund, and another, less continuously built-up area forming a roughly parallel but narrower belt about 8 miles (13 km) further south. Cologne is the centre of a smaller, more uninuclear type of conurbation. There is a growing tendency for all these conurbations to link up to form a West German megalopolis.

derivative manufacturing industries, notably iron, steel, heavy engineering and heavy chemicals, and the spread of modern communications (canals, railways and roads). The main part of the conurbation extends from Duisburg (*see* Fig. 102), the Rhine port (population *c.* half a million), to Dortmund (*c.* 650,000), and includes Oberhausen (*c.* 260,000), Mülheim (*c.* 190,000), Essen (*c.* 725,000), Gelsenkirchen (*c.* 370,000) and Bochum (*c.* 360,000). Altogether, this area has a total population of nearly 6 million. Not far to the south is another, narrower and less continuous urban belt, extending from Düsseldorf (*c.* 700,000) to Hagen (*c.* 200,000) by way of the textile centre of Wuppertal (*c.* 420,000), while south again,

[*Courtesy: German Embassy*

FIG. 102.—Duisburg: a Ruhr port. This photograph shows part of the Rhine and an industrial area in the southern quarter of Duisburg, the great Rhine port. On the river there are barges and tugs, symbolising the heavy traffic on this waterway. Factories reach back from the waterfront; those shown here include iron blast furnaces, mills (*Niederrheinische Hütte*) turning out heavy iron and steel products, chemical works and a copper smeltery.

within 6 miles (10 km) of each other, and only about the same distance from Wuppertal, are Solingen (*c.* 175,000) and Remscheid (*c.* 135,000). The whole region, excluding outlying parts west of the Rhine, covers only about 1,000 sq. miles (2,500 km), but houses at least 8 million people, far more of whom live close to their work than is usual in Los Angeles.

Though it includes patches of good agricultural land, the Ruhr is dominated by rows of houses, blocks of flats, industrial plants, collieries, and commercial premises. Like many other conurbations, it has proved highly vulnerable to aerial attack, and dangerously dependent upon outside sources for most of its food and raw materials. It suffers from industrial and residential obsolescence and from an out-of-date, costly, congested transport system. Coal-mining has shifted northwards, but the total output is declining in favour of imported petroleum, a development which is attracting new petro-chemical industries to the area. The conurbation as a whole, however, like the conurbations of northern England, suffers from a lack of new, rapidly expanding industries, and from a shortage of employment opportunities for women. A Ruhr planning authority (established in 1920) is endeavouring to seek more industrial diversification, and is developing a strategy for opening out the core area (Duisburg–Dortmund) by creating new residential areas in the less densely peopled tract south of the Ruhr River, and by persuading industrial firms to move northwards into the roomier Lippe valley, westwards beyond the Rhine and eastwards beyond Dortmund. It is also aiming to build new roads, including motorways, and to safeguard existing green areas of limited extent as recreational grounds. Unfortunately, it has no authority over the area embracing Düsseldorf, Solingen and Remscheid, which is subject to another planning body.

MEGALOPOLISES

The American Megalopolis

As long ago as 1915, Geddes (*op. cit*) pointed out that the built-up area of Greater New York was rapidly approaching Philadelphia and Boston. He went on to say: "The expectation is not absurd that the not very distant future will see one vast city-line along the Atlantic coast for five hundred miles." Over forty years later, Professor Jean Gottman* was able to state that Geddes' future had arrived. He found then in existence a "super-metropolitan" region extending, as a union of conurbations, along the U.S. Atlantic seaboard, "from a little north of Boston to a little south of Washington," and including such urban clusters as New York, Philadelphia, Baltimore, their satellites, and their attached suburbia (*see* Fig. 103). Even where rural land still existed, it was mostly occupied by city-working, non-farming people. Gottman correlates the spread of this "megalopolis," as he called it, with the development of overseas trade and

---

* In his article, "Megalopolis," *Economic Geography*, Vol. 33, 1957, and in his book, *Megalopolis*, Twentieth Century Fund, New York, 1961.

the competitive role played by a number of seaboard nuclei all of which strove to share it, the use made of each individual nucleus as a springboard for interior settlement, and the advance of manufacturing.

The megalopolis forms America's "Main Street." It extends for 600 miles (1,000 km), and concentrates over half of the U.S.A.'s industrial and commercial power as well as possessing the best-equipped universities

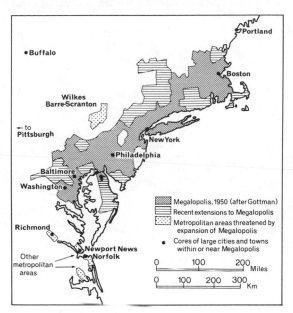

FIG. 103.—The American Megalopolis. This continuous urbanised area, called the "Megalopolis" by Jean Gottman, contains some of the most populous cities in the United States and also a large number of smaller urban centres. The overall population density should not, however, be exaggerated: it is less than the average density of the Netherlands, England and Belgium, for there is, in fact, a surprising number of open spaces within the megalopolis.

and libraries, and the most influential newspapers and periodicals. It accommodates nearly 40 million people and includes 5 million cities, one of which—New York—has well over a third of the total population in its agglomeration. Already this belt of urban settlement—knitted together by railways and freeways—is pushing northwards to take in Portland, southwards to take in Norfolk and Newport News, and—via such towns as Reading, Harrisburg and Pittsburgh in Pennsylvania, and by way of the already thickly peopled Hudson–Mohawk gap—is approaching such Great Lakes cities as Buffalo, Cleveland, Detroit and even Chicago.

Other Megalopolises

Outside the United States, there are similar signs of the coming linkage of million cities and conurbations. In the Netherlands, for instance, the existence of a semi-annular conurbation (*see* Fig. 104) has been recognised for some time, and it is now conjectured that in the not very distant future it may well merge westwards with the industrial areas of Belgium

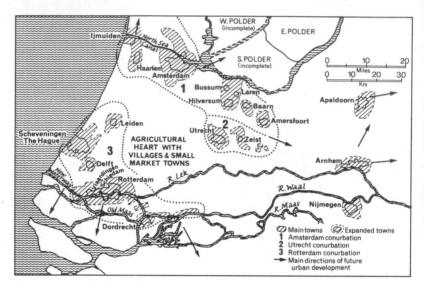

FIG. 104.—Randstad Netherlands. This map shows the tendency for the development, within the Netherlands, of an annular or ring city. At present it is discontinuous and may be regarded as consisting of three separate conurbations. Within a generation it may, if its growth is unchecked, virtually link up with Belgian and French Flanders to the south-west and with the Ruhr and Rhineland to the south-east.

and the conurbation of north-eastern France, and eastwards with the Greater Ruhr to form another giant agglomeration of which the major urban areas will be divided from each other only by suburban houses and gardens, out-of-town shopping centres and new, low-spreading factories, city recreational areas and small intensively worked farms. This zone, which may ultimately spread to reach Paris and Hanover, is little more than 200 miles (320 km) long and contains fewer large cities than the Washington–Boston axis, but it already has an average population density of well over 500 per square mile outside existing cities.

In Britain, the Clydeside conurbation is nearing the smaller one centred on Edinburgh, and the development of a U-shaped megalopolis round the southern Pennines is already evident. The latter embraces a number of major and minor conurbations: West Yorkshire, Sheffield–Rotherham, Nottingham–Derby, West Midlands, the Potteries, South-east Lancashire and Merseyside. As long ago as 1915, Geddes suggested the existence of "Lancaston," an almost continuous line of towns between Liverpool and Manchester. The growth of towns and motorways in the tract of country between this future megalopolis and Greater London (already the city of "Londbirm" is envisaged) suggests the probability of this English "coffin-belt" or "hour-glass," as it has been called, linking up—across the narrow Straits of Dover, shortly to be tunnelled—with Randstad Holland and the Ruhr, and thence via the Rhineland and Lorraine with the cities of Milan and Turin. The only real break in this zone of dense urban population, about 800 miles (1,280 km) long and accommodating over 80 million people, would then be the Swiss Alps.

Another megalopolis is forming in Japan. Referred to already as the Tokaido Megalopolis, it comprises an industrial and commercial belt encompassing Tokyo–Yokohama, Nagoya, Kyoto, Osaka and Kobe (all million cities, expanding, unfortunately, over Japan's most productive agricultural areas). These urban concentrations are all joined together by the fast Tokaido Trunk Line of Japanese Railways. The total population is 45 million (45 per cent of the country's total population). Through suburban expansion it is growing rapidly: by more than 10 per cent between 1960 and 1965, compared with a national average growth of 5.2 per cent. Already there are signs of an extension westwards along the shores of the Inland Sea to Kitakyushu, Japan's most recent million city.

Chapter XV

The Material Structure of Cities

THE SHAPE OF CITIES IN GROUND-PLAN

THE shape of towns and cities—often more obvious on the map than on the ground—is by no means uniform or regular. Variations are born of different sites, communications and history.

On fairly flat, firm, undifferentiated land, a town might be expected to conform to a roughly circular ground-plan, growth proceeding by the gradual addition of concentric rings, as has happened to a large extent in

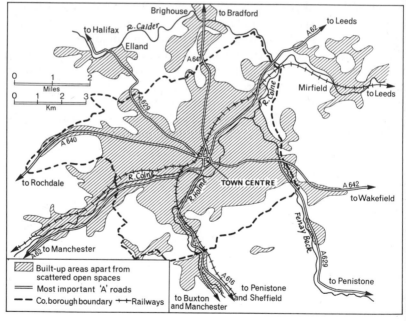

FIG. 105.—The stellate plan of Huddersfield. Like many other towns, especially those at the convergence of two or more valleys carrying roads, Huddersfield has tended to assume a stellate or star-shaped form. Even along roads not confined within valleys, *e.g.* the Rochdale, Halifax and Wakefield roads, built-up prongs project outwards between green wedges and zones of sparse settlement.

FIG. 106.—Whitby: the harbour and East Cliff. The estuary of the River Esk at Whitby is set between steep cliffs. On the east side, shown here, there is a sharp ascent to St Mary's Church (of Norman origin) and the Abbey (of Anglian origin), both of which appear on the skyline. The buildings between the river and the cliff-top huddle close together and, following the contours, manage to climb some distance up the abrupt hillside.

London. In the case of a port, we should expect an approximation to a semi-circular plan, possibly with some pulling out of the waterfront zone to make way for new commercial, industrial, residential or recreational needs, so that the ultimate shape may somewhat resemble that of a bowler hat with its brim forming the waterfront, as at Liverpool.

Even towns on undifferentiated terrain, however, rarely assume the shapes expected. Building frequently follows the laying down of communications, mainly rail and road, and lags in the spaces between these transport routes. Hence many towns assume a star-shaped, or stellate pattern. Especially is this the case when a number of steep-sided valley-ways converge, as, for example, in Huddersfield (see Fig. 105). Where there is only one valley and only one important through route, a linear shape is characteristic. Many small industrial towns in the Rossendale Forest (e.g. Whitworth and Darwen) and in South Wales (e.g. Tredegar and Ebbw Vale) conform to this pattern. There are other examples of linear towns in gaps in the Chalk downlands of south-eastern England (*e.g.* Berkhamsted and High Wycombe), in the Wupper valley (West Germany) and in the Swiss Alps. In the latter case, growth is particularly noticeable on the sunny (*adret*) sides of east–west valleys, the shaded southern (*ubac*) sides having fewer buildings. The inhabitants of towns

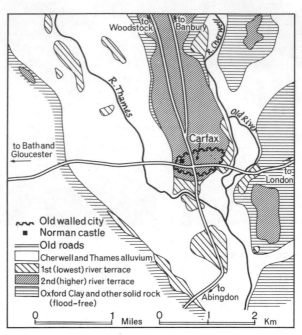

FIG. 107.—Oxford: a dry-point site. Medieval Oxford was built on a relatively high gravel terrace (20–25 ft (6–8 km) above normal Thames level) between the Thames and the Cherwell crossings. It has chiefly spread northwards along the terrace, but also downwards in other directions on to a lower terrace (only 5–10 ft (1·5–3 m) above normal river level). These lower parts of the city are still flooded from time to time. Carfax—the centre of the city—is located where old north–south and east–west roads meet.

thus confined are fortunate in having quick, though steep, access to the open spaces above.

Steep slopes do not always prohibit settlement; rows of houses follow the contours at places such as Whitby (*see* Fig. 106) and Hebden Bridge in Yorkshire. But they generally severely restrict it and promote asymmetrical development. Marshes, too, may at least initially deter builders, as they did, for example, in Paris, which was long confined by the "Marais" on the north bank of the Seine. Similarly, Oxford was for a long time restricted to the higher gravel terraces rising about 20 ft (6 m) above the present flood-plains of the Thames and Cherwell, with their clayey sub-soils (*see* Fig. 107). Most of central Belfast stands on "slobland"—once estuarine mud-flats at the head of Belfast Lough. Marshes, however, can be drained to allow building to take place and to halt preferential growth in selected directions. Streams and rivers, too, need no longer hinder the builder—they may be bridged, diverted, or culverted underground—and even steep-sided valleys, if not too deep, may be filled in. Who can now recognise the former Shoreditch, Westbourne, Holborn and Fleet Rivers in London?

On large rivers, the built-up area often spreads much more widely on one side than on the other. There are many reasons for this disparity: *e.g.* the incidence of gentler relief on one side, the relative firmness and dryness of opposing banks, and the direction from which the main roads and railways stem. (Other reasons were suggested on p. 130). Thus Cairo, Vienna, Hamburg and Philadelphia occupy mainly the right banks of their respective rivers, while Moscow and Calcutta favour the left banks.

Most towns and cities now sprawl outwards and rarely end abruptly. Hence the distinction between town and country is blurred and what the Americans described as a "rururban" belt evolves. Most medieval towns, however, especially those which were planned for strategic purposes, were sharply confined within their walls, at least until the rise of extra-mural faubourgs, which themselves, however, were often enclosed within extended walls. Many towns occupying naturally defensive sites were also decisively severed from the surrounding country. They include Athens and other Mediterranean acropoles which did not spread down from their hill-tops until times became more settled. Cities within meander loops, *e.g.* Durham (*see* Fig. 57), were for long protected and bounded by rivers. In other cases, land ownership has sometimes, at least temporarily, limited the expansion of a town in a particular direction, though such obstacles have often been leap-frogged and subsequently either built over or converted into public parks.

VARIATIONS IN LAND USE WITHIN TOWNS

Though geographical entities, except where they form parts of conurbations, towns are structurally heterogeneous. Their buildings vary in size, shape, height and arrangement, and also in age and function,* and their populations vary in density, social status, and—often—in racial

* The function, form and arrangement of buildings is often referred to as "urban morphology."

origin. There is, however, an element of order in these groupings and it is often possible to identify what may be called "urban regions," each of which may be roughly, if not wholly, distinguished by age, functional specialisation and population structure in the same way as entire towns. The oldest part of the town, still perhaps containing remnants of centuries-old buildings and street patterns, is generally in the centre, the newer parts progressively further and further out. Working-class houses frequently stand cheek-by-jowl with the older factories, which often line canals and railways and rarely abut on the higher-class residential zones. The main shopping streets, business premises and public buildings occupy central locations and only slightly invade residential areas. Structures such as schools, churches and public-houses have a much more scattered distribution than most buildings, and are often interspersed with dwelling-houses, as are those shops, *e.g.* grocers' and confectioners', which satisfy everyday wants. Complications are introduced in cases where a town, in its urban expansion, has incorporated former villages which may then act as sub-centres, *e.g.* for shopping and entertainment.

It is possible, therefore, to divide a town into a number of areas which are more or less distinctive in themselves and which differ from adjacent areas in their material and human character.* Thus industrial zones, poor and better-class housing areas, commercial and administrative districts can usually be identified. But it would be wrong to assume that these regions are static: people move not only from one housing area to another, but also leave a town altogether, to be usually replaced by "comers-in". The better-class houses of one period (*e.g.* Victorian villas) may become the professional offices, nursing homes, students' lodgings or workshops of another. Factories and rows of houses which have become run-down may be replaced by blocks of flats, offices or playing fields. Structural and functional change and population mobility are as characteristic of urban settlements as spatial differentiation.

THEORIES OF URBAN GROWTH AND THE EVOLUTION OF FUNCTIONAL ZONES

In attempts to explain the origins and development of urban zones based on the functional attributes of "Western" cities, three principal theories have been propounded:

1. *The concentric theory*, first suggested by E. W. Burgess as an explanation of the urban regions of Chicago (R. E. Parks and E. W. Burgess, *The City*).

* The identification of such "urban regions" is often more meaningful than the recognition of administrative and ecclesiastical divisions such as wards and parishes.

2. *The sector theory*, as postulated by Homer Hoyt (in *The Structure and Growth of Residential Neighbourhoods in American Cities*).

3. *The multiple-nuclei theory*, as proposed by C. D. Harris and E. L. Ullman (in "The Nature of Cities," reproduced in *Readings in Urban Geography*, edited by H. M. Mayer and C. F. Kohn).

These theories are examined in the following sections.

1. The Concentric Theory

In his study of the urban morphology of Chicago, Burgess expressed the view that a large city tends to expand outwards along a broad front, each zone growing by gradual colonisation of the next outer zone. At any one time, a number of more or less concentric zones may be envisaged,

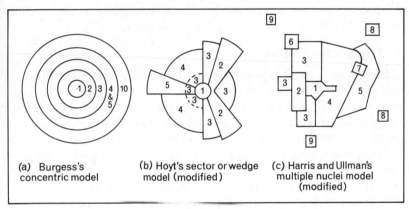

(a) Burgess's concentric model

(b) Hoyt's sector or wedge model (modified)

(c) Harris and Ullman's multiple nuclei model (modified)

FIG. 108.—Models of urban structure. No actual town fully conforms to any of these models, but most show in their structure elements of each. 1. Central business area; 2. wholesaling and light industry (including Burgess's slums); 3. low-class housing (interspersed with factories in Burgess's model); 4. middle-class housing; 5. high-class housing (including many suburbs, especially in Burgess's model); 6. heavy industry; 7. outlying subsidiary business district; 8. outer suburban housing; 9. outer suburban industry; 10. wealthy commuters' zone.

giving inland cities an annular structure (*see* Fig. 108) and cities along waterfronts (such as Chicago) a semi-annular structure. Burgess's zones, travelling outwards, are as follow: (i) a central area, or Central Business District (C.B.D.),* known in Chicago as the Loop; (ii) a zone of transition and perhaps of "urban blight," with congested slums and unstable immigrant populations, but often supporting minor commercial premises

* This is a term used by American geographers and sociologists. The ordinary person often refers to the "downtown" area, just as English people speak of the "city" or "town" in a restricted sense.

and light industries which have invaded the area from the C.B.D.;
(iii) a zone of factories and adjacent workers' dwellings and apartment
houses, where land values, as in zone (ii), may now be declining; (iv) a
better-class, suburban residential belt, with more substantial, newer,
houses, occupied by relatively stable families; (v) a commuters' ring,
30–60 minutes' travelling time from the city's nucleus, and consisting of
well-separated, well-to-do, mainly detached houses in a semi-rural setting.
This zone may also incorporate old villages not yet completely attached
to the city, and dormitory towns; land values are lower than in the
C.B.D. but are markedly rising, and there is often space for new, hori-
zontally-spread factories.

It should be noted that Burgess's concentric zones are applicable only to
"Western" cities of the type found in Europe, Anglo-America and
Australasia. In other continents, there are more wealthy homes in central
areas, and there are often external slums ("shanty towns").

2. The Sector Theory

Burgess was careful to point out that his annular pattern was in reality
imperfect. He recognised the distortions which variations in terrain and
routeways bring, and was not unaware of the way in which social sectors,
e.g. the Negro belt of Chicago and the upper-class residential area
immediately north of the Loop, overlooking lakeside parks, could modify
his concentric model. Homer Hoyt, by contrast, regarded the main
elements of growth as being based on the outer growth of sectors rather
than rings (*see* Fig. 108). He recognised, like Burgess, the existence of a
C.B.D. and of different classes of residential areas, but visualised the latter,
once they had arisen near the city centre, as spreading outwards in
broadening wedges. He considered that new developments gradually
come to reproduce the character of earlier developments in the same
sector. His arguments were supported by the varying rents charged in
different parts of large cities, which he observed changing outwards, not
laterally in concentric zones, but axially in wedges, one wedge, perhaps
because it occupied more attractive terrain, having higher average rents
than the adjacent one. He also identified a sector devoted chiefly to
wholesaling and light manufacturing, much of the latter carried on in
small workshops or on the upper floors and in the rear portions of commercial premises.

3. The Multiple-nuclei Theory

Harris and Ullman, while agreeing that a city may show both elements
of concentric zoning and also sectors of change, argued that most large

cities contain a number of subsidiary centres whose separate outward growth complicates the growth of a city from one central nucleus as postulated by Burgess and Hoyt. Their theory can certainly be applied to those cities which, in their expansion, have engulfed a number of villages and small towns, each continuing to act as a minor node within the agglomeration (*see* Fig. 108). It may also be applied to many colonial cities in Asia and Africa, which have at least European and native nuclei. In other cases, it must be acknowledged that certain functions, *e.g.* heavy and noxious industries, tend to seek waterfront and railside locations, and to be segregated from good housing areas, while lighter industries, *e.g.* clothing, profit from cohesion and from more central locations. The more desirable sites, capable of bearing high rents, are pre-empted for the highest class of housing. Once nuclei for various city activities have been established, Harris and Ullman believed they would be confirmed and would expand by accretion to form distinctive land use regions.

None of the three models outlined above exactly fits an actual city, each of which has its own individual morphology. Nevertheless, they serve as guide-lines towards the understanding of particular towns, most of which embody elements of each. Towns grow by outward accretion, which generally proceeds both from the main nucleus and from secondary nodes, while axial growth, too, is often evident, especially along roads and railways springing from the centre. Industry, commerce, residence and other functions, all have their own requirements, and sort themselves out to form distinct units. This sorting, however, may be interfered with, *e.g.* by the deliberate creation of new suburban factories and shopping centres away from traffic congestion, noise and dirt, and by the introduction of local authority housing estates in random areas previously devoted in the main to middle-class residences.

Recently, many "gradient studies" have been undertaken, and graphs drawn, in further attempts to discover to what extent there is order in the social and material arrangement of towns. Though no acceptable model has yet resulted, it has been found that there are relationships between time-distance from a city centre and, for example, land values, road traffic densities, population and housing densities, juvenile delinquency rates, the proportions of land used for commercial purposes, changing building heights, and so on. Most of the quantitative work concerning these gradient analyses has confirmed the varied findings of Burgess, Hoyt, Harris and Ullman.

CENTRIPETAL AND CENTRIFUGAL TENDENCIES

The processes of outward extension and internal change common to all developing cities (known in the U.S.A. as "sequent occupance") are subject to both centripetal and centrifugal forces. The former, less marked than they were before the widespread use of the motor-car, result in concentration, the latter in dispersion.

As C. C. Colby has pointed out,★ factors favouring the operation of centripetal forces, which attract some urban functions to the central parts of cities, include: (a) certain site attractions, e.g. a waterfront or a convergence of routeways; (b) functional magnetism, which leads one theatre or cinema to attract another for the convenience of both management and patrons, and clothing shops and warehouses to attract garment makers; (c) functional prestige, conferred, for instance, on a doctor with a Harley Street address; (d) human nature, e.g. the desire to be at the centre of things, the inertia which leads some people to cling to sites no longer suitable for residence, and civic pride which may find expression in the erection of prestigious administrative buildings even in the centre of quite small cities.

Factors encouraging the outward movement of urban functions include: (a) the more open character of land away from the crowded centre and the availability of more space for horizontal building and for car parking; (b) the frustrating congestion of traffic, the noise and the high incidence of air pollution in the centre; (c) the lower cost of land and lower rent charges of the outer urban zone; (d) the growing obsolescence of property in the central areas; (e) the human desire to live and work in healthier and more congenial environments—to be half in the country and half in the town.

The flight from the centre of cities began in Britain early on in the the nineteenth century when land in the centre became too precious for re-housing, and when the dangers of cholera epidemics resulting from insanitary congestion were realised. At first, only the wealthy could move far from their work, but the introduction of mechanised city transport and rising living standards later allowed the less well-to-do also to adopt a suburban life. It is now chiefly such commercial services as are in greatest need of central sites and best able to pay for them which seek town and city centres, while residence and industry, largely under the influence of motor transport, show an increasing tendency to move further out. High-class houses become established most often on airy,

★ "Annals of the Association of American Geographers," Vol. 23, 1933, reprinted in *Readings in Urban Geography*, edited by H. M. Mayer and C. F. Kohn.

fairly high ground (where it exists), industry on lower, flatter ground near railways, main roads, canals and docksides. Many of the poorer housing areas, now decaying, adjoin factories near which they were established when it was necessary for the working classes to walk to work.

THE CENTRAL AREAS OF TOWNS AND CITIES

The buildings near the central area of a large town often cluster round an ancient cross-roads (*e.g.* Carfax at Oxford), an important bridge (*e.g.* at Newcastle) or an old market-place (*e.g.* at Huddersfield). In old towns dating from medieval times (*e.g.* in English cathedral cities), these buildings are amassed heterogeneously among an intricate maze of streets, but in planned towns, especially in the United States, they more often form square or rectangular blocks separated from each other by a recti-linear road pattern. While a few old buildings may remain in this core area, most of them have been replaced on several occasions, even in the New World. New roads may have been recently cut, or widened and perhaps re-aligned, but—even in cases where there was heavy areal bombing in the Second World War—street patterns have undergone much less change than the buildings which line them.

The core area (or C.B.D.) contains the principal business premises of a town: its chief shopping streets,* banks and other offices, its departmental stores and nearly all its specialised shops. Those who work in this area serve the entire community and also the surrounding countryside, while those shops and offices which lie outside the town centre are fewer in number and more scattered in their distribution and simply serve small sections of the populace.

Public buildings such as the town hall or civic centre, public library and art gallery, the general post office, the chief hotels and places of enter-tainment, and often newspaper offices, gather within the central area. The outer limits, especially in Europe, are marked by less intensive forms of land use, by less imposing buildings of lower average height, by the appear-ance of motor-car dealers and garages, storage buildings and workshops, old houses (once, but rarely now, homes of the wealthy) converted to professional and other uses, and a congeries of low-grade restaurants and small shops. Bus and railway stations are often located on the margins of the C.B.D., and also perhaps university buildings and technological institutes.

Commercial premises throng in city centres because, until at any rate

---

* In most towns, central shopping areas account for about 40 per cent of the town's total retail trade.

the last few years, those parts of the built-up areas were the most accessible to the urban and extra-urban population as a whole, and also because only such establishments could afford the very high rents charged for such desirable central sites. Central offices benefit, too, from various ancillary services concentrated in the central area, *e.g.* those of lawyers, accountants, bank managers and advertising agents. The existence of cafes, tobacconists, newsagents and hairdressers, generally just off the main streets, where rents are lower than along the main thoroughfares, is an outcome of the large turnovers which may be achieved, even by small retailers, in an area more crowded with pedestrians during the day than any other part of the town.

Buildings within the central area, especially in North America, are often multi-storeyed, and may reach skyscraper proportions, owing to the very high land values placed on exceptionally competitive sites. They are also generally multi-functional. Shops usually occupy the ground floors so that their window-displays may tempt passers-by. Higher floors, for which somewhat lower rents are charged, are usually tenanted by professional workers and office staffs, or even by people not concerned with essential central services, *e.g.* clothing manufacturers, printers, bookbinders and storage agents (*see* Fig. 145, p. 331).

In the largest cities, the central services may be grouped into segregated quarters, each principally devoted to a specialised function. Thus in London there is the City (the financial core), Westminster (the administrative area) and the West End (the main shopping and theatre area). (Originally, the City of London was a mercantile town, the City of Westminster simply the seat of the Royal Palace and Abbey.) Even more specialisation is found in certain areas, *e.g.* many newspaper offices are clustered in Fleet Street, banking houses in Lombard Street and tea merchants in Mincing Lane. On Manhattan, there is a financial quarter in the south, a shopping and entertainments area further north. Paris has a distinct governmental area, separated from the city's own administrative centre, a commercial area dominated by large stores and luxury industries, a cultural complex and an entertainments sector.

Since 1945, the pace of change in central areas, always rapid, has accelerated. The reasons are various: (*a*) in many European countries, war damage and the obliteration of entire building blocks has necessitated widespread rebuilding; (*b*) in virtually all advanced countries save the Soviet Union the private motor-car has become so commonplace that existing city centres have become choked with traffic, so denying them the accessibility which is their lifeblood; (*c*) "urban blight," marked by obsolescent and vacated buildings, high but falling land values and rents, has set in on the peripheries of central areas. There have therefore been growing demands for a spate of "urban renewal." Most cities have plans, in most cases at least partially implemented, for the erection within their central areas, of newer, taller buildings, broader streets, and pedestrian precincts. One of the finest examples of the latter is to be found in Rotterdam (*see* Fig. 122, p. 276); in England a notable one was pioneered by Coventry.

In the past, as well as in the present, shopping areas have often been re-sited, perhaps as a consequence of the increasing importance of arterial roads compared with ways to the railway station. In Newcastle, for example, Grainger Street, leading to the Central Railway Station, yielded place as a shopping street to Northumberland Street, a continuation of a main road leading north from a modern Tyne Bridge. In Bradford, Market Street, leading to Forster Square Station, gave way to Broadway.

Recent plans for reducing the volume of motor transport and easing the traffic flow in city centres are essential for there have already been serious losses in land values and in some American cities the C.B.D.s are already degenerating into "dead hearts." The growth of population and purchasing power in the outer zones, the desire for easier traffic circulation and increased demands on space, coupled with the extension of communication by telephone (reducing the need for face-to-face contacts) have already combined to encourage the outward movement of some retailing and office premises. By and large, residential populations have long since fled from the centres of Western cities, which have become more and more workshops rather than living-spaces. They are now dead on Sundays and at night except in the "bright-light" districts round places of entertainment. Urban renewal programmes must attempt to maintain these central areas as living organisms during the rest of the week.

INDUSTRIAL AREAS IN CITIES

Some manufacturing is carried on in most towns. Where it is a dominant function, and carried on in big factories, it is usually concentrated on or close to important routeways. Thus many factories line navigable rivers, canals, railways or the seafront. They have recently become more numerous alongside arterial roads. Heavy industries, requiring bulky raw materials and in some cases also producing bulky commodities, have the greatest need of cheap transport facilities. They may also require large quantities of water both for processing and for the removal of effluent. Some, too, emit air pollutants and noxious fumes. Hence heavy industries are often sited by the sea or a large river generally some distance away from all but the meanest, deteriorating dwelling-places and slums, *e.g.* along the

Thames estuary east of London (Fig. 83), in the New Jersey marshes near New York and on the Calumet waterfront south of Chicago. Smaller and more specialised industries (*e.g.* light engineering, textiles, food-processing and furniture) are quite satisfactorily placed alongside roads and railways, where they are more often interspersed with the terraced houses of their employees (*e.g.* in the Lancashire and Yorkshire mill towns). The lightest,

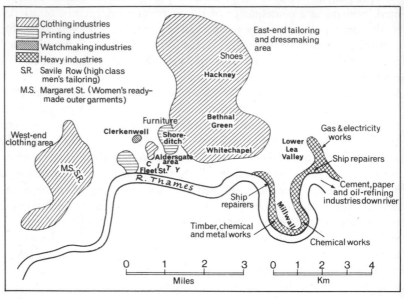

FIG. 109.—London: some industrial distributions. Clothing and printing industries are common to the inner parts of many metropolitan cities. Heavier and more noxious industries, which may also, like the chemical and electricity generating industries, consume large quantities of water, often have waterside locations well removed from both the central commercial areas and the better-class residential districts. Compare Fig. 83.

cleanest and quietest industries, using little machinery but demanding considerable manual skill are those mainly concerned with the luxury trades, *e.g.* bespoke tailoring, dressmaking, jewellery manufacture and watch-repairing, along with printing and publishing. Such occupations are most conveniently carried on in small workshops in or near city centres, where they often occupy rear premises and upper floors, as in Paris, New York and London (*see* Fig. 109).

New factories are now being built on cheap, relatively flat land on industrial estates just outside urban settlements, and in their own grounds in outer suburban areas. They are usually low-spread structures, their approaches are often pleasantly landscaped, and they are well provided with car parking facilities.

HOUSING AREAS IN CITIES

The few remaining "town houses" of Western cities, mostly built for the well to-do in the eighteenth and nineteenth centuries, are often now unfashionable and therefore converted into flats or remodelled for professional purposes (*e.g.* as doctors' and dentists' surgeries, private hotels, nursing homes and offices). Apart from these, the majority of residential properties decrease in age but increase in size, cost and garden space with distance from the inner urban zones. Slums and sub-standard houses, including, in Britain, many back-to-back dwellings and regimented bye-law terraces,* are still found in most industrial towns, where they are often overlooked by the multi-storeyed factories which provided employment for most of their occupants at the time when they were erected. The poorest of these inner areas, with their "twilight housing," show higher crime rates and more overcrowding than the outer areas. Their inhabitants show more physical and mental defects, are more addicted to alcoholism and immorality, and are of lower economic status than those of suburban areas. Houses in such areas are now being extensively demolished and most of the poor families which occupied them are being re-housed either on suburban council estates (where housing densities are much lower), or in high blocks of flats built in *situ* (*see* Fig. 110).

Once the railway came, but even more since the motor-car appeared, people have been increasingly housed in "suburbia," which in most cities advances further and further from city centres as new, better-spaced houses replace the old. In London, evacuation from the historic City began early: in 1851 the population was 128,000, but it was less than 5,000 in 1961. The County of London has been losing numbers since 1901, when the population was 4½ million. It is now less than 3,200,000. Even the outer ring of the conurbation is now beginning to show a reduced population growth as the wealthier people hop over the Green Belt and take up residence in the "exurbia" of dormitory towns and "stockbroker belts," with their loose clusters of villas and extensive grounds.

Suburbs, Mumford's "non-city," castigated by him as a "collective attempt at private living," whose people "work anywhere and live nowhere," are now becoming more extensive than the cities which spawned them. Indeed, between 1919 and 1939, the area occupied by

* The *Public Health Act* of 1875 recommended the adoption of bye-laws which laid down minimum room sizes, back-spaces, street widths and so on.

towns and cities in Britain doubled, and in the U.S.A., where there is more private transport as well as more space, it multiplied even more. In France and the U.S.S.R., multi-storeyed living and high urban densities have been more traditional than in Anglo-Saxon countries and neither Paris nor Moscow have such extensive suburbs as London and New York.

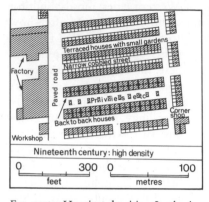 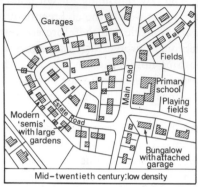

FIG. 110.—Housing densities. In the inner zones of industrial cities many housing areas remain densely populated, though demolition is gradually producing a loosening-out of such congested urban tracts. Far lower building densities are found in newer estates which have generally been laid out further from city centres. The gross density in the first of these maps is about 25 houses per acre, in the second only about 4 (net densities are closer to 30 and 7 respectively).

Suburbs in large cities expand and gain in population not only through migration from more central urban areas but also through immigration from country districts and smaller towns. Suburban growth is often preferential, and most frequently takes place along and close to significant lines of road transport, and round suburban railway stations. Since motor-cars can move freely along minor streets, there is no particular disadvantage now in filling up the spaces between the main traffic arteries in those high-class suburbs where most people possess motor-cars. The scenically attractive areas, and the less smoky zones, generally the western parts of cities in western Europe (facing the prevailing winds) gain at the expense of less desirable areas, but since sites and houses in such favoured tracts command higher prices, social segregation results.

NEIGHBOURHOOD UNITS AND REGIONAL SHOPPING CENTRES

In themselves, suburban housing areas offer little in the way of shops or social facilities or workplaces. Because of these deficiencies, in which they stand in marked contrast to the inner zones of towns, and also in contrast to villages, the idea of "neighbourhood units" is gaining ground, and has been introduced into most New Town plans. Such areas—which may house up to 10,000 people—are designed to include a varied range of shops, at least a primary school, church and chapel, and perhaps also a public park and community hall or adult education centre.

[*Courtesy: United States Information Service*

FIG. 111.—A shopping plaza near Washington, U.S.A. Most large cities in the United States now possess extensive out-of-town shopping centres, designed to serve a motorised public. They are very destructive of the countryside and are contributing to the decay of city core areas, for car parking on the scale shown here is impossible in "down-town" shopping districts.

Another recent development—springing largely from suburban mobility as compared with the traffic crawl of city centres—is that of the regional shopping centre, generally located at a significant route node, and often including a large supermarket, and perhaps even a Woolworth's, as well as plenty of space for parking motor-cars. Already such centres are achieving success: sales figures are expanding much more than those of central shopping centres.

The idea of developing regional shopping centres first took hold in the U.S.A., and it became popular in Britain in the mid-1960s. For example, a shopping centre was opened at Cowley in 1965 to help relieve some of the congestion in the heart of medieval Oxford. It includes two spiral car parks and is being used not only by people from the city's rural hinterland, but also by motorists travelling along the outer by-pass from North Oxford. In the U.S.A. some of these out-of-town shopping centres cover more than 100 acres (40 ha) and are accessible to nearly half a million people within a driving range of only twenty minutes. The newest of them offer as many as 10,000 car spaces. The stores themselves, and perhaps also office buildings, hotels, cafés, theatres and children's playgrounds, are gathered together in covered pedestrian malls. There are notable examples near Minneapolis, Boston, Seattle, Detroit and Washington (*see* Fig. 111). Besides these shopping centres, round which it is expected houses may later cluster, there are now many arterial highways in the U.S.A. which provide drive-in banks, restaurants and cinemas which motorists may visit without leaving their cars. In these cases, development is taking on new forms, but it is sometimes contributing almost as much to urban sprawl as the now largely condemned and therefore discarded practice of erecting private houses alongside such roads without filling in spaces between them: a practice known as "ribbon" development.

OPEN SPACES

All towns, even within their inner zones, are to some extent broken up by the occurrence of open spaces in the form of streets, roads, railways, market-places, car parks, temporarily derelict land (resulting, in most cases from recent slum clearances and the demolition of obsolescent buildings), private and public gardens, recreational parks and playing fields, school playgrounds and in many cases even patches of woodland and farmland.

Many historic towns contain urban tracts which are not subject to the operation of a market economy and are not usually at the disposal of the highest bidder. They include the precincts of medieval castles, *e.g.* at Richmond (Yorkshire); abbeys, *e.g.* at York; cathedrals, *e.g.* at Chichester; and the surrounds of royal palaces, *e.g.* in London. Most of these open spaces are available for public enjoyment, and are pleasantly secluded from the worst of traffic noises, smells and activity. Public parks, *e.g.* St James's Park and Hyde Park in London, Central Park on Manhattan, the several lakeside parks of Chicago, and Princes Street Gardens in Edinburgh, are among other open enclaves which interrupt the zonal arrangements of towns, and which sometimes act as divides between different functional regions. Some of these islands of quiet are unsuited to building, but most are preserved from it by deliberate municipal policy.

In cities such as Paris and Vienna, old lines of fortification have been successively broken down to make way for broad, tree-lined boulevards. London has a particularly green appearance owing to the existence of numerous large town gardens usually bordered by Georgian or earlier residences. They are particularly notable in Bloomsbury. Here are embodied some of Ebenezer Howard's Garden City notions, where samples of town and country are happily blended in an urban settlement.

THE RURURBAN FRINGE

Beyond the main built-up areas of large cities, as we have seen, there is usually a tract of land which may contain not only new shopping clusters, dormitory villages and towns, occasional modern factories, often only one storey high, and scattered, expensive houses with large gardens, but also playing-fields, golf courses, colleges and universities, airports, sewage works, hospitals and expanses of farmland used mainly for market-gardening and the production of milk. These varied land uses are all closely associated with the town of which they are characteristic. They mark the intervention of a transitional zone between town and country which is still tributary to the town if not wholly part of its built-up area.

Chapter XVI

The Population Structure of Towns

THE HUMAN RESOURCES OF TOWNS

To geographers, as well as sociologists, the people who live and work in towns, or who visit them for shopping, amusement, instruction, medical attention, and so on, are an essential part of urban studies. It may, in fact, be argued that towns are even more the people who inhabit and benefit from them than the buildings and thoroughfares which materially distinguish them.

The smooth working of a town as an entity depends partly on the efficiency of its municipal services, including transport, but even more on the extent to which its citizens are willing to regard themselves and to act as a united community. If they are rigidly compartmentalised by their social, economic, ethnic and political affiliations, the town will consist merely of a collection of segregated units superficially joined together by streets and buildings, and it will not function satisfactorily.

VARIATIONS IN URBAN POPULATION DENSITIES

Both rural and urban population densities vary from country to country. The highest rural densities, reaching 2,500 to 4,000 per square mile in parts of Java, Egypt, the Ganges and Yangtse deltas, may be compared with urban densities of 700,000 in Victoria (Hong Kong) and 450,000 in parts of central Calcutta and Old Delhi. Western cities have much lower densities: Paris, one of the most congested, reaches nearly 90,000 per square mile, *i.e.* more than twice the density of the County of London. Britain's worst industrial slums rarely reach 200,000 per square mile (*c.* 300 per acre), and in the New Towns the residential districts average only about 50 per acre, gross densities being less than 10 per acre.

Industrial cities, especially the older ones, generally show higher densities than resort centres and dormitory towns. Many towns in northern England, with a high proportion of working-class citizens, are more crowded than the newer towns of southern England, though, of course, much depends on how generously town boundaries are drawn when examining relative densities.

Within a single Western city, the central area normally has very few residents, and has, indeed, been referred to as "an extending crater" (by A. E. Smailes in *Towns and Cities*). But densities are high immediately beyond this "crater," and then generally decline outwards towards the newer, better-class suburbs. The steepness of the population gradient varies along different radii, especially if the town has a "sector" structure (*see* p. 240), and may be modified further by the existence of sub-centres which have their own retailing and perhaps industrial districts. Nevertheless, the newer, outer parts of Western cities always show lower densities than the inner and older parts. Non-Western cities present a different pattern: densities are high near the centre, where the wealthier people live, perhaps in the same buildings as their shops and workshops, and they are also high on the fringes, where the poorer people and rural immigrants dwell, often in modern slums. Only recently, as transport has improved, have some of the upper-class begun to move out into Western-type suburbs.

In the inner core of a Western city competition for business premises is keen. Land values are high, and few people can afford to reside there except those rich enough and zealous enough to enjoy to the full the social and cultural life of a city centre, such as those who occupy, for instance, the still fashionable and well-maintained Georgian town houses of central London. To some other groups, central houses, or at least rooms, may be either essential or highly desirable, *e.g.* to hoteliers and caretakers, and to employees in restaurants, theatres and cinemas who work late at night. The inner cores of most cities, however, remain population deserts during the darkest hours, though flooded with people during the working day. Chicago's central business district, for example, has barely 6,000 permanent residents, but its buildings accommodate nearly a million workers during office hours.

Inner residential areas support large numbers of poorly-paid people at high densities because such residents can neither afford to buy much land nor to pay high transport costs. They rarely possess private motor-cars and they need to be within a short distance of their work. They often occupy small nineteenth-century terraced houses built at a time when large gardens were regarded as exclusive to the rich. Some, *e.g.* in Glasgow's Gorbals, are accommodated in tall apartment houses which have degenerated into miserable slums, others in sub-standard back-to-back houses. As these are demolished in the interests of hygiene and good living, their residents may be rehoused in newer blocks of flats, *e.g.* the pre-war Quarry Hill flats in Leeds, and the post-war Park Hill flats in Sheffield (*see* Fig. 112), for such people may still prefer to live close to their neighbours. Building high does not necessarily increase housing densities as the need for light, open spaces and traffic mobility now demands that individual blocks are well separated from each other.

[*Courtesy: City Architect, Sheffield*]

Fig. 112.—Park Hill Flats, Sheffield. Like most large towns and cities, Sheffield has undertaken a number of post-war urban renewal projects. Among them, slum clearance and rehousing have loomed large. Under the Park Hill scheme, illustrated here, nearly 1,000 flats and maisonettes have been provided on a cleared hillside above the Midland Railway station. Movement within the flat-blocks is only in part by vertical lift, for the hill-slope contours allow all but the top floor of the four to ten storey blocks to be directly accessible at one end from ground level. Within, decks run the whole length of the irregularly aligned buildings: these decks provide room for children to play and for adults to meet; they are open to the sky on one side and allow for extensive views. Within easy reach of the city centre, the development nevertheless has its own shops, public houses, social amenities and playgrounds, and its surrounds have been to some extent enhanced by landscaping.

On modern council estates, usually erected further from the city's central area than flat-blocks, and designed to accommodate not only older, displaced families, but also new ones, population densities are much lower than in a city's inner housing zone. Land is generally cheaper and there is often room, even on authority estates, for a semi-detached layout, for both kitchen and flower gardens, and perhaps also for garages. Still lighter densities are usually achieved on private estates, and especially in upper-class suburbs where space-consuming bungalows and other detached houses are characteristic. Here, on the urban periphery, low land values encourage a lower intensity of land use than is customary near town centres. Here, too, where housing densities are least, the affluent can not only afford to buy large tracts of land to match their opulent houses, they can also afford to pay the price of a longer journey to and from work, and to own their own motor vehicles.

RURAL AND URBAN SOCIAL GROUPINGS

Rural societies are relatively homogeneous and static. Urban societies are more heterogeneous in occupation and social habits, they are supported by weaker kinship and community ties, and they are more mobile. Rural people are accustomed to make daily journeys from home to field, weekly journeys from farmstead to market. Urban movements are more complex: there are often longer and less direct journeys to work, different journeys to shops and entertainment. House removals, including those from one town to another, are more frequent among townspeople. Urban incomes show more variety than rural ones; they range from very high to very low, and are reflected in a more intricate class structure.

Occupation and social status are commonly revealed by the kind of residential area a family occupies. In Liverpool, for example, over half the unskilled and semi-skilled workers live in the inner housing zone, only a quarter in the outer, while half the professional workers reside in the outer zone, only about 6 per cent in the inner. There are comparable differences between one town and another. In Bradford, a typical large industrial town, over two-thirds of the workers are manual employees, whereas in Ilkley, a nearby dormitory town, the figure is only one-third. Higher income groups tend not only to move from the inner to the outer zones of towns, but also from the older, often stagnating industrial cities into newer, expanding towns and peripheral commuter districts.

THE AGE COMPOSITION OF TOWNS

Urban and rural areas vary considerably in the age composition of their populations. In both advanced and developing countries, the typical movement of young, vigorous and ambitious adults from rural into urban areas creates imbalance, the towns being supplied with a high proportion of people in the 20 to 30 age group, the country villages being left with large numbers of the less enterprising workers and of old people. The latter are often joined by other old people who, upon retirement, at least in developed countries, often leave the town for the country. In some dispersal areas, e.g. regions of difficulty such as the Central Massif of France and the Highlands of Scotland, the exodus of young adults and their children is so large that village schools close down and farms are abandoned. If, however, the migrations are predominantly from over-crowded areas of agricultural poverty, *e.g.* southern Italy, then rural under-employment is reduced and the remaining farmers—perhaps in consequence able to enlarge their holdings—may thus be able to improve their living standards.

When towns cease to attract rural migrants, perhaps because their industries contract, their populations tend to show a rising average age.

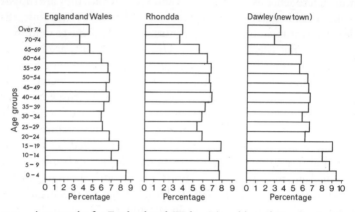

FIG. 113.—Age-graphs for England and Wales, Rhondda and Dawley (1966 sample census). Rhondda has fewer people in the 0–14 and in the 20–29 age-groups, and more in the 40–64 groups than the country as a whole. Dawley shows less imbalance than East Kilbride, but had 35 per cent of its population in the 0–19 group, and only 10·5 per cent in the over-65 group in 1966. Contrast Rhondda: 30 per cent and nearly 13·5 per cent respectively.

In extreme cases, for example in the declining coal-mining towns of the Rhondda, the 55 to 69 age group has become larger than the 20 to 34 group (*see* Fig. 113).

New towns, such as those round London and Glasgow, attract in particular young married couples with children, who may set up their first homes there and value the spaciousness these planned settlements provide. Aged people are in a marked minority since they are hard to move, and the later middle-aged are generally old enough to have already bought their own houses in the overspill city and are therefore unwilling to move. While England and Wales as a whole shows the following age group percentages (1966): 30.9 in the 0 to 19 age group, 31.4 in the 20 to 44 group, and 12.4 in the over-65 group, East Kilbride, a Glasgow over-spill town, had in its early years about 40 per cent of its population in the first group, 50 per cent in the second, and only 2 per cent in the third. Many urban settlements in Africa, Asiatic Russia and tropical Asia have similar age compositions, the 20 to 40 male age group being particularly large.

Because most seaside resorts and spas are favoured by retired people, they generally support more than the average number of old people, while university towns have an excess of young adults. A single large city shows many age composition variations within its different parts. Near the centre, for example, there is often a "rooming district," with accommodation for college and university students, nurses and office-workers, especially where there remain large Victorian houses which it has been easy to convert into apartments. In these districts there is a preponderance of single men and women aged 18 to 30, whose older landladies swell the number of females in the higher age groups. In the poorer housing areas, dominated by working-class communities, there is usually a high percentage of young married people and their children, a pattern repeated on most authority estates where accommodation is often allocated according to the number of children in the family. The age-pyramids of private estates usually reveal a high proportion of smaller early middle-aged families, while better-class housing areas are more narrowly based, but display a distinct late-middle-aged spread.

THE SEX COMPOSITION OF TOWNS

Even if we ignore the fact that in most countries there is some disparity in the numbers of men and women (*e.g.* in England and Wales, where there are about 107 females to 100 males, males predominating in age groups, 0 to 19 and 25 to 34, females in all the others, and especially in the oldest), towns vary greatly in sex composition. In military towns, naval bases, mining towns and those mainly concerned with heavy industry, there is an excess of males, while in service towns, *e.g.* holiday resorts,★ small market towns, and centres of light industry, *e.g.* textile towns, females outnumber men. Women are also more numerous in certain good residential areas within easy reach of city offices and shops and in such London boroughs as Hampstead and Kensington where more domestic servants than are now usual are employed.

In the developing areas of tropical Asia and Africa, it is largely, at first, young adult males who migrate from country to town, but because there is often less work for women than men in rural districts, it is common later for women to join their menfolk when the latter have become established in satisfactory employment. Early disparities are particularly noticeable in very large towns where greater changes in modes of life are called for,

★ In Worthing females outnumber men by 3 to 2.

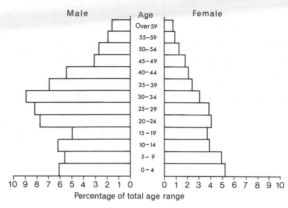

Percentage of total age range

FIG. 114.—Age- and sex-groups for Calcutta. Calcutta is not unlike many large cities in the developing countries which are now experiencing rapid urbanisation. There are fewer females than males in every age-group, and young and early middle-aged men are the most numerous of all the groups. Contrast the small fraction of the total population over 59 (less than 2½ per cent) with the percentage (*c.* 19 per cent) for England and Wales.

and adjustment is less easy. Thus in Calcutta (*see* Fig. 114), men exceed women by more than 175 to 100, while in Indian towns of about 50 to 100,000 population they outnumber women by only about 120 to 100.

FERTILITY AND MORTALITY IN TOWN AND COUNTRY

Fertility is generally higher in rural areas than in urban, and farming populations usually produce larger families than city, especially large city populations. This is perhaps because: (*a*) rural houses are often larger than town houses; (*b*) in the country even small children can usually help with daily chores; (*c*) towns provide more diversions; and (*d*) towns-people are usually better educated and more conversant with birth control methods. In the New Towns of advanced countries, however, fertility rates may be as high as in rural areas for, as we saw above, New Towns tend to have a large number of young women of child-bearing age while rural areas often have an excess of old people.

Higher levels of urban fertility are reached in some countries and towns than in others. These variations appear to be due to differences in occupational, social and industrial structures. For example, industrial towns in northern England, central Scotland and South Wales all show higher fertility rates than the towns of south-eastern England. Foreign-born, especially coloured groups, are generally more fertile than native-born, certainly in Britain, probably because such citizens are very conscious of their minority status and also because they take into the new country the demographic habits acquired in the old.

In many of the towns of developing countries, as in early nineteenth-century Europe, urban mortality rates have tended to be higher than rural ones. The slums of cities such as London, Manchester and Essen were for long both "child and adult cemeteries," for social overcrowding combined with inadequate sanitation gave free play to the spread of such epidemics as cholera. In 1841, the expectation of life in London was only 36 years, in Manchester 26 years, compared with 41 for England and Wales as a whole. Both towns were still periodically ravaged by cholera. Country-men migrating from rural Africa and Asia into the swelling towns and cities not only find themselves too often huddled together in insanitary shanty towns but they are also very prone to such diseases as influenza, tuberculosis, bronchitis and alcoholism. They are also inclined to adopt less nutritious diets, and many therefore fall prey to various deficiency diseases.

Just as the adoption of hygienic measures and the improvement of medical services in Western cities gradually lowered mortality rates to those of rural areas, so health standards are rising in African and Asiatic cities, in some cases to a more satisfactory level than in country districts because doctors and hospital services are concentrated in the cities. In such advanced countries as the United States, the highest death rates are generally found in the smaller towns, which have all the drawbacks of close-knit groups among which epidemics may easily spread, but lack the best medical skills and health services.

In England and Wales, all the large conurbations except London (a special case, where the best medical staffs in the country are available) have higher mortality rates than elsewhere. The older coal-mining and industrial towns of northern England—more crowded and less attractive to the medical profession—are much more lethal than the more widely dispersed, cleaner towns of south-eastern England, just as the humid, cloudy, less rewarding farming areas of highland Britain show higher death rates than the richer farmlands of lowland Britain.

ETHNIC VARIATIONS WITHIN TOWNS

Many large towns have a congeries of people differing in language, religion, nationality and racial characteristics. These differences, while helping to enrich the life of a town and perhaps adding strength to its cultural endowment, pose obvious problems of adaptation, integration and assimilation. This may result, especially when the differences are

[*Courtesy: United States Information Service*

FIG. 115.—Chinatown, San Francisco. San Francisco boasts the largest oriental population of any city outside the Far East. Here, in "Chinatown," where most of the orientals live, there is a mingling of Eastern and Western architecture, dress and street signs; The Chinese "hand laundry" has now given way to a modern self-service laundry, bicycles and rickshaws to motor-cars and parking meters.

wide, in either imposed or voluntary segregation, *i.e.* the virtually complete confinement of individual groups to particular sectors of the town (*see* Fig. 115).

Chicago and New York furnish good examples of large cities with mixed populations. In both, the poorest immigrant groups at first find the only accommodation they can afford is in rooming districts near the centre, generally in large houses originally occupied by wealthy residents but now divided up into small apartments. Here they settle down in extremely high densities. In Chicago, the oldest immigrant groups (mainly Germans, Scandinavians and Irish) have long since left this now dilapidated, congested area. They have become assimilated as Americans and are dispersed throughout the whole urban area, including the outer suburbs. Their places near the Loop have been taken by later immigrants (*e.g.* Italians, Czechs and Russians) many of whom are now moving out in their turn to form less segregated groups, mainly in the somewhat better working-class zone. Negroes, who first began to migrate into Chicago from the southern States at the end of the First World War, and now number nearly a million, cluster in a north-south belt about 4 miles (6 km) long, half a mile (0.8 km) wide on the south central side of the city. Their expansion beyond this unkempt coloured zone is very difficult because of white intimidation and lease restrictions. Nevertheless, as the Negroes prosper, the more affluent gradually infiltrate southwards, to take over, at first piecemeal, property abandoned by whites. Their erstwhile neighbours then in turn slowly retreat before their advance, so allowing the highly segregated Black Belt to extend itself. The family houses thus transferred to Negro occupation are then usually converted into apartment units into each of which are crowded several coloured families. Besides the Black Belt, Chicago has a small, segregated China-town, and a number of less rigidly defined areas known as Little Italy, Little Wales, the Jewish Ghetto and so on.

In New York, as in Chicago, there remain many "foreign quarters," especially on Manhattan's lower east side, and in Harlem, where the city's worst slums are to be found. In these areas gather the more indigent of the recent arrivals, many of whom fail to find employment and go on relief. Harlem, the segregated Negro quarter, covers about 3 sq. miles (8 sq. km) and houses nearly half a million Negroes, who have their own businesses, entertainments and places of worship, as in Chicago's Black Belt. Pressing on the Negro quarter, which is now spreading towards Central Park, is an expanding area occupied chiefly by recent immigrants from Puerto Rico, most of whom are ill educated, semi-skilled and, like the Negroes, confined to poor areas. There are also in New York very large numbers of Irish citizens (more than in Dublin), and Italians (more than in Rome). Neither of these national groups suffers much from discrimination. They have been part of the city's population for a long time, and are fairly widely dispersed, though there do exist, for social and linguistic reasons, certain compact settlements of Italians, mostly of peasant origin and little education, and similar groups of Greeks and other southern Europeans. Half the Jews in the United States live in New York, and there are far more there than in Jerusalem. Half the total have their homes in Brooklyn, where they retain many of the social customs their forebears brought in from the Old World.

NATIONAL, RELIGIOUS AND LINGUISTIC VARIATIONS AMONG URBAN POPULATIONS

Where towns include among their populations peoples of diverse nationalities, creeds and languages, there is a marked tendency for distinctive groups to separate out from the rest, sometimes owing to prejudice among the dominant community and the discriminatory policies it adopts, sometimes owing to a natural social desire to live with one's compatriots, who speak the same tongue, attend the same church, and share similar social habits.

Among the most distinctive groups the Jews have preserved their separate urban communities, partly because of the social ostracism which Christians and followers of other faiths have often exercised, and partly because of their own continuing desire to preserve their identity and oppose assimilation whatever their economic status. "Ghettoes" have long been characteristic of East European and other towns, including several in the New World, e.g. Chicago and Montreal. In England, there are large numbers of Jews in Manchester and Leeds, where they are largely employed in the garment trades; most are limited to specific parts of these cities, though, like other groups, they gradually spread outwards as they prosper and as the areas they have made their own deteriorate in condition and depreciate in value.

In the old Moorish towns of Spain (e.g. Valencia and Granada), not only were there separate Moslem and Jewish sectors, there was also a distinct Christian quarter. After the conquest of the final remnants of the Moorish kingdom in 1492, the towns were largely Christianised, but the Moors were allowed to occupy new quarters outside the walls. The Jews, some of whom accepted Christian conversion, at least tacitly, were permitted to remain in their own district, though their numbers declined under persecution. In many towns in the Near East and in North-west Africa, small Christian and Jewish communities are segregated from the larger Moslem ones, while in India there are exclusive social groupings of Hindus and Mohammedans. In Northern Ireland, people from the predominantly Roman Catholic quarters of towns such as Belfast and Londonderry often clash with Protestant elements, who, in the main, live in different streets, especially in the poorer areas.

The problem of language is acute in Eastern Canada (especially in

Quebec) and in Belgium. Montreal and Quebec, while predominantly French, have their English sectors and institutions, while Brussels has both Walloon and Flemish speakers. Brussels is, in fact, a bilingual island in a Flemish sea; as it expands southwards it enters Walloon territory, and so enlarges the linguistic problem, already reinforced by the fact that the Flemish-speaking element is mainly Roman Catholic and conservative, the Walloon element chiefly anti-clerical and socialist. Historically

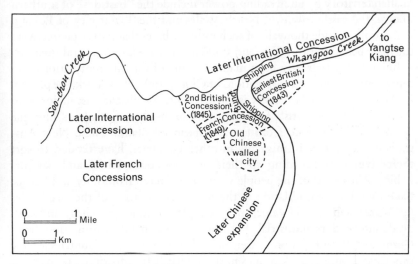

FIG. 116.—British, French and Chinese settlements in Shanghai. Shanghai, situated on the Whangpoo Creek leading into the main estuary of the Yangtse, has grown into the most populous city and the pre-eminent port and manufacturing centre of China. It owes much of its rise to the trade and settlement concessions granted to Westerners in the mid-nineteenth century, when it became a Treaty Port. On the Bund were built the many-storeyed offices of the great banks and insurance companies. The old Chinese city was walled in the fourteenth century.

superior and more influential, the Walloons are now numerically inferior to the Flemings. The rivalries between these two legally equal communities are increasingly expressing themselves in riots which threaten the unity of the Belgian nation.

In many countries, virtually dual or triple cities have grown up side by side owing to the settlement in the same locality of people of different national origins. When, for example, some centuries ago, German pioneers pressed eastwards into Slav territory, military strongholds and trading forts were established, with separate German and Slav sectors (along with Jewish ghettoes). Similar policies were adopted by the British when they established plantation towns in sixteenth- and seventeenth-century Ireland, and by both British and French in their colonial towns in Asia and Africa, where the segregation of imperialist and native communities was motivated by both hygienic and political considerations. In Shanghai, twin British and French settlements were founded down-river from the ancient Chinese walled city (*see* Fig. 116), while a normal feature of the more important Indian cities came to be the British appen-dages laid out in clean civil and military lines. Other planned towns sown in alien territory by an invading power include the "bastides" of southern France, the castle towns of North Wales and the Tartar city of Peking. It was only outside the walls of such military bases that native people were for long permitted to reside and trade in their own extramural quarters.

Reference has already been made to some of the different nationalities represented among the populations of Chicago and New York (*see* p. 261). In Australia national diversity is more recent. While the vast majority of Australians have British forbears, most post-war immigrants into the large cities have come from the European mainland. These New Aus-tralians, like urban immigrants in other countries, have tended to sort themselves out according to their incomes, occupations and national habits. Thus most of the people who have entered from Italy and Greece have found accommodation in the more central areas of the large cities *i.e.* in areas where land values may be high but housing is cheap and low-grade, and where industrial works are near at hand. Immigrants from Germany, Poland and other Central and West European countries, on the other hand, mostly seek homes in somewhat better districts, and disperse themselves more. The best suburbs, *e.g.* the seaside residential areas of Melbourne and Brisbane, have the highest proportion of British-born stocks (Peter Scott, "The Population Structure of Australian Cities," *Geographical Journal*).

SKIN COLOUR AS A SEGREGATING FACTOR IN TOWNS

Different ethnic groups have come to be most noticeably segregated in Western cities when they have differently coloured skins. Disharmony and tension are at a maximum in the United States and in South Africa, where they are not infrequently expressed in race riots, and at a minimum in Latin America, especially in Brazil, where frequent intermarriage has produced a wide range of colour variations, and where it is only of slight advantage to be white.

In American and South African cities the white element is always dominant, the coloured subordinate. In the U.S.A., Negroes form the only large minority group (over 10 per cent of the total population), but, although present in large numbers in many cities, they are everywhere outnumbered by whites. In South Africa, on the other hand, Negroes form a clear majority of the whole population, and there are also considerable numbers of other racial groups, almost equally despised by most of the whites, *i.e.* Cape Coloured and Indian. In Johannesburg, it is the African Negro element which is most numerous; in Cape Town, the Cape Coloured; in Durban, the Indian, with the African a close second. The South African Government's avowed object is to confine these non-white communities to their own rigidly defined urban areas, though of course there has long been in operation a natural process of separation. The rapid growth of African immigration into Johannesburg brought chaos; tumbledown slums such as Sophiatown developed, especially in the 1940s and 1950s, and were a reproach to the city authorities. They became notorious for their insanitary living conditions, their disease, immorality, illegal brewing, gang warfare and lawlessness, and are now in the course of demolition. In their place, the Government is mass-producing cheap but decently constructed durable houses in an area set aside for African occupation on the south-western side of the city. The strict apartheid policy remains.

Since the Second World War the immigration into Britain of large numbers of British citizens from the "Coloured Commonwealth" has caused concern to many white people in the cities they have most often chosen to enter, despite their value in industry, hospitals and transport services, and the gaiety they have added to the grey streets by their dress. No form of legal segregation is practised, but the newcomers nevertheless tend to separate themselves from native-born British people, not mainly through their fears of white intimidation but chiefly through their need of cheap housing, the greater social satisfaction they derive from living close together, their similar customs, and—in the case of Indians and Pakistanis, and West Africans—their shared language. The official policy is aimed at dispersal and eventual integration with native-born people. Schooling is helping this process, though the education of many coloured children in schools shared by lighter skinned boys and girls presents its own problems, which are particularly acute in Wolverhampton (over 10 per cent of whose schoolchildren are of immigrant origin), Birmingham (nearly 9 per cent), Derby (8 per cent), Warley, Leicester and Huddersfield (over 7 per cent), Bradford and Nottingham (nearly 7 per cent).

Several British ports have long had coloured districts in their dock areas, *e.g.* Limehouse in London and Tiger Bay in Cardiff. The entry of large numbers of coloured people into inland towns and cities is a new phenomenon. These immigrants tend to settle, at first, in the older residential districts between the central business areas and the suburbs, i.e. in "twilight" areas, formerly dominated by large, middle-class houses, but now occupied by the poorer working classes. Gradually, as in North America at an earlier date, they become more stable and, as their earnings improve, they migrate outwards towards the inner margins of the more open suburbs, where they occasionally inflame white prejudice. There is, as yet, little social intermixing of coloured immigrant and native-born British, and more inter-community tension exists than between native-born and, for example, Irish and Italian incomers.

Chapter XVII

Urban Problems

TOWNS have always had their problems of commissariat, of housing and social adjustment, layout, fabric decay, hygiene, defence, government and so on. A number of these problems have already been broached in this book. As towns have multiplied in number and grown in size, and continue to do so, their problems have augmented, and new ones have appeared. It is our task in this chapter to examine some of these problems, old and new, and to suggest how at least a few of them may be eased.

FOOD AND WATER SUPPLIES

As we saw in Chapter V, towns could not come into being until the surrounding countryside was capable of providing a food surplus. Nowadays, with modern transport and large farm surpluses in many parts of the world, towns generally have little difficulty in obtaining food, even from far-distant lands. Developing countries, however, may lack the capital to give all their townsfolk an adequate diet, and even in developed countries there are sporadic, temporary shortages owing to failures in economic planning, poor harvests, dock strikes and traffic hold-ups occasioned by excessive snow, floods and so on.

The problem of water supply is more permanent and applies specifically to cities. It is becoming increasingly serious even in advanced countries which certainly have no problem in paying for the water they consume. The root of the problem lies in the fact that 98 per cent of the Earth's surface water is contained in the salt oceans and in ice-caps. The remainder is unevenly distributed and often polluted. Over half is needed for agriculture, about a third for industry, 10 per cent for domestic use.

Many cities, especially in developing countries, lack a clean supply of fresh water. In India, for example, less than a third of the urban population has access to pure water, and the main reason why such diseases as cholera are endemic to such cities as Calcutta is because potable water is so scarce. Even when people are provided with purified water for drinking, they usually wash themselves and their clothing in contaminated supplies.

Most large cities have to seek water from distant sources. New York is in part supplied from reservoirs in the Catskills 100 miles (160 km) away but still runs short during occasional droughts. Its Water Board is now investigating the comparative costs of adding to its supplies by building a large desalination plant run by atomic energy or piping water from reservoirs 600 miles (960 km) away. Los Angeles is in an even worse position. Four-fifths of its water is at present brought by aqueducts from the Owens valley in the Sierra Nevada and from the River Colorado, the rest from local wells. The city is now considering whether to tap the Columbia River, 800 miles (1,290 km) away, or—like New York—to undertake the large-scale, expensive, desalination of offshore sea-water.

The demands made on water by urban industries, power-stations and domestic premises are growing at a much faster rate than the growth of population. In England and Wales, for example, 700 million gallons of water were provided by public undertakings in 1900, 2,500 in 1967. It is expected that the latter figure will double by A.D. 2000. Many wells are yielding less than they did, river pollution is a continuing evil, and the remaining water resources—mostly in thinly-peopled highland areas of abundant rain—are far from many consuming centres. In their search for additional reservoir sites, Liverpool and Birmingham are facing growing opposition from Welsh Nationalists; Glasgow, examining potential sites in the Scottish Highlands, and Manchester, seeking more sources in the Lake District, encounter resistance from bodies concerned with the preservation of the natural beauties of the countryside, especially in areas designated as National Parks and nature reserves. In 1963 the British Government set up a Water Resources Board to investigate future needs and to advise on what action should be taken to meet them. *Inter alia*, it is examining the feasibility of constructing barrages across Morecambe Bay, Solway Firth, the Wash and the Dee estuary in order to provide new freshwater lakes comparable with Lake IJssel in the Netherlands.

URBAN SPRAWL

As we have seen, cities tend to grow outwards and—at least in the developed world—to extend their housing areas at lower and lower densities as the distance from the centre increases. Suburban villadom is particularly extensive in the United States and Australasia, but even in such small countries as Britain which have more stringent planning controls, urban sprawl, accelerated by the growing use of the private motor-car, is consuming more and more good agricultural land. In

Europe as a whole, population in the urban fringes grew about two and a half times as fast as in more central housing areas between 1940 and 1950, and five times as fast between 1950 and 1960.

In Japan the area covered by towns and cities already amounts to a fifth of the cultivable area, for settlements, like farmland, prefer flat or gently sloping ground. In England and Wales, the proportion of urban land doubled between 1900 and 1960 to occupy 11 per cent of the total area; by 2000 the percentage is likely to be 16, a comparatively modest increase made possible by the acceptance of higher building densities than

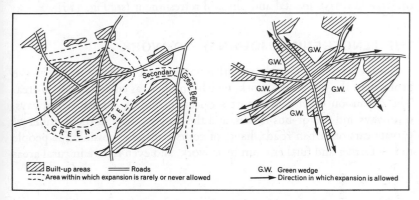

FIG. 117.—Green belts and green wedges. The idea of green wedges is now gaining more acceptance: in the case of a large city the preservation of such rural tracts allows people living near city centres to reach the open country more quickly than is possible under a green belt policy.

those of the 1930s (R. H. Best, "Recent Changes and Future Prospects of Land Use in England and Wales," *Geographical Journal*). Such an increase, while reducing the amenity value of much of the more accessible countryside, need not, however, result in a reduction of British food supplies because, (*a*) further agricultural intensification is still possible, (*b*) private garden produce is by no means negligible.

In its attempts to limit urban sprawl, Britain—in common with some other countries—has introduced "building high" schemes, the preservation, where practicable, of green belts round its large cities, and the planning of New Towns (*see* Chapter XVIII), designed mainly to house "overspill" populations.

As David Thomas has pointed out (in "London's Green Belt: the Evolution of an Idea," *Geographical Journal*), proposals to limit the spread of London were made as early as Elizabeth I's reign. The demand for some control over its unabated growth was quickened when Ebenezer Howard and his "garden city" followers advocated green belts round all Britain's major cities with a view to preserving agricultural land and providing recreational spaces, but no fully prepared scheme was launched until 1935. Nearly 30,000 acres (12,120 ha) have now been acquired for the maintenance of a 10-mile (16-km) wide Green Belt round the capital. Other urban authorities have taken up the idea. Occasionally, however, some building has been permitted in such open areas, and the idea is growing that a series of green wedges might be preferable for they would allow more people the chance of easy access to the open country from which they could derive mental and physical refreshment (*see* Fig. 117).

THE LENGTHENING JOURNEY TO WORK

Closely connected with suburbanisation and urban sprawl is the problem of the journey to work, which lengthens as cities increase in area. The expansion of city transport services, including suburban railways, tramways and motor-bus routes, and the post-war rise in the number of private cars on urban roads, have, of course, made it possible for people to live further and further from their work, and even to live in rural areas

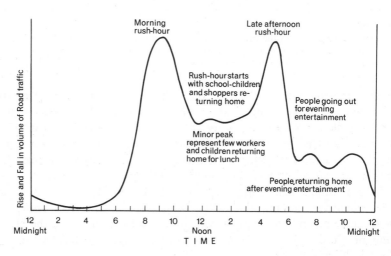

FIG. 118.—The day's travel peaks in England. In most countries the volume of traffic on urban roads is much greater at times when people are going to and from work than at other periods. In England the morning rush-hour is normally about 8–9 a.m., the afternoon rush-hour about 4.30–5.30 p.m. The spread of works canteens and school dining facilities during the last thirty years has reduced the numbers of people now going home for lunch.

while working in urban settlements. The growth in the number of people employed in service occupations, especially in city offices, however, has further multiplied the number of commuters, most of whom move to and from work at about the same time. Hence, the "rush hour" has become a problem both for people and transport undertakings (*see* Fig. 118). People waste time and money on travel, and become excessively fatigued and frustrated, while transport authorities keep in reserve large amounts of capital equipment and pay only partially productive labour in order to serve the public as well as possible at peak hours. The convergence of people on city centres creates almost insoluble traffic problems, and it has become so difficult for people to reach offices and

[*Courtesy: Royal Danish Ministry for Foreign Affairs*

FIG. 119.—Copenhagen: transport by bicycle and street-car. Copenhagen, the capital of Denmark and a city larger then either Stockholm or Oslo, suffers, like other million cities, from traffic congestion in its central area. Unlike many large European cities, however, a high proportion of the workers in this low-lying, almost flat, city still find it convenient to travel in and out by bicycle or tram-car. The photograph shows a rush-hour scene in one of the city streets.

shops in the central area in their own cars that 90 per cent of workers in central London, for example, reach their destinations by public transport. A higher proportion of people reach Manhattan by car from places round New York because this city has more motorways and, perhaps, a less efficient rail system. In Amsterdam and Copenhagen large numbers travel to work by bicycle and tram (*see* Fig. 119), but beyond a radius of 10 miles (16 km) most use rail.

Daily journeys between the central area of cities and the suburbs or satellite towns are not the only ones made. There are also transverse or lateral and circumferential journeys, especially perhaps between different parts of polynuclear conurbations. Besides journeys to work there are movements concerned with shopping and entertainment, the former concentrated in the afternoons, the latter in the evenings. There are even journeys from cities to places outside (*e.g.* to smaller towns, regional shopping centres and new country factories), but the "reverse commuters" who make them cause no great problem and their journeys to work are usually shorter than those of city workers.

The commuting distance varies with the magnetic power of the city centre. London, for example has a commuting range of more than 70 miles (113 km), including the whole of Essex, Sussex and Kent. In New York, people who work in Manhattan spend, on average, about an hour travelling to work each day; workers in Birmingham about three-quarters of an hour, in smaller English cities about half an hour.

As R. E. Dickinson has pointed out (*op cit.*) a number of very large firms (*e.g.* Philips in Eindhoven) have reached the stage where it is becoming uneconomic to bring in more labour by private coach over long distances, and have begun to establish branches in smaller towns.

TRAFFIC IN TOWNS

In recent years the problem of the growing volume of road traffic has claimed more public attention than any other urban problem. It contributes in large measure to the changing face of those central areas upon which routes converge; it leads to the demolition of buildings and the displacement of city populations which stand in the way of road improvement schemes; it is a cause of urban noise, air pollution and frayed nerves; and it is responsible for the establishment, in less congested rururban areas, of out-of-town shopping centres, light industrial works, hotels and office blocks.

City traffic has, in fact, grown to such proportions that modern planners are accused of designing new towns and adapting old ones to

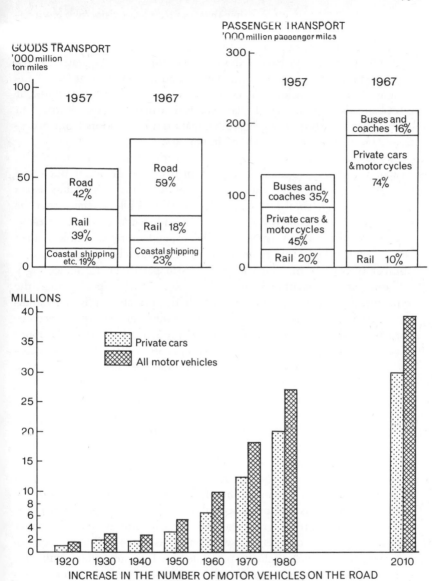

FIG. 120.—The growth of road transport in Great Britain. The rapid increase in the use of roads for both freight and passenger transport during the decade 1957–67 is illustrated by these graphs. Private cars are chiefly responsible for the congestion which increasingly slows down transport on urban and inter-urban roads.

accommodate the motor-car rather than to provide a satisfactory environment for people. As Colin Buchanan has stated (in *Traffic in Towns*), there are clearly limits to the volume of traffic a town can accept. Within these limits a town can have a civilised environment, comparatively free from undue noise, air pollution, danger and the unpleasant visual intrusion of motor vehicles. If a town is prepared to accept more traffic, it must be ready to permit costly, large-scale destruction and reconstruction of the townscape and to segregate the main traffic corridors from pedestrians, and from their work, shops and houses.

In 1964, there were about 12 million road vehicles in circulation in Britain, *i.e.* nearly five times as many as in 1934, and Professor Buchanan believes the figure may reach 40 million by 2010 ("Britain's Road Problem," *Geographical Journal* (*see* Fig. 120)). While agreeing that the motor-car has undoubted advantages (*e.g.* independence of movement, manoeuvrability, ability to enter buildings, and more adaptability than aircraft and vehicles on fixed rails), it has undoubtedly produced a number of evils from which large towns in particular are increasingly suffering. In combination with the expansion of urban populations, the areal spread of built-up land (of which the private car is the "arch-sprawler"), the spawning of taller and taller office blocks built to accommodate the growing number of service workers, and Europe's inheritance of numerous winding, narrow streets dating from earlier times, the motor-car has recently provoked much argument about its place in a changing world, and the ways in which its advantages can be fully realised without the wholesale destruction of all that is best in the urban environment.

A number of palliatives have been adopted from time to time with a view to easing the traffic problem. They include the introduction of staggered working hours, the use of one-way streets, traffic lights, zebra crossings, parking meters; and even load-spreading (*i.e.* the use of all streets as traffic arteries), but none of these is fully effective. Specially-designed motorways and purpose-built outer ring-roads to divert traffic away from cities are of greater value. Also helpful are primary inner ring-roads, skirting city centres, with terminus parks at the junctions of incoming roads. Such a scheme is planned for Leicester, which will have in its central area, improved motor-bus services, more taxis, and a mono-rail, but no private cars (*see* Fig. 121). In 1965, Leeds attempted a modified form of this scheme. Known as "park and ride," it was an attempt to induce incoming motorists to leave their cars in suburban parking spaces and to transfer, at low cost, to small express motor-buses for their journeys into the town centre. The plan was abandoned because motorists

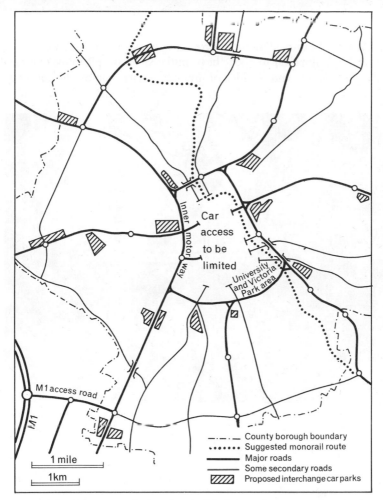

Car
access
to be
limited

Inner motorway

University
and Victoria
Park area

M1 access road

M1

1 mile

1km

—·—·— County borough boundary
•••••• Suggested monorail route
———— Major roads
———— Some secondary roads
▨▨▨ Proposed interchange car parks

FIG. 121.—The Leicester road plan. Devised in November 1964 as a major contribution to the alleviation of the urban traffic problem, the Leicester plan may be
regarded as a model from which other cities may learn how to mitigate their
own road congestion pains.

still preferred to complete their journeys in their own cars and to risk
finding room in city parks.

However, improvements in public transport could make a real contribution to easing the traffic problem. Services could be extended and
accelerated if private cars, most of which carry single commuters, were
effectively deterred from entering city centres. Many cities (*e.g.* Tokyo,

Philadelphia, Buenos Aires and Montreal) have recently followed the example set by London (the pioneer), New York, Paris, Chicago, Berlin and Moscow, in tunnelling underground railways. Others, following the lead set by Wuppertal in 1901, have initiated or are planning overhead roads and railways, and the idea of minibus services run on the automatic

[*Courtesy: Netherlands National Travel Office*

FIG. 122.—The shopping precinct in Rotterdam. The "Lijnbaan," Rotterdam's post-war, arcaded shopping centre from which vehicular traffic is excluded, is a model of its kind. It has more beauty than most retail precincts and particularly reflects the Dutch love of flowers. In the background of the photograph is the old City Hall, one of the few monumental buildings to escape bomb damage during the Second World War.

moving-belt principle is being canvassed. Multi-storeyed car-parks are becoming commonplace in towns, and useful experiments in the production of small, efficient, electrically driven motor-cars are being made in attempts to reduce the volume of urban noise and air pollution.

Pedestrian precincts are a feature of most new towns and of many reconstructed older ones and it is now accepted planning practice to segregate pedestrians from vehicular traffic by building footways and motor roads at different levels, despite the high costs involved (*see* Fig. 122). Urban roads of motorway standard which cut swathes through

[*Courtesy: United States Information Service*

FIG. 123.—The motor-car in Los Angeles. This photograph illustrates the kind of complex, multi-level urban freeway system that characterises the sprawling city of Los Angeles. Traffic movements are indicated by the white lines traced out by vehicle headlamps during a time-exposure at night.

towns are a feature of Berlin, Brussels, Stockholm and many American cities, especially Los Angeles. It would seem preferable to construct such freeways alongside rather than through cities so as not to destroy their intimate character and not to make traffic movement so easy as to be useless to the towns through which the roads pass. As much as two-thirds of "downtown" Los Angeles is occupied by streets, roads, garages and car-parks—a grievous loss to the city's civic amenities and also to its rate rolls (*see* Fig. 123).

URBAN DECAY AND RENEWAL

Though many towns, especially in Europe, still possess historic cores, the replacement of obsolete and decaying buildings has been a continuing process. More attention is now being devoted to this task than previously, partly because the areal bombing so many towns underwent during the Second World War provided an unusual opportunity for widespread renewal projects.* Moreover, there has recently been a change in public opinion on the subject of what constitutes decent living standards.

The areas most in need of renewal are clearly the central areas of towns and their inner, working-class residential areas. Renewal of the former usually entails the erection of multi-storeyed office blocks, the delineation of pedestrian precincts well equipped with a variety of shops, the straightening and widening of roads, the provision of open spaces, and perhaps also the construction of town houses and of buildings required for cultural and recreational purposes. Renewal of working-class areas involves the clearance of slum property and either the demolition or improvement of sub-standard, "twilight" housing, and the replacement building of city flat-blocks and suburban estates.

Apart from costs, one of the major difficulties town-planners have to face in devising satisfactory urban renewal projects is the harmonious integration of the old and the new. Most towns have a number of buildings of architectural and historic interest whose preservation on aesthetic and cultural grounds is generally held to be desirable. How should these structures be best fitted into the new townscape? The problem is obviously acute in certain historic towns such as York, Bath, Winchester and Oxford in England, which contain entire quarters of historical importance and for this reason attract thousands of tourists each year. Already in these cities there are disfiguring elements: branches of multiple stores, with the same fascias repeated in all towns whatever their age and character, the garish advertisements displayed in the windows of supermarkets, and the introduction of mock-Tudor and mock-Georgian buildings among genuine period pieces. Somehow new streets and structures must be so designed that they tone in with the old. Even too much street-widening and re-alignment† may be offensive to people intellectually and emotionally attached to a city's individuality, to its alleys, arcades, flights of steps and roof-lines. There is an obvious danger that modern planners and architects, restricted by costs, may—like chain-store directors—reproduce in their urban renewal schemes city centres which look alike whatever their geographical, economic and cultural environment.

---

* The fact that a number of these schemes, e.g. in Germany and Japan, were ill-conceived was mainly owing to the urgency of the need to rehouse people and re-establish factories, and to the shortage of capital needed to finance large-scale projects.

† Buildings are replaced much more often than street patterns are altered, partly because of legal difficulties concerning thoroughfares, and partly because of their various subterranean service communications.

AIR AND WATER POLLUTION

Air and water pollution—environmental evils ever since mankind first mastered fire and buried its dead—became particularly serious in industrial towns and cities in the nineteenth century when the burning of coal became more common, urban populations grew, and factories spread. The public have, however, become increasingly aware of the character and evils of pollution and —despite the exacerbation of the problem caused by the internal combustion engine—some alleviation has been achieved in many countries since the Second World War as a result of legislation and improved technology.

Pollution is at a maximum during a continuous period of temperature inversion,* fog and still air when the air at ground level is hemmed in. It was stated in the 1966 volume of the *Clean Air Yearbook* that the petrol engines of motor vehicles pour 5 million tons of carbon monoxide into Britain's atmosphere every year. Diesel engines account for another 80,000 tons. Coal burning produced 1,200,000 million tons of smoke, of which three-quarters came from domestic chimneys, 800,000 tons of grit and dust, 4,500,000 tons of sulphur dioxide. That such quantities of pollutants are harmful to public health may be illustrated from examples taken from such industrial centres as Liège, Donora (near Pittsburgh), New York and Los Angeles. In two foggy days in Liège in December 1930, 63 people died from respiratory troubles. Another 20 died in Donora in October 1948, and thousands more became ill. New York suffered severely in both November 1963 and again in November 1966. Although people with heart, lung and other respiratory ailments were advised to stay indoors, 200 deaths resulted from the first period of high smog incidence, 80 during the second. Los Angeles is said to be shrouded for 100 days every year with smog, the principal causes of which appear to be the gaseous emissions from electricity power-stations and motor exhausts.

In Britain, a *Clean Air Act* was passed in 1956. It prohibited the emission of dark smoke from chimneys, and required local authorities to establish both smokeless zones (in which no smoke would be allowed) and larger smoke control areas (in which the amount of smoke would be restricted). Since then, though it is true that less and less smoke producing bituminous coal has been burnt, too few authorities have completed their control programmes. At high cost, factories have installed smoke arrestment plants, and have raised their chimney stacks to remove sulphur dioxide and

---

* Temperature inversion, *i.e.* when the air at low levels is colder than it is higher up, and when calm and foggy weather cause the air at ground level to stagnate.

other wastes from the surface air. In the siting of new factories more attention is being paid to the prevailing wind and to the distribution of population, and district heating from central combustion plants is being introduced into some housing areas. In Los Angeles, all new cars and lorries are being fitted with exhaust-control systems, and in New York a watch is being kept on poisonous fumes from public and private incinerators and from metal-burning plants.

Besides being a menace to public health, air pollution defaces buildings and statues, corrodes metal window frames and affects the growth of trees and other vegetation. The visual effect of water pollution is, however, more obvious. Seas, lakes and rivers are all tainted with pollutants, largely as a result of emptying into them industrial and agricultural effluents and domestic sewage. By no means all municipal sewage and industrial sewage is fully treated before it enters seas, lakes and rivers, and as a result aquatic life in general, and commercial lake and river fisheries in particular, suffer greatly. Lake Erie, for instance—a source of water-supply for millions of people as well as factories—has now become a vast public sink. While most of the waste which has entered it descends to the bottom, to become increasingly toxic, the algae which it fertilises consume so much oxygen that too little now remains in the lake to nourish more than a fraction of the fish which once abounded in it. There are, too, signs that the pollutants are beginning to rise to the surface, so endangering more of its aquatic life. The Lake of Zürich is already said to be a dead lake. The lower Seine in 1900 had fifty species of river fish, now only a few diseased eels, while the River Tees, seventy years ago a notable salmon river, is now deserted by these fish.

As with air pollution, however, water pollution is—again at considerable cost to factories—being brought under control. Many factories have long been accustomed to recirculate the water they use for processing. Now they are being obliged to reduce the percentage of noxious effluent entering the rivers into which they empty their waste, and rivers in most industrial countries are consequently slowly becoming cleaner. More effective sewage plants are also being built as a contribution to the campaigns for clean water, though complete purification costs much more than some governments are prepared to spend. Even in favoured cities such as Paris not all buildings are linked to sewage systems.

WASTE DISPOSAL

Even to rid the environment of its most toxic gaseous and liquid effluents is, as we have seen, costly and far from easy technically. There is growing concern also about the increasing volume of waste in more solid form. Much is, of course, disposed of in dust-bins, but the vehicles which take it away often consign it to unsightly naked tips, which are not always free from health hazards.

Some refuse is burnt, some pulverised and then dispersed over cultivated ground. Many of the worked-out gravel pits round London became receptacles for rubble produced by wartime bombing. Elsewhere old

FIG. 124.—Spoil-heaps near Buxton, Derbyshire. The surroundings of Buxton, a tourist centre, are disfigured by limestone quarries, limeworks and spoil-heaps. This photograph, taken within a mile of the spa, somewhat resembles in appearance pictures of the china clay spoil-heaps near St Austell, Cornwall, though here the waste deposits have been largely flattened.

mines have been used for similar purposes. In places such as Chicago and Rio de Janeiro much refuse has been dumped into Lake Michigan and the Atlantic respectively, and coastal boulevards laid out on land thereby reclaimed.

The slag heaps and spoil heaps of mining and quarrying areas (Fig. 124) stand witness to the difficulties of getting rid of large quantities of solid waste, but some public authorities are now planting these excrescences or else levelling them to make new land for housing and recreation. Motor-car scrap-yards have now arrived to offend the eye, and only recently has adequate machinery been developed to reduce these discarded products into fully shredded material (see Fig. 125). Plastics litter is a growing menace, especially in the form of bottles and food containers, often left

FIG. 125.—A motor-car scrap-yard. The problem of waste disposal in and close to large towns grows more acute despite modern methods of reduction and regeneration of discarded material. Eyesores like this are becoming increasingly common near urban highways.

behind in picnic areas and parks and on beaches. Most plastics materials can be burnt, but P.V.C., which is coming into greater use, cannot, except at great cost, without producing new kinds of pollutants. It does not decompose like most material, nor can it, unlike waste paper (of which again there are increasing quantities) be satisfactorily salvaged and re-used. Is society eventually going to be strangled by its motor-cars or smothered under its own refuse?

THE LIMITATIONS OF LOCAL GOVERNMENT

It is now generally agreed that local government units in most countries are too restricted in area to permit entirely satisfactory administration. They generally pre-date the arrival of motor transport, and they were in too many instances devised when urban populations were much smaller than they are today and before large numbers of people now living in rural areas were as closely tied to towns by their work and many of their leisure pursuits. In England, where the so-called urban areas (county boroughs, municipal boroughs and urban districts) are divorced administratively from the rural districts,* there is undoubtedly a case for the

* For some purposes municipal boroughs, urban and rural districts are subject to control by the administrative (not geographical) counties, and therefore have less power than county and county borough authorities.

administrative linkage of towns with their rural hinterlands, (as was the case in ancient Greece, with its city-states, and in Danish England, with its Midland shires based on a county town or borough). There is perhaps even a case for the establishment of democratically elected regional councils, based on regional capitals, which could take major decisions on such matters as social and economic planning, water supplies, transport co-ordination and the broad field of education, while more localised authorities could retain their present powers with regard to such subjects as cleansing, housing and welfare and health services. The new Greater London Council has recently been established on this basis, while the powers of individual London boroughs, now reduced in number from 95 to 52, were curtailed. Perhaps, however, the G.L.C. should have been awarded powers over a wider area than the capital itself, for its problems can only be effectively handled if proper consideration is given to the surrounding region.

In all conurbations, it would certainly seem advisable to establish one major authority and to reduce existing town councils to the status of minor authorities. As matters stand, it is difficult for present urban councils to adjust (*i.e.* extend) their boundaries to conform with a town's spatial and demographic expansion. Time lags are caused mainly through the prejudicial attitudes of jealous neighbouring authorities, which are always ready to fight absorption even when it is seen to be socially and economically sound. County authorities, of course, oppose the expansion of county boroughs because they depend for much of their income upon borough overspill.

While, however, large regions might be more effective administratively than the existing small ones, and would certainly be easier for the central government to negotiate with, there is some justification for the view that local representatives know the needs and aspirations of their own people better than regional councillors would, and that if rural areas were integrated with large towns for local government purposes their interests might be neglected.

Large regions have, of course, from time to time been established, *e.g.* in England, France and Germany, but generally only for *ad hoc* purposes. Examples include the war-time Civil Defence regions of England and Wales, the later Standard Regions established by the Treasury and used by several ministries, and the present regions of Britain served by Economic Planning Councils and Boards (*see* Fig. 72). All of these, however, have been or are under central bureaucratic control, and have no democratically elected representatives.

The Maud Report

Central governments are not blind to the archaic character of local government units. In 1968, for example, a step forward was taken when a new single county borough was created on Tees-side to take over work previously shared between Middlesbrough C. B., Stockton M. B., Redcar M. B., Billingham U. D., and other units (*see* Fig. 126). In the following year, a general reform was advocated in England by the Commission on Local Government, under the chairmanship of Lord Redcliffe-Maud, which published its recommendations in June (*see* Figs. 127 and 128). The main proposals are as follows: (*a*) the election of provincial councils in place of the present Economic Planning Councils, with the task of determining regional stategy and planning; (*b*) the abolition of the present county councils, county boroughs and urban and rural district councils; (*c*) the creation of three large "metropolitan authorities" (based on Birmingham, Liverpool and Manchester, in addition to the Greater London Council) and fifty-eight "unitary authorities." Within this broad framework a new pattern of smaller, more local councils, including village councils, is recommended. The powers of these purely local councils, however, would be minimal: they would act as sounding-boards for local opinion, and would share with the larger authorities in the provision of selected services (*e.g.* the provision of houses and the improvement of highways) but only to a limited degree.

The Government's conclusions about these suggested reforms were embodied in a White Paper published in February 1970. In general, the

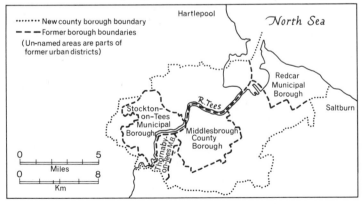

FIG. 126.—The new Tees-side County Borough. The new Tees-side County Borough was established in 1968 in order to rationalise the existing administrative subdivision of an area with considerable physical, industrial, commercial and social unity. Under the Maud proposals the further extension of this new county borough under a unitary authority is recommended.

FIG. 127. The Maud proposals: northern England. If the Maud proposals are carried into effect, town and country will be brought much closer together administratively during the next few years. Halifax and Huddersfield will have populations of only 195,000 and 207,000 respectively, but most unitary authorities will support at least 250,000 people. It will be noted that the West Yorkshire conurbation has not been selected as a future metropolitan area.

Maud proposals were welcomed and regarded as broadly acceptable, but two additional "Metropolitan authorities" were recommended: (a) West Yorkshire, covering roughly the West Yorkshire conurbation and its rural appendages, and (b) South Hampshire, comprising Southampton, Portsmouth, South-east Hampshire and the Isle of Wight. The Government expressed the view that in West Yorkshire there were too many interlocking problems for a number of separate unitary authorities to handle individually. It also felt that the rapid growth of population and industry in the Southampton and Portsmouth areas—where a large new Solent City is envisaged—necessitated a similar two-tier authority for the entire South Hampshire region.

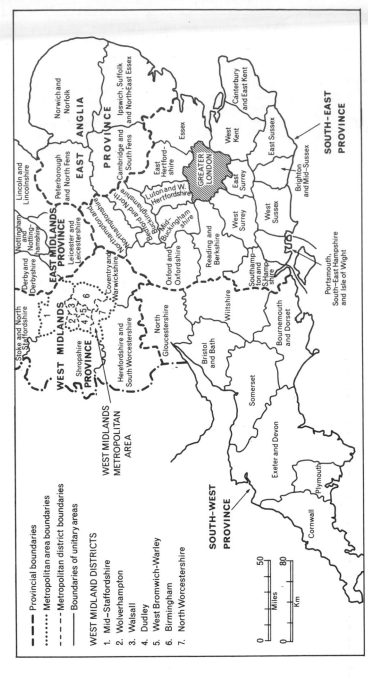

Fig. 128.—The Maud proposals: southern England. The "provinces" marked on this map and on Fig. 127 may be compared with the major divisions of England shown on Fig. 72. Which units seem to be the most satisfactory from a geographical point of view?

Chapter XVIII

Town-Planning, Old and New

EARLY TOWN-PLANNING

THOUGH most towns have developed spontaneously and gradually into urban settlements, as we saw in Chapter V, some have been conceived and planned from the outset as urban units. Even unplanned towns now generally incorporate in their material fabric at least planned sectors.

Historically, the plan most commonly approved of was the grid-iron or chequerboard. Often ascribed to Hippodamus of Miletus, who laid out Piraeus and Rhodes in the fifth century B.C., it was an economical design which had already been used at Harappa and other ancient cities, but was popularised by the Greeks. It became common in the Middle East following Alexander's conquests, and was widely used by the Romans both in their military camps and in their colonial towns (*e.g.* Turin, Tours, Chichester, Cologne and Saragossa), where elements of it are still visible.

Many of the planned towns of medieval Europe reveal in their streets and sometimes in their buildings the essentials of the chequerboard plan. Examples include Hull and Winchelsea in England, Edward I's castle towns in Wales, the French military bastides, and the fortified places established in eastern Europe by the Teutonic knights and German colonisers between the twelfth and fourteenth centuries. The same rectilinear plan was later adopted in Anglo-America, where nearly all the towns still conform to this regular layout.

The grid-iron plan is simple to follow both on the map and on the ground. It allows of easy land measurement even by untrained surveyors, it provides for easily constructed buildings of the most economical and adaptable shape, and it facilitates the subdivision of properties. Unfortunately, it pays no regard to topographical variations, lengthens diagonal journeys and makes for a monotonous townscape. Nowadays, it also hinders traffic movement because there are so many intersections.

In their planning of princely cities and autocratic enclaves, Renaissance and Baroque architects introduced a new design: the radial or wheel plan, beautifully illustrated in many seventeenth- and eighteenth-century

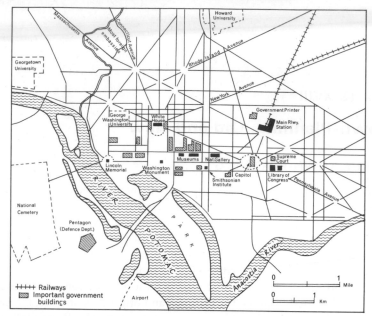

FIG. 129.—Washington, D.C.: central street plan. Like most carefully selected capital cities springing from nearly virgin sites, the central parts of Washington were carefully planned. The work was entrusted to Charles l'Enfant, and includes, in the typical eighteenth-century manner, systems of radial avenues leading from the more important edifices: in this case the Capitol, seat of Congress, and the White House, home and office of the President. The principal hotels, shops and theatres lie north and east of the White House. Washington has now spread far beyond its originally authorised bounds, and even beyond the District of Columbia, and parts of its layout follow the rectilinear pattern common to most American cities (*cf.* Fig. 47).

creations, *e.g.* Versailles, parts of Paris and St Petersburg, Karlsruhe (*see* Fig. 39), Nancy and Washington, D.C. (*see* Fig. 129). Each of these places incorporates at or near the centre a palace or kindred edifice commanding wide perspectives in several directions. Concentric circular roads were often added, to produce a spider-web or radiocentric pattern. The broad avenues of such cities form excellent processional ways on ceremonial occasions. This type of plan is not generally popular nowadays since it produces extreme traffic congestion at the centre.

TOWN-PLANNING IN BRITAIN AFTER 1700

In Britain, the eighteenth and early nineteenth centuries were marked by a number of excellent achievements in town-planning. Most of them, unfortunately, though aesthetically very elegant and in some cases magnificent, were confined to wealthy cities and high-class residential areas. Examples are numerous in parts of London, in such spas and resorts as Brighton, Scarborough, Cheltenham, Bath and Sidmouth, and in Edinburgh New Town. Less graceful, more utilitarian, but still piece-meal planning produced many of the working-class and factory districts of industrial towns, especially after the bye-laws of 1840. Every room in these houses had a window and every house a small yard, but not until 1875 was every new house provided with a back access and minimum dimensions laid down for street widths. These minima, unhappily, were usually taken as standard requirements by a majority of builders, who have left behind a legacy of straight, narrow thoroughfares fronted and backed by virtually uniform, drab rows of terraced houses.

There were, however, a number of affluent industrial employers who, chiefly in the nineteenth century, proved sufficiently enlightened and concerned for the welfare of their workers to engage architects to draw up plans for "model villages" and towns. Thus in 1785 David Dale began work on the cotton town of New Lanark, a task continued by his more famous son-in-law Robert Owen in 1816. In 1852, Sir Titus Salt provided Saltaire, near Bradford, for those employed in his alpaca works. George Cadbury moved his cocoa and chocolate works from central Birmingham to Bournville in 1879 and housed his employees in a much more romantic and greener environment than the classical layout of Saltaire provided (*see* Fig. 130). William H. Lever created Port Sunlight in 1886, another settlement in the romantic idiom, for employees in his soap works. In 1895 the owners of Bolsover Colliery had the less attractive Creswell built for their miners, and in 1905 Sir Joseph Rowntree had New Ears-wick, near York, erected. Several similar developments took place in other countries, *e.g.* at Pullman (Illinois), Agenta Park near Delft (Nether-lands) and Noisel-sur-Seine (France). Some of these model villages and small urban settlements are now undergoing "face-lifts" to bring them up to mid-twentieth-century standards of convenience and amenity.

More significant to modern planners than the ideas which resulted in the founding of settlements simply for the "hands" of benevolent employers was the "Garden City movement," an emotional reaction against the ugliness and dirtiness of expanding industrial towns, led by Ebenezer Howard. It was inspired, like Bournville, Port Sunlight and New Earswick, by the romantic notion that towns ought to combine rural as well as urban elements, and should provide a pleasant, healthy environment for workers in a variety of occupations. It was first given practical form as a balanced community project in Letchworth Garden

City, 37 miles (59 km) from London. Letchworth dates from 1903 and incorporates, within a carefully delimited area, separate industrial, commercial, recreational and low-density residential areas, a discrete functional zoning which still finds favour among town-planners. Welwyn Garden City, nearer London, was launched in 1919 as a similar venture by

[*Courtesy: Cadbury Bros.*]

FIG. 130.—Bournville. A model village which helped to pave the way for the Garden Cities of Letchworth and Welwyn, Bournville was built by George Cadbury in the 1890s for the comfort and convenience of his employees after he had moved his factory from the overcrowded central part of Birmingham into the outskirts. He paid attention not only to the layout of individual houses, but also to the provision of gardens, grass verges, trees, recreational spaces and community buildings. Bournville contains no uniform rows of houses, but a harmonious pattern is apparent, not unlike that which distinguishes many private housing estates developed in suburban England in the 1930s. The "village" is now in the hands of a trust, and not all its inhabitants work in the Bournville factory.

a private company and was the forerunner of similar "pretty" settlements in other advanced countries. To these Garden Cities were added numerous tree-garlanded, spacious, middle-class Garden Suburbs (notably Hampstead). Such residential districts unfortunately lack local industry and usually possess few social amenities. Their emergence as semi-urban forms led the more receptive and progressive local authorities to improve their own standards of housing and layout, and, between the wars, in England and in Europe, many council estates incorporated a number of Garden City features in their tracts of semi-detached housing.

TWENTIETH-CENTURY TOWN-PLANNING LEGISLATION IN BRITAIN

From the passing of the first British *Town-Planning Act* of 1909 to the consolidating *Town and Country Planning Act* of 1962, the tasks of town-planning has devolved on local authorities, that is, at the present time, counties and county boroughs. Large-scale town-planning, however, cannot now be satisfactorily accomplished unless the needs of the area surrounding the town (*e.g.* for transport and industry needs, and hospital and educational provision), and even the needs of a neighbouring town, are taken into account. Hence the central government has slowly come to realise the value of regional planning within a national framework. In 1965 it established Regional Economic Planning Councils and Boards to examine regional problems and suggest solutions. But these bodies, unlike local councils, do not consist of democratically elected members, and their duties—to determine the broad objectives of economic development in each region—carry no executive power. Authority for the planning of existing towns remains with the counties and county boroughs, subject, of course, to various central government departments, in particular the Ministry of Housing and Local Government, the Ministry of Transport and the Board of Trade.

THE AIMS OF TOWN-PLANNERS IN RELATION TO COMMUNITY NEEDS

Since virtually all development in both town and country in Britain is now subject to planning permission, it is important to be aware of the principles which guide the work of those to whom the changing shape of towns is entrusted. To be effective, the work of town-planners must be based on adequate mapping, social and economic surveys, and on statistical analysis. Town planners must approach their problems both analytically and synthetically, and must use the expertise of architects, engineers, sociologists and other specialists. They must also concern themselves not only with the needs of the town but also with the requirements of the urban hinterland.

If town-planners are considering the future of an established settlement, they have to study how it can be adapted to modern demands without full-scale reconstruction; if they are designing a new town, they must see that both economic and social needs are satisfied, that convenience is served and that visual beauty and harmony are achieved.

To be wholly successful, large-scale town-planning must aim at producing a balanced and aesthetically pleasing environment which should generate in its inhabitants a genuine attachment to the place and to their neighbours. Account should be taken of the physical landscape of slopes, rivers and valleys, and the town should be so adapted to them that it appears to spring naturally from the ground. Residential areas should have satisfactory housing densities, and provision should be made for all age-groups and for both married and single people. The proportion of people who prefer to live in tall flats rather than in low-rise dwellings should be determined. In New Towns, supplies of water, gas and electricity have to be ensured, drainage systems have to be installed and accessible and attractive town centres have to be designed. The amount of land to be devoted to industry, housing, commerce and open space has to be decided as well as the location of these functional areas. To come to terms with the motor vehicle, attention has to be given to the alignment and width of roads, to public transport facilities, and to the feasibility of separating vehicular traffic from pedestrian routeways.

NEW TOWNS IN BRITAIN

Britain's First Post-War New Towns

Informed opinion in the 1930s averred that the undesirable outward sprawl of London—which had long been a menace both to its inhabitants and the surrounding countryside in peacetime, and was likely to prove a particularly vulnerable target in wartime—had somehow to be halted. The establishment of a Green Belt was advocated and also the rehousing of a proportion of its population beyond this *cordon sanitaire*. The extensive bombing of London in the war years confirmed this opinion, which was further strengthened by the publication, in 1944, of Professor Patrick Abercrombie's Greater London Plan, which recommended both the maintenance of an effective Green Belt round the existing conurbation and the establishment, at a distance of about 20 to 30 miles (32 to 48 km) from Charing Cross, of eight New Towns, each to accommodate about 50 to 60,000 people. The Reith Report on New Towns came in 1946, and was followed in the same year by the *New Towns Act*, which authorised the appropriate Government Ministries not only in England, but also in Wales and Scotland, to decide on suitable locations for new towns both in the London area and outside. The Act made provision for the creation of Development Corporations to acquire designated sites, to have plans

FIG. 131.—British New Towns. This map should be examined in conjunction with Fig. 99. Among the major conurbations, West Yorkshire is notable in that it is not yet associated with any New Town developments.

drawn, and to build these new settlements with money provided by the Treasury. A similar Act was later passed by the Northern Ireland Parliament.

The first New Town to be thus designated was Stevenage, in November 1946. Like the others which followed (the first four round London, four of the next eight elsewhere—*see* Fig. 131 and table, p. 294), it was to be a complete town (*i.e.* a balanced community unit) with its own commercial and administrative centre, its own industrial, residential and recreational areas, schools, churches, and so on. It was not to be merely a dormitory centre for the accommodation of commuters (*see* Fig. 132).

Towns under Development Corporation	Date designated	Approx. pop. at designation	Original pop. target	Latest revised target	Area served	Main purpose for which town was designated
Stevenage	Nov. 1946	7,000	60,000	150,000	Gtr London	London overspill
Crawley	Jan. 1947	4,500	56,000	120,000	Gtr London	London overspill
Hemel H'stead	Feb. 1947	21,000	60,000	80,000	Gtr London	London overspill
Harlow	Mar. 1947	4,500	80,000	130,000	Gtr London	London overspill
Newton Aycliffe	Apr. 1947	600	20,000	45,000	Durham	Housing dispersed workers on existing indust. estate
East Kilbride	May 1947	2,500	50,000	100,000	Clydeside	Glasgow overspill
Peterlee	Mar. 1948	200	30,000	—	Durham	Rehousing miners
Hatfield	May 1948	8,500	25,000	30,000	Gtr London	London overspill
Welwyn G. City	May 1948	18,500	50,000	—	Gtr London	London overspill
Glenrothes	June 1948	1,100	30,000	75,000	Fifeshire & Clydeside	Housing workers in new colliery; later Glasgow overspill
Basildon	Jan. 1949	25,000	100,000	106,000	Gtr London	London overspill
Bracknell	June 1949	5,000	25,000	60,000	Gtr London	London overspill
Cwmbran	Nov. 1949	12,000	35,000	55,000	South Wales	Better housing for workers on industrial estate
Corby	Apr. 1950	15,700	40,000	80,000	East Midlands	Housing local steel-workers
Cumbernauld	Dec. 1955	3,000	50,000	100,000	Clydeside	Glasgow overspill
Skelmersdale	Oct. 1961	10,000	80,000	—	Merseyside	Liverpool overspill
Livingston	Apr. 1962	2,000	70,000	100,000	Glasgow & Edinburgh	Glasgow overspill
Dawley (Telford)	Jan. 1963	21,000	55,000	220,000	W. Midlands	W. Midlands overspill
Redditch	Apr. 1964	31,500	70,000	90,000	W. Midlands	W. Midlands overspill
Runcorn	Apr. 1964	28,500	70,000	100,000	Merseyside	Liverpool overspill
Washington	July 1964	20,000	60,000	80,000	Tyneside & E. Durham	Tyneside & Sunderland overspill
Craigavon	July 1965	40,000	100,000	180,000	N. Ireland	Belfast overspill & economic development of N. Ireland
Antrim	July 1966	3,000	30,000	—	N. Ireland	Econ. development. of N. Ireland
Irvine	Nov. 1966	30,000	70,000	85,000	Clydeside	Glasgow overspill
Milton Keynes	Jan. 1967	40,000	250,000	—	S.E. England	London overspill and immigration into S.E. Region
Peterborough	Aug. 1967	81,000	175,000	>200,000	S.E. England	London overspill and immigration into S.E. Region
Ballymena	Aug. 1967	18,000	70,000	—	N. Ireland	As Antrim
Newtown	Dec. 1967	5,500	13,000	70,000	Central Wales	Economic growth of Central Wales
Northampton	Feb. 1968	120,000	220,000	300,000	S.E. England	As Peterborough
Warrington	Apr. 1968	75,000	>200,000	—	S.E. Lancs. & Merseyside	Manchester overspill
Leyland–Preston–Chorley		253,000	400,000	>500,000	Lancashire	Manchester overspill
Towns under County Council						
Killingworth	1959	310	17,000	20,000	Tyneside	Tyneside overspill
Cramlington	1963	7,700	48,000	62,000	Tyneside	Tyneside overspill

[*Courtesy: Stevenage Development Corporation*
FIG. 132.—Stevenage New Town: the centre. Stevenage, the first British New Town (designated November 1946), now has a popular shopping mall, a small part of which is shown here. It is free from vehicular traffic and offers some shelter to pedestrians. The supermarket, the branch of Woolworth's, and various chain stores are typical. The planners' concern for pleasant surroundings is suggested by the fountain.

Fourteen New Towns were designated between 1946 and 1950. Most incorporated an existing village or small town which already possessed some basic services, *e.g.* water supply, sewerage and electricity, and an attempt was made to avoid building on the best agricultural land. The combined populations of these early New Towns, *c.* 130,000 at the outset, have now reached nearly 750,000. Some have attained their original target populations and have been handed over to the New Towns Commission, which attends to their upkeep and the development of their property, and has the power to improve general amenities and to acquire additional land; a few have obtained urban district status. Many have had their original target figures raised, for the population of Britain is still mounting and the containment of urban sprawl in large cities has not ceased to be desirable.

The early New Towns, such as East Kilbride (illustrated in Fig. 133), were built on the neighbourhood principle, each neighbourhood unit provided, like a country village, with its own school and place of worship, a small shopping centre and a few social facilities. Their plans owed much to the experience gained at Letchworth and the early Welwyn Garden City, but most of them have a less formal geometric layout and lower housing densities, even though they include flat-blocks as well as low-rise dwellings. Housing areas are separated from industrial zones, but not

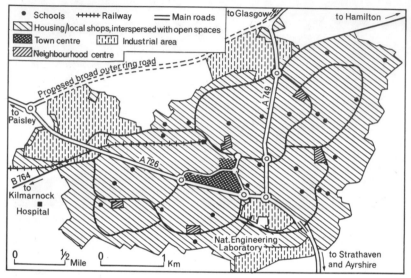

FIG. 133.—Plan of East Kilbride. East Kilbride, the first New Town outside the London area to be designated, was designed, like its predecessors, on the neighbourhood principle. In May 1947 its population was only 2,500, by 1969 it exceeded 60,000. In the same year more than 160 firms were employing labour, there were 18 new schools and 180 new shops.

widely divided from them. Major road nets have been designed to skirt rather than thread the neighbourhood units, but the necessity of providing the latter with secondary roads and with links to the town centre has not been overlooked. Within the central area, where architectural virtuosity has found most scope, some separation of vehicles and pedestrians has been achieved, as in some older cities which have recently been given a "face-lift."

British New Towns of the 1950s and '60s

Cumbernauld, the only new town to be designated in the 1950s, represented a departure from what seemed to have become standard town-planning practice. This town, designed mainly—like East Kilbride earlier—to accommodate part of Glasgow's overspill, was planned on far more compact lines, with higher housing densities and no division into neighbourhood units (*see* Fig. 134). In 1967 it received an American award for the best example in the world of community architecture. Throughout Cumbernauld, a pedestrian can walk from his home to the centre without crossing a motor-road and the road accident rate is said to be only a quarter that of the national average.

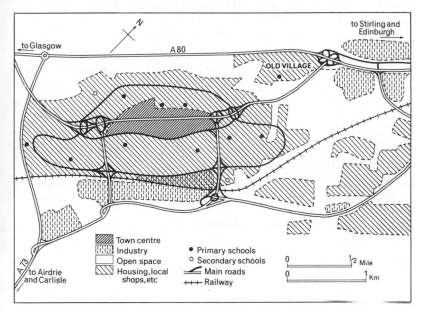

FIG. 134.—Plan of Cumbernauld. Cumbernauld was the first of the "second genera-tion" of New Towns to be designated. It is further from Glasgow than East Kilbride and has found it easier to establish its own identity. Its design departs from the neighbourhood principle and therefore its centre is likely to become more lively than that of East Kilbride. Its population in 1955 was about 3,000; by 1969 it approached 30,000. It was then accommodating 64 firms, 12 schools and nearly 50 new shops.

Of the twenty or so New Towns designated in the 1960s, which include three in Northern Ireland and the first coastal one (Irvine in Scotland), most are being built on sites further from "overspill" cities. Their plans show more variety, some, for instance, adhering to the neighbourhood principle, others rejecting it. Higher housing densities have become more acceptable, more provision has been made for public transport, and there has been, as in Cumbernauld, a much greater emphasis on the separation of pedestrians and vehicles. Far higher population targets are aimed at, especially at Milton Keynes in the south-east region, at Craigavon (Northern Ireland) and at Dawley. The latter, originally planned to take only moderate pressure from the West Midlands conurbation, is to be enlarged to incorporate the neighbouring towns of Wellington and Oakengates, and may reach 250,000 people by A.D. 2000. It has been re-named Telford. The latest New Town—based on an amalgam of Leyland, Preston and Chorley—may rise to half a million and may eventually provide north Lancashire with a metropolis important enough to balance Merseyside and Manchester in south Lancashire.

Cramlington and Killingworth, north of Newcastle, differ from other New Towns in that they are being built, not by Development Corporations appointed by Westminster, but by the Northumberland County Council. Though small, they are models of their kind, with piped television (no sprouting aerials), underground telephone lines and attractive recreational areas, based, at Cramlington, on what had previously been disfiguring pit spoil heaps, and, at Killingworth, on a lake occupying a former mining subsidence area. Other recently designated New Towns, notably Peterborough, Northampton and Warrington, are being grafted on to what are already quite sizeable towns with well-developed central areas and social amenities.

The Social and Economic Character of British New Towns

While the majority of British New Towns have been or are being built to check the further spread of very large cities and to reduce their congestion, some have been designated for other reasons. Newton Aycliffe, for example, was originally planned to house in pleasant surroundings workers on an existing industrial estate whose homes were scattered in a number of small, dreary villages, while Peterlee was intended to rehouse pit-workers in a declining colliery area of equally miserable villages, and to provide alternative employment. Glenrothes in Fifeshire was planned to accommodate the workers in a large new colliery, but when the impending closure of this pit was announced only a few years after the town had been designated, the Development Corporation had to turn its attention to the provision of other employment. Cwmbran, in South Wales, was designated for the purpose of providing better living conditions and more employment opportunities for heavy industrial workers and their families. It was hoped that the creation of Newtown, in Central Wales, and its later expansion might stimulate the general economic growth of an area suffering from depopulation.

Much industry has already been attracted into all the New Towns, for they provide not only land for up-to-date factories, but also room for industrial expansion and for extensive works car-parking, a growing volume of reliable, well housed labour, mostly of early mature years, and —usually—rapid access to major roads and railways. Most of the New Town industries are light and therefore provide jobs for both men and women and many belong to the "growth" category. Skelmersdale, for example, has attracted works turning out television tubes, lorry trailers and stockings; Cramlington a new factory operated by the Wilkinson Sword Company; Killingworth the headquarters and research laboratories of the Northern Gas Board, and the new headquarters of a world-renowned electrical engineering company; Runcorn the Department of Health and Social Security's statistical division and computer; Stevenage the Platignum Pen Company; Bracknell the headquarters of the Meteorological Office; East Kilbride the National Engineering Laboratory and a ladies' garment factory; Craigavon a large plant belonging to the Goodyear Tyre and Rubber Company. Where the pre-existing settlement was dominated by one industry (e.g. Corby by steel, Hatfield by aircraft manufacture, Runcorn by chemicals), the Development Corporations are providing alternative employment.

While most residents in New Towns find better housing and a healthier environment than in the old, many complain that the provision of social amenities, and, to some extent, shopping facilities, lags too far behind the supply of houses and industries. They feel that rents are too high, and that there is a lack of variety in housing and in social classes. Especially when they have come from large cities, they find a lack of homeliness and a dearth of meeting-places. They miss the bustle and activity of older towns, and are slow to gain an attachment to their new surroundings. Gradually, however, as more and more migrants join them, community loyalties and social integration develop, and complaints dwindle. A few New Towns now run their own newspapers, social amenities are being expanded, and more recreational facilities (e.g. swimming pools) are being introduced. The "New Town Blues" tend to disappear after a few years.

Further New Towns will be designated, not only for overspill purposes, but with the intention of catering for general population growth. Many will doubtless be built where they can act as "growth points" and so stimulate the development of regions into which there has recently been little immigration. They will thus aid the dispersal of industry and perhaps lead to a more uniform distribution of the country's population. Some of these future towns may be very large, e.g. the one suggested for the Southampton-Portsmouth area (a new Solent City), the one suggested for Humberside (incorporating Selby), and others recommended for the

Tay and Severn estuaries. The provision of a city within a Dee barrage has been mooted, and even one floating or anchored on the North Sea. Fears are being expressed (*e.g.* in Blackburn, Burnley and Wigan) that such new cities as Preston–Leyland–Chorley may prove so attractive as to draw away not only their own people but also some of their most progressive industries, and thus accelerate the decline which they have been striving to stave off ever since their cotton and coal-mining industries began to shrink in the 1930s. There are "Old Town" as well as "New Town Blues."

EXPANDED TOWNS IN BRITAIN

By the *Town Development Act* of 1952, it was made possible for a local authority to tackle its overspill problem in a new way: by arranging with the authority responsible for a smaller town to accept some of its families (*e.g.* those on council housing lists and those occupying slums and substandard houses in need of demolition). By this method, many of the largest cities, especially London, Glasgow, Birmingham, Manchester–Salford, Liverpool and Bristol, have been able to relieve part of their housing problems and make possible a more extended programme of inner urban renewal without adding unduly to the extent of outer urban sprawl. Many of the transfer agreements have been made with nearby small towns (*e.g.* Salford with Worsley, Liverpool with Ellesmere Port, Bristol with Keynsham), but others have been concluded with towns further away from the overspill town. For example, London has agreements with Swindon (80 miles (128 km) away) and with King's Lynn (90 miles (144 km) away), Birmingham with Weston-super-Mare, Glasgow with Inverness and Berwick.

Under these expanded town schemes, the recipient authority benefits as well as the exporting authority, for the former not only gains in labour and rateable value, but often also by attracting new industries, some of which, of course, may be recruited, along with workers, from the exporting city. Agreements between large cities and country towns of moderate size (*e.g.* between London and Luton or Swindon) are usually more successful than those between large cities and very small ones, for the latter, despite government grants, have few of the financial resources needed to effect sizeable population transfers, and also inadequate social and shopping facilities to serve a greatly expanded population. In large towns, transferred populations can usually settle down more quickly. There are already some industrial firms which can easily attract auxiliaries, and in general more potential for economic growth, especially when they are close to motorways and other major communications. They can, therefore, if expanded, make a useful contribution to the Government's plans for a better dispersal of industry and a less uneven population distribution.

It is not always easy, however, to match housing and employment in expanded towns, and of course the ingress of large numbers of people from other cities creates initial tensions. There exists, too, the potential development of urban sprawl which may, if the expansion programme is not carefully controlled, lead to some of the evils from which the exporting city is itself endeavouring to escape.

NEW TOWNS OUTSIDE THE BRITISH ISLES

Many examples of planned New Towns outside Britain have already been given in this book (*e.g.* in Chapters IX and X), but the main purpose

[*Courtesy: Fotokronika Tass*

FIG. 135.—Akademgorodok, Western Siberia. This New Town was deliberately founded by the U.S.S.R. in 1960 to accommodate a population exclusively devoted to scientific research. Its population is almost entirely young and of uniformly high intelligence. It has fifteen scientific institutes, a university, and boarding schools restricted to children with outstanding intellectual ability.

for which they have been built has often been political or economic rather than social. Political consideration have led to the founding of a number of new capital cities, *e.g.* Brasilia, Canberra, Islamabad and Chandigarh; new ports have been recently built at Eilat, Ashdod and Tema; Schefferville and Magnitogorsk were established to house new mining communities; many towns in Soviet Asia have been founded for strategic and commercial purposes; the new Dutch polders contain pioneer farming communities; and the French Government in 1964 embarked on a ten-year plan for the construction of six new holiday resorts on the Languedoc coast.

[*Courtesy: Swedish National Travel Association*

FIG. 136.—Vällingby, Stockholm. Vällingby is the best known of a number of residential satellites recently built round Stockholm, to which it is linked, like the others, by underground railway. The photograph shows part of the main shopping precinct and pedestrian mall, and an example of a block of flats.

One of the most unusual of these New Towns is Akademgorodok, 20 miles (32 km) from Novosibirsk in Soviet Asia (*see* Fig. 135). It is almost unique in that it was founded by the Soviet Government purely as an educational and scientific centre. Part of the Siberian forest had to be cleared before it could be built. It now houses 50,000 people, including several hundred competitively selected, exceptionally gifted, scientifically inclined children who are accommodated in a large boarding school. The town contains several ordinary state schools, a University and fifteen major scientific institutes staffed by top rank Russian scientists and technological research workers. It provides a wide range of social and shopping services and its inhabitants and their achievements are expected to foster the whole country's interest in the development of the Soviet's Asiatic territories.

More comparable with the majority of British New Towns are the satellite towns recently planned in Finland and Sweden. Only 6 miles (9 km) from Helsinki is the beautifully planned Garden City of Tapiola, a modern representative of the movement which gave Britain Letchworth and Hampstead Garden Suburb.

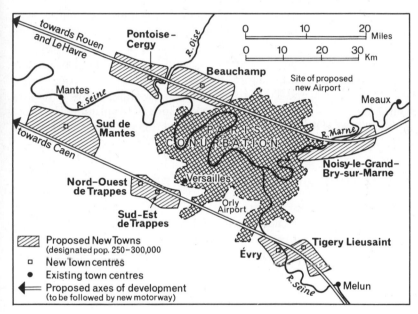

FIG. 137.—Paris, A.D. 2000. Many large European cities are now engaged in planning for the year 2000. The developments envisaged for Paris include the establishment of two roughly parallel axes of development, north and south of the Seine. It is expected that they will account for an important share of the estimated addition of 6 million to the population of the Paris region between 1968 and 2000. At present there are 8 million.

Centred on Stockholm, a city which houses 800,000 people within its boundaries, a planned metropolitan structure is now approaching completion with the construction on its outskirts of a string of partially self-sufficient units containing between 10 and 25,000 people. The best known of these satellites, nearer the capital than the first generation of New Towns round London, are Vällingby, north of the city (*see* Fig. 136), and Farsta, to the south. Both are linked by fast underground railway (20 to 30 minutes' run) to the centre of Stockholm, and each is well equipped with a major shopping and cultural centre, office and light industrial employment, ample car parking space and high density residential areas comprising both tall blocks of flats and lower, single-family dwellings. Vällingby's town centre has been built above its underground railway station, and is not only restricted to pedestrians but is also approached by pedestrian streets, thereby reducing traffic congestion.

Other countries which have recently embarked on New Town projects with a view to limiting the previously unbridled outward growth of metropolitan areas include France. Here, it is planned to build at least eight new settlements beyond the main commuter range of the capital, Paris (*see* Fig. 137). Provision is being made for each of these new towns to house 250 to 300,000 people. New "overspill" towns are now also arising near Tokyo and Osaka, Lahore, Sydney and Adelaide, Chicago, New York, Washington and Toronto, Milan, Warsaw and Cracow, and in the Ruhr industrial area, among other places. Much of the planning involved in the creation of these towns derives from British experiments and experience.

THE FUTURE OF TOWNS AND CITIES

Urban populations are growing rapidly in all countries, and the question as to how such additional numbers are to be contained is becoming more acute. We have already seen that in Britain both green belt and new and expanded towns policies have been adopted to control the unrestricted outward distension of large cities, but despite these plans most of the dwellings in post-war Britain have in fact been built in the suburbia of existing towns. Should the number of New Towns continue to multiply, and, if so, where should they be located, how big should they be, and what form should they take? Should the main emphasis be placed on the controlled expansion of selected towns in "growth" regions, or should more funds be allocated for the creation of more houses and factories in stagnating or declining industrial towns which are not yet "oversize"?

Town-planners, of course, exercise their minds chiefly with problems of form, and have often presented blue-prints of ideal cities. Most of these embody proposals for future expansion, for cities do not remain static. Most planners aim at limiting the volume of traffic congestion while maintaining easy links between people and countryside, residence and work, homes, shops and entertainments. Among the many ingenious suggestions which have been put forward for future urban plans, the following are among the most common (*see* Fig. 138):

1. *Satellite and radial plans.* Here, round the main town centre, a number of individual units are grouped, each having a similar measure of self-sufficiency. To reduce the flow of traffic between the satellites and the

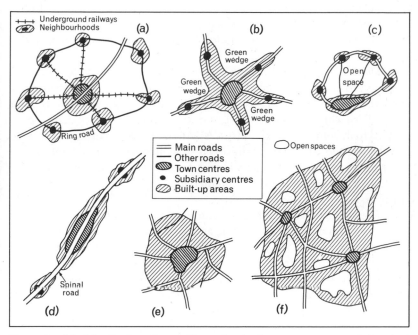

FIG. 138.—Models of urban forms. These sketch-plans suggest some of the views town-planners hold about the ideal form which a new town should take, or according to which the growth of an existing town may be controlled. (*a*) Satellite or neighbourhood plan. (*b*) Stellate or radial plan. (*c*) Circuit linear or ring plan. (*d*) Beaded linear plan. (*e*) Core or compact plan. (Here the average height of buildings will normally be higher than in other towns with similar populations.) (*f*) Dispersed plan. (Here each centre has its own particular group of functions which distinguishes it from the others.)

main city centre, underground railways or other forms of efficient public transport are provided. Stockholm's planning is assuming this form and, there are many elements of it in Greater London's plans, though here the main centre has already been allowed to grow much too large. The radial plans being partially adopted for the future development of Copenhagen are broadly similar, stress being placed in this case on highly intensive growth along virtually the whole length of a number of major radial highways, and on the maintenance of open spaces between these axes of development.

2. *Linear plans.* Here, growth is envisaged along either side of a spinal road, industrial zones perhaps on one side, on the other shops and offices, with housing beyond, and—further still from the major road—recreational areas, all joined together by minor routeways. Such a plan gives easy access to open land and allows of virtually unlimited expansion. But—unless a beaded form, consisting of a number of town centres, is adopted—the town is likely to become so elongated that some parts become too distant from the main centre.

3. *The ring city.* In essence, this plan is similar to the last except that the dominant road is now circular. Ideally, a number of towns are strung out along the circumferential road, the interior of the ring being left as open space. Each cluster can again grow outwards, one node perhaps being allowed to develop as a major city. A system of roads crossing the centre may be devised to provide additional links between the several nodes. These nodes would be especially useful if each were permitted to develop specialised functions. Randstad Netherlands shows obvious elements of this plan.

4. *The core city.* This type of city allows of the maximum amount of building within the smallest possible area, and depends more upon vertical than upon horizontal movement. In its extreme form it might be a 2-mile (3-km) high structure, embodying car parks, shops, places of amusement, and so on, all in the same compact block, and would conserve more land for other purposes than any other surface urban form. The fear of heights and the dread, that many people have, of prolonged enclosure, poses problems for advocates of this type of city.

5. *The underground city.* Cities built underground would certainly preserve the greenery of the countryside, but health hazards militate against their complete realisation. When, however, underground railways and roads are quite feasible, there seems to be no valid reason why some workplaces and major shopping centres should not be located underground as well as on the surface; they are, in fact, being laid out in Osaka, Tokyo and other Japanese cities.

6. *The dispersed city.* This plan—suggested by Frank Lloyd Wright, among others, in his "Broadacre City," and partially realised in Los Angeles—is the antithesis of the core city. It is the most lavish as regards space, and lacks a close central nucleus. Dispersed units—here housing, there government buildings, in another place shops and factories—need to

be incorporated, but they are widely scattered, separated by broad open spaces, and joined by a continuous network of wide roads. The current development of out-of-town shopping centres and industrial estates reveals dispersion in practice. A fully dispersed city may be envisaged as producing an aesthetically pleasing "rururban" environment, but it would lack the intimacy and vitality one normally values in a city, and would add greatly to the erosion of truly rural, agricultural land.

Chapter XIX

Urban Fields

It has already been pointed out in this book (notably in Chapter V) that there has always been a close relationship between a town and the country round it. Every town owes much of its sustenance to the patronage of the surrounding area—its "urban field"—which supplies it with a proportion of its workers and shoppers and others who wish to take advantage of its cultural, recreational, professional and health services. The town thus acts as a collecting, marketing and general service centre for a wider area than the town itself covers. It crystallises the social character of a whole region. It is also the main agency through which external influences are disseminated to the smaller settlements within its ambience.

Not all writers use the term "urban field" when referring to the area served by a town and from which the town derives so much of its business. Some, likening all towns to commercial ports, prefer the term "hinterland," or the German "Umland," while others favour "sphere of influence," "tributary area," "catchment area" or "city region." The use of the latter term, though common to planners, is to be deprecated, for some writers also use it when referring to a particular quarter or zone of a town. Peter Schöller (in *Aufgaben und Probleme der Stadtgeographie*) differentiated between the "umland," which he described as the area within which communications with a town are close and constant, the "hinterland," where communications are less frequent, and the "zone of influence" where communications are exceptional and may cover only such items as the itineraries of commercial travellers or visits to urban hospitals. This attempt to define more precisely the terms most writers use loosely when referring to "urban fields" has not, however, been accorded wide recognition.

PRIMARY AND SECONDARY URBAN FIELDS

Though Schöller's attempt to distinguish between the various terms used to describe the service area of a town has not received general acceptance, it is nevertheless true that virtually all towns have more than one field. Certainly their contacts with the surrounding area diminish in intensity as distance increases, until a zone is reached whose people are more conveniently served by another town. In the sphere of central government, entertainment, luxury goods of the highest value, and certain specialist functions (including those of a financial and medical character), London and Paris, for example, serve the whole of their respective countries, but on a lower level of services their urban fields are restricted to their own regions: south-east England (on the lowest level simply the London Basin) and the Paris Basin. Thus a large political capital undoubtedly has both a primary and a secondary field. On a smaller scale, a regional capital such as Newcastle-upon-Tyne also possesses at least two fields: the primary one in this case would be the Tyneside conurbation, the secondary one would include virtually the whole of Northumberland and Durham, and probably also the Yorkshire portion of Tees-side.

THE SIZE AND SHAPE OF URBAN FIELDS

It was shown in Chapter X that the chief function of market towns, commercial cities and regional capitals is to provide services for people living in the surrounding area. Such "central places" are regularly visited by farmers and their wives for marketing their surpluses, for shopping, entertainment and professional consultations. Their older children may attend school there even if there is a primary school for their younger ones in the local village. The larger the central place, the larger the service area. Hence, as was explained in Chapter VI, in a homogeneous area there is a marked tendency for the growth of a hierarchy of settlements based on a hexagonal lattice of urban fields.

Places such as industrial towns, mining towns and tourist resorts are not central places, and their relations with the surrounding rural area are usually rather weak. Therefore—although they have to some extent come to act as service centres—they are not generally regarded as fully equipped central places (they may, for instance have comparatively small shopping centres), and their urban fields are usually much smaller than those of commercial towns of the same size. The proportion of "basic" to "non-basic" workers (see p. 152), however, is not necessarily much lower since the manufactured articles an industrial town produces are not usually made simply for the town itself, and the clientele upon which a resort town depends is drawn from a very wide area beyond its municipal boundaries.

The size of a town's sphere of influence depends not only on its main function and on its position in the central place hierarchy, but also on other factors. In areas of low population density, for example, service areas are often extensive but support few people, while in areas of higher density they are usually small but support comparatively large numbers of people. Distance from other towns of comparable importance and the extent to which a town acts as a traffic node also affect the magnitude of its catchment area. Thus towns within a conurbation, *e.g.* Halifax in West

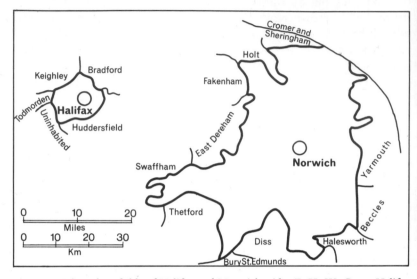

FIG. 139.—The urban fields of Halifax and Norwich. *After F. H. W. Green.* Halifax has a population of close on 100,000, Norwich one of about 120,000, but their urban fields are quite disproportionate in extent. Norwich, the only large town between Cambridge and Yarmouth, is the most important market centre of an extensive agricultural region; Halifax is dwarfed by other near-by industrial towns, such as Bradford and Huddersfield, and simply caters for the central needs of people living in industrial and farm villages close to it.

Yorkshire or Bolton in South-east Lancashire, have urban fields of very limited size, partly because they are chiefly manufacturing towns, not central places, and partly because they are only minor route foci in areas dominated by much larger commercial cities. Though these towns are not greatly different in size from Norwich and Oxford, for instance, their urban fields are absurdly small compared with those of Oxford and Norwich. Their catchment areas are, however, densely populated on the whole and include industrial as well as agricultural villages (*see* Fig. 139).

Large towns usually include within their total urban fields a number of smaller urban fields. Thus a small country town provides a weekly market and perhaps also a cinema, secondary school, bank, doctor's surgery, and solicitor's office for the needs of the rural community immediately tributary to it, but for the satisfaction of more specialised and more occasional needs, *e.g.* hospital treatment, higher educational facilities and luxury shopping, the people living not only in this small urban field but also in the parent town itself may well look to a larger settlement.

One urban field is not rigidly divided from another. There are clearly zones of overlap whose people may regularly visit more than one town. Their choice depends partly upon the kind of services each town provides, and partly upon their respective accessibilities. Obviously many people will visit one town for some purposes, the rival town for others. In a single village family, for example, the man may work in one town, his wife may prefer to shop in another and their children may go to school in a third.

Comparatively few urban hinterlands assume the neatly shaped hexagon postulated by Christaller (*see* pp. 118–119). Some are elongated in the direction of important roads, and some broaden out near railway stations. Others are affected by the geographical location of neighbouring, competing towns. Others may be restricted in one direction by topographical barriers, *e.g.* a mountain range or a sea coast.

THE RELATIONS BETWEEN A TOWN AND ITS TRIBUTARY AREA

R. E. Dickinson (*op. cit.*) has divided the principal regional associations of a city into four categories:

1. Trade relations, which provide a series of trading areas growing out of different trading activities, *e.g.* retailing and wholesaling. It may be noted here that individual shops have their own catchment areas, wider in the case of stores selling furniture, carpets, jewellery and expensive clothes than for those retailing sweets, tobacco and newspapers, and other everyday articles.

2. Social relations, which produce a social area comprising people who seek to benefit from the various entertainments and cultural activities a town provides.

3. Commuting relations, which produce an area of settlement round a town and perhaps a series of dormitory towns, and also a zone of movement through which people pass on their way to and from work. This area may also include small resorts and recreational land to which townspeople repair for bodily and mental refreshment.

4. Agricultural relations, which lead to the development of particular kinds of farming near a city, which itself acts as a convenient market.

Characteristically, dairy-farming and market-gardening activities, the latter in part in glasshouses, as near Brussels and London, are often associated with city margins, for milk and vegetables not only deteriorate quickly, they are also fairly bulky commodities which are demanded daily at cheap prices by city shoppers.

There also exist, of course, industrial relations between towns and their spheres of influence. Some urban factories are concerned with processing raw materials produced, at least in part, within the urban field *e.g.* meat-packing plants, dairies, egg-packing plants, sugar-beet refineries, canneries, lumber mills, textile finishing and piece-dyeing works, and steel works. Other city industrialists produce goods largely sold within the town itself and its immediate hinterland (*e.g.* agricultural machine makers, printers, local newspaper publishers and bakers).

THE DELIMITATION OF URBAN FIELDS

Most students of urban geography agree that virtually all towns and cities have more than one urban field. The area served by a city hospital, for example, differs from that served by a city shopping centre or a technical college. Yet to most researchers these various areas are sufficiently coincident for a composite urban field to be identified, even though—as is always the case with geographical regions—its boundaries are zonal rather than linear. Owing to the more widespread use of the private car, however, the movements of people into a central town either from the surrounding rural area or from a smaller town are increasingly multi-directional, people visiting different towns for different services. There are also nowadays more varied movements and attachments based on social class, age, sex and other social differences. Hence D. Thorpe (in *The Geographer and Urban Studies*) and others argue that it may be more useful to study the intensity of a number of urban fields rather than to concentrate on the means whereby a single field may be delimited.

Whether one attempts to discover, map and justify an area which one may label "the urban field of City X," or whether one is content to elucidate and map the variety of urban fields related to a particular town, certain meaningful indices have to be selected to see how far a town and the area contiguous to it are associated. Among the most commonly used indices are the following: (*a*) newspaper circulations, (*b*) public transport services, (*c*) retail and wholesale deliveries, (*d*) higher educational catchment areas, (*e*) commuter range. It will be useful to discuss each of these criteria before referring, more briefly, to others.

The Newspaper Circulation Index

High-ranking towns publish both morning and evening newspapers, towns of moderate size publish evening ones only, while small towns find customers only for weekly ones. All these newspapers contain "district" news as well as town news, and therefore serve to link together the interests of those living in both the town and the urban field, and to foster their community spirit. The sphere of influence of a newspaper is ascertainable by: (a) studying the district news columns to see from which villages items are included (weekly newspapers are especially valuable for this purpose), (b) examining the source of the small advertisements (for instance in the "Houses for Sale" or "Occupations Vacant" sections), (c) inquiring from the publishers the circulation area, or—if details are not readily or comprehensively available—investigating from newsagents in outlying districts the sales of the newspaper in question compared with those of competitive organs published in other towns. (Less than 50 per cent sales of the selected newspaper may be taken as marking the approximate outward limit of the town's primary sphere of influence if there is only one rival newspaper in the field).

It has been suggested that the use of the newspaper circulation index is most useful in areas where towns are widely spaced and where the country is not, like Britain, dominated by national newspapers, but the method works well enough even in Britain because evening and weekly newspapers are locally, or at most, regionally, orientated (see Fig. 140).

Urban Fields and Transport Services

To F. H. W. Green* and his disciples, the most meaningful method of determining a town's urban field is through the study of the timetables of local motor-bus services. By this means, Green was able to produce maps of England, Wales and Northern Ireland, showing the primary fields of all towns which in the late 1930s (Northern Ireland) and 1940s (England and Wales) had at least one regular market-day bus service serving no place larger than itself. The field, of course, was defined as the area in which a particular town was the most accessible centre, and which would, therefore, be the principal place visited by people seeking services not available in their village (Fig. 140).

---

* F. H. W. Green wrote a number of articles on this subject. They include: "Town and Country in Northern Ireland," *Geography*, Vol. 34, 1949; "Urban Hinterlands in England and Wales: An Analysis of Bus Services," *Geographical Journal*, Vol. 116, 1950; "Bus Services in the British Isles," *Geographical Review*, Vol. 41, 1951; and a review in the *Geographical Journal*, Vol. 132, 1966, of a map of Southern England, *British Bus Services*, compiled and drawn by J. C. Gillham, and published in 1965.

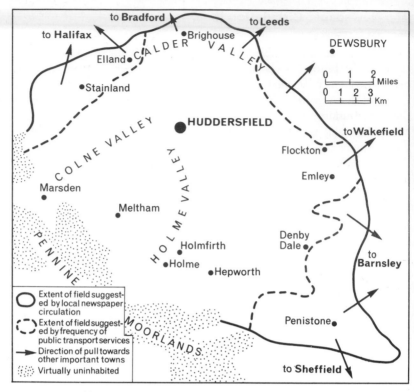

FIG. 140.—Huddersfield's urban fields. Towns do not possess clearly defined urban fields. This map shows the approximate spheres of influence of Huddersfield based on the circulation of the *Huddersfield Examiner* (daily and weekly editions) and on the relative frequency of motor buses entering the town compared with neighbouring central places in 1969. Along the periphery of Huddersfield's urban fields, people are also drawn to other West Riding towns, notably Halifax, Bradford, Leeds, Dewsbury, Wakefield, Barnsley and Sheffield.

While Green's technique is fairly straightforward and has been successfully applied in a few other countries, especially the Scandinavian ones, critics have raised certain objections to it: (*a*) population movements based on data provided by motor-bus timetables do not necessarily reflect a pre-existing social pattern; the latter, in fact, in at least some cases, *e.g.* the formation of an evening class, is produced by the existence of transport services; (*b*) the growing use of the private car reduces the general reliance of motor-bus timetables to the movements of country people as a whole, most of whom are now independent of public transport and are able to travel much more freely in a variety of directions, although Green himself found that although the motor-bus had lost ground to the motor-car since he did his work in England and Wales, J. C. Gillham's 1965 maps (*see* footnote above) of bus centres and urban hinterlands in southern England differed only in detail from his own maps drawn fifteen years earlier, and in fact confirmed his own researches; (*c*) Green's work, confined to market town level, fails to show how the sphere of influence of a large city embraces at a specialised level that of a number of small towns. (All Green's urban fields are small in area—averaging 81 sq. miles (170 sq. km) in England and Wales—and, because of the method he adopted, they cover simply the immediate hinterlands of his bus centres.)

A study of the number and frequency of late buses leaving a particular town for external destinations gives some idea of the numbers of people in outlying areas who are able to take advantage of the cinema and theatre performances, concerts, lectures and other functions held in a town in an evening, and provides supporting evidence for the extent of a town's urban field. In the same way, early morning services may be studied with advantage to help determine the range within which workers are drawn into a town each day.

The use of railway time-tables is less satisfactory than the use of motor-bus timetables for the determination of a town's urban field. So many local railway lines have now been "axed" that except in the case of very large cities with well-used suburban services, comparatively few people now travel regularly and often by rail to the most accessible town. People in a small town, however, may well visit a larger one by rail, but their visits are normally infrequent and serve simply to demonstrate part of a large town's secondary sphere of influence.

Retail and Wholesale Services and the Urban Field

High-ranking towns act as important centres of wholesale distribution as well as retail trade, and have more highly specialised shops and more departmental stores than low-ranking towns. But even the latter are regularly visited by shoppers who cannot find all they want in village and sub-centre stores. It is clearly impossible to find out with any certainty the home addresses of people buying from town shops, but the area within which city stores may make weekly deliveries (especially of foodstuffs) gives a reasonable indication of the urban field. Certain developments are, however, reducing the value of this retail index: (*a*) the growth of out-of-town shopping centres and supermarkets; (*b*) the unequal facilities for parking for car-shoppers in rival towns; (*c*) the replacement of many delivery vans by travelling shops which make regular village tours.

Large cities with more than an average proportion of a country's wholesale trade generally possess very large urban fields. For this reason, their shopping facilities and other services are highly developed since firms setting up in business have to consider not only the population of the town in which they intend to open their premises, but also the population of the urban hinterland, which may well be five or six times that of the town itself.

Educational Catchment Areas

Large villages possess primary schools, but secondary schools and technical colleges are generally confined to urban settlements. The catchment area of a secondary school (especially grammar school) which draws pupils from a fairly wide expanse (see Fig. 141) provides a town with an educational field which is likely to differ somewhat in size and shape not only from the town's shopping field, but also from that based on the homes of students attending the same town's technical college (if it has one). Educational indices, moreover, are not of general application: many county boroughs accept in their schools, if not in their colleges, only pupils who live within the narrow borough boundaries. Schools close to administrative county boundaries, of course, have their catchment areas severely distorted.

The Commuter Range of Towns

Though R. E. Dickinson (op. cit.) avers that the journey to work is one of the "most meaningful criteria" for defining the range of influence of a service centre, it cannot be used with any precision since each office-block and industrial works in a town has its own individual commuter range which differs from the rest. If, however, say, in a particular village or dormitory more people leave their homes for work in one town than in others, it may be justifiable to include such a minor settlement within that town's urban field. How to obtain this information would present problems in most countries, e.g. in England, where no official statistics exist which might enable one to relate work-place to home address.

Miscellaneous Criteria used for defining a Town's Hinterland

The extent to which people outside service centres visit a town for hospital treatment or make visits to cinemas, football grounds and other places of entertainment, cannot, unfortunately, be easily or directly computed. Membership of various community organisations which commonly have their headquarters in towns, e.g. Boy Scouts and Girl Guides District Associations, may provide useful information. At one time the areas covered by Poor Law Unions consisted of market towns and their

FIG. 141.—The catchment area of Ermysted's Grammar School, Skipton. This map
has been compiled from figures kindly supplied by Mr D. T. Edwards, Senior
Geography Master, Ermysted's Grammar School. It shows the homes of all the
day boys in the school in September 1969, together with those of a small number
of boarders (chiefly from the upper Wharfe valley and Littondale) for whom
motor-bus services are inadequate: there are 434 pupils in all. It is evident that the
urban field of Skipton as a school catchment centre includes rural Airedale above
Keighley, rural Wharfedale above Ilkley and a largely urbanised area north of
Colne (Lancashire) to the south-west, including Barnoldswick and Earby.

primary urban fields, but local government units today, as explained on pp.
282–283, more often isolate towns from their hinterlands than otherwise.
The ecclesiastical parish organisation of the Church of England, based on

village and tributary area rather than on town and tributary area, is of no more help in our study than diocesan groupings, but the circuit arrangements of the Methodist Church—district associations of churches sharing groups of ministers and having their principal places of worship (and superintendent ministers) in particular urban centres—may be of value in tracing urban fields as defined by religious data.

In some countries, the range of local radio stations and the number of telephone calls made between a town and other places have been used to determine and map urban fields. In India, geographers have even plotted the extent to which literacy rates decline with distance from a city.

Whatever results these various indices produce—and it is always worthwhile experimenting with new ones—it is obvious that when undertaking market research or planning industrial development and effective local government areas, planners should take into account the size, shape and character of urban fields.

STUDY QUESTIONS

1. Review the factors affecting the growth of "million" cities in *either* intertropical areas *or* the southern hemisphere.

2. Select a "million" city in each of *three* continents. Describe the locations and chief functions of each of your selected cities.

3. Discuss the distribution of million cities in *either* Japan *or* the United States *or* India.

4. New York, Tokyo, London, Buenos Aires, Shanghai, Los Angeles and Calcutta are among the twelve largest cities in the world. Select any *four* of these cities and in each case analyse the geographical factors which have contributed to its eminence.

5. Discuss the factors which have contributed to the growth of very large cities in *either* China *or* Latin America.

6. Select any *two* conurbations in Great Britain, Discuss their location and industrial character and state the ways in which they differ from each other.

7. Write a short geographical account of a conurbation outside Great Britain.

8. What is meant by the word "megalopolis" as used by present-day geographers? Give examples of this urban form.

9. What centripetal and centrifugal tendencies may be observed in towns? Give reasons for such movements.

10. Explain the following terms: (*a*) twilight housing; (*b*) urban blight; (*c*) rururban fringe; (*d*) slab block.

11. Discuss the site of any housing estate near your home. How far does it act as a neighbourhood unit?

12. What are the advantages and disadvantages of living (*a*) near the central area of a town; (*b*) in suburbia; (*c*) in a small hamlet?

13. Name *three* towns or cities of diverse ethnic, linguistic or religious character, and discuss the problems which may result from the close contiguity of such varied population elements.

14. What are the disadvantages of living in a town containing *either* a high proportion of old people, *or* a very disproportionate number of males?

15. Analyse *three* of the major problems from which large cities suffer. Can you suggest how they may be overcome?

16. Explain what is meant by urban renewal. What considerations need to be borne in mind when replanning the central area of a town?

17. Discuss the Maud proposals for local government reform in so far as they may affect your own town or rural settlement.

18. In what respects is town and country planning of concern to a geographer?

19. For what reasons may it be desirable to preserve the inner core of a town? Using specific examples where possible, suggest ways in which preservation or piecemeal renewal may be best undertaken.

20. Comment on the distribution of New Towns in Britain. If there were a proposal to build a New Town within 20 or so miles (30 km) from your home, what site would you choose, and why?

21. What factors would you take into account in planning a New Town once the site had been chosen?

22. What are the advantages and disadvantages of a New Town compared with an older one?

23. Is it better to expand an existing town or to build a new one?

24. Describe and draw a map of the town you would like to see planners design.

25. Explain and illustrate by specific examples the term "hinterland" as applied to both commercial ports and large inland towns.

26. Discuss *three* methods by which the extent of a town's urban field may be determined. Apply these methods to your own town, or, if you live in a rural area, to the town you most frequently visit.

27. How far is the meaningful region of today the one dominated not by natural unity but by a very large city?

28. Using specific examples, discuss the relations between towns and (*a*) the areas immediately surrounding them; (*b*) more distant areas both in the home country and outside it.

Part Four

FIELD-WORK

Chapter XX

Field-work in Relation to Rural and Urban Settlements

M OST of the material in this book is based on field studies of particular settlements, rural and urban, and most of it can be checked and supplemented by further such studies, many of which are well within the capabilities of intelligent sixth-formers.

The value of such field-work is obvious. It not only gives reality and actuality to the study of settlement geography, and so acts as a corrective to the many generalisations one finds in a book like this; it also provides an opportunity for acquiring useful standards of comparison against which information gleaned in other ways, especially by reading, may be measured. It provides excellent training in thoughtful observation, and in recording by cartographical and other means the data required by the settlement geographer, and thus helps to create the sound foundation upon which the structure of human geography as a whole may be erected. It also gives the student an opportunity for seeking out some of those causal relationships which are fundamental to his subject.

Most students live in a town and nearly all the rest in villages close to urban settlements. Distance therefore imposes no difficulty—as it does in so many branches of human and physical geography—in carrying out field surveys *e.g.* of village sites and forms, town plans and urban morphology.

It may be claimed that such field-work, if well done, can hardly help but give the student an increased awareness of his own environment and an expanding interest in it. It may go further, and inspire him with a critical sense of civic pride, so that he may be more acutely concerned, for example, about the implications of a new town plan, a project for village expansion, or a scheme for a new motorway. It may even enlarge his aesthetic sense and assist him to do what he can to preserve what is beautiful and what may be threatened by an urban renewal project, especially if he lives in a historic town. Thus the geographer, through his knowledge, judgement and expertise, should be able to play his part in the realistic assessment of any programme for the future development of his own village or town which officialdom may put forward.

THE FIELD STUDY OF A FARM

The most profitable single settlement to study in the field is the farm—its house and other buildings in particular, but also its fields and the work involved in making them productive. By the study in depth of such a small unit of settlement, useful comparisons may be made with others of a contrasted kind such as are published in the "farm studies" surveys of the Association of Agriculture.

Items which merit attention in the field study of a farm include its site in relation to relief and geology, the sun, wind and water, and its situation with respect to roads, railways and markets. The age and function of all the buildings should be noted as well as the materials (traditional or otherwise) of which they are made. Their spatial arrangement should also be examined, and a large-scale, fully annotated map drawn to show this arrangement (*see* Fig. 142). Newly erected buildings—which may be a sign of current prosperity—should be inspected to find out what purpose they serve and whether they are constructed of the same materials as the old. Any cruck buildings which may still exist are worth a special note: they indicate that farming has been carried on on the same site for at least 350 years. The position and use made of outlying buildings (*e.g.* the barns or laithes in Yorkshire Dales pastures) should not be overlooked, especially if one is trying to trace the historical geography of farming.

When studying the fields attached to the farm, it is important to observe their shape and size, for these provide clues to the age of enclosure, and perhaps also to the way in which they are worked. Their boundaries, save in parts of the Fens, are generally distinguished by some particular feature: generally walls where there is building material to hand, hedges in most areas of clay and shale, occasionally more modern post and wire fences. Gate fastenings and stiles are often interesting as they vary from one part of a country to another.

The convenience of the fields to the farm buildings, the way they are drained and their varied soils★ are important in so far as they affect the farming pattern, and field names may furnish a key to an earlier pattern. To discover the use the farmer makes of his fields and the organisation of his year's work programme necessitates a number of visits to the farm spread through the seasons. If some of the land is arable, the crop rotations

★ Soil profiles should be studied with the aid of either a spade or soil auger, acidity tests applied and the texture examined.

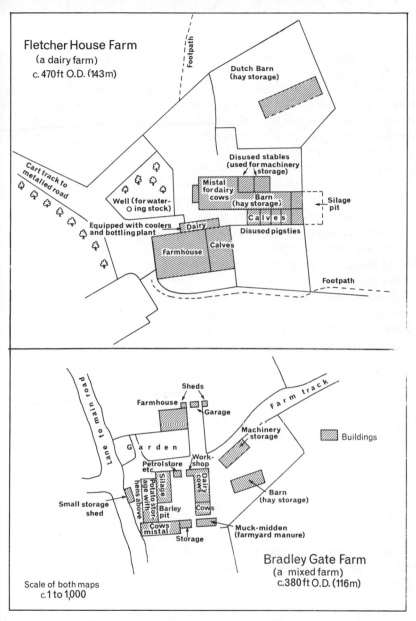

FIG. 142.—Farm buildings near Huddersfield. Each of these farms is near the edge of the Huddersfield County Borough. Their buildings—nearly all of local sandstone—are scattered and vary considerably in both layout and function.

adopted by the farmer and the use he makes of his varied crops must be inquired into; if the land is partly or wholly in pasture, the kind and number of his livestock, his arrangements for winter feeding, lambing and calving, and so on, the products he derives from them, and the markets to which he sends his surpluses, must be taken into account. The average distance of his various fields (e.g. orchards, vegetable plots, pastures and arable land) from the farmhouse in relation to the time the farmer spends on them, may be significant. What machinery there is on the farm, what fertilisers and pesticides are spread, what (if any) labour additional to that of the family is employed, should all be investigated.

Amenities and problems exist on all farms and should receive the field worker's attention. Is there a piped water supply? Is electricity laid on, and if so, is it generated on the farm itself or obtained from the grid? Are there any particularly difficult weather problems, e.g. the incidence of frost on a fruit farm, the liability to flood of low-lying fields, the occurrence of heavy winter and spring snows on a livestock farm? Which pests and diseases are troublesome? Is the land threatened by urban sprawl or New Town developments?

Attempts should be made to find out from the farmer in what ways his farming pattern has changed, whether he has any special plans for the future, and how far the kind of farming he has adopted has been affected by government policies and subsidies, and by the absence or presence of a nearby urban settlement.

All farms vary to some extent, even in the same area. It is preferable to make a field study of a typical one rather than of an unusual one, and best of all to examine contrasted ones in different physical environments. Though the chief object may be to examine a farm as a unit of settlement, the farm buildings and the farming pattern are so interwoven that the understanding of the one can only be satisfactorily undertaken if some study is also made of the other.

THE FIELD STUDY OF A VILLAGE

Like a farm, a village should be considered not simply as an isolated settlement complete in itself, but also as an element in a larger geographical area. Its relations both with the land close to it and with a nearby town are equally significant in shaping its economic and social character.

The local and regional setting of a village may be examined cursorily on a map or aerial photograph, but more completely from a carefully selected viewpoint. A perambulation of its streets and surroundings will add to the field worker's knowledge of its site in relation to relief (includ-

THE USE OF GEOGRAPHICAL FRACTIONS FOR MAPPING TOWN OR VILLAGE BUILDINGS

Suggested scheme:

Numerator: **Abc**   **A**=main function of building
Denominator: **xyz**   **b**=sub-division of functional type
                        c=no. of storeys
                        x=materials used for building walls
                        y=materials used in roof construction
                        z=age of building

Details of scheme:

Numerator: **A**=main function, *e.g.*

H=house or other dwelling; **F**=factory or workshop; **W**=warehouse or other storage-place; **T**=transport building; **R**=retail shop; **O**=office; **P**=public building; **C**=café, inn or other place of refreshment; **E**=place of entertainment, *e.g.* cinema, theatre, club; **D**=doctor's or dentist's surgery; **S**=school or other educational centre.

b=sub-divisions of **A**, *e.g.*

H1=residential hotel or boarding-house; **H2**=block of flats; **H3**= terraced house without gardens; **H4**=terraced houses with gardens; **H5**=detached house or bungalow.; **H6**=semi-detached house or bunga-low; **P1**=town hall; **P2**=public library; **P3**=art gallery; **P4**=museum; **P5**=church; **P6**=chapel; **P7**=community hall

c=no. of storeys, *e.g.* 1, 2, 3, 4. (If more than 9, this figure may be placed in brackets to avoid confusion.)

Denominator:

x=walls, *e.g.*

1=stone; **2**=brick; **3**=concrete; **4**=pebble-dash; **5**=cement; **6**= timber; **7**=half-timber; **8**=cob; **9**=other (e.g. glass and steel). (If the walls are of more than one material, the appropriate figures may be placed in brackets.)

y=roofs, *e.g.*

1=stone slats; **2**=slates; **3**=flat tiles; **4**=pantiles; **5**=thatch; **6**=timber; **7**=corrugated iron or asbestos.
(A small letter could be added to indicate shape of roof, *e.g.* **a**=gable; **b**=hip; **c**=flat.)

z=age, *e.g.* (i) simple method: **1**=pre-Victorian; **2**=Victorian and early twentieth century; **3**=inter-war years (1918–39); **4**=post 1945.

(ii) more complex method: **1**=pre-Tudor; **2**=Tudor (1485–1602); **3**=seventeenth century and Queen Anne (1603–1713); **4**=Georgian, Regency, etc. (1714–1836); **5**=Victorian (1837–1900); **6**=Early twentieth century; **7**=Between Wars (1918–1939); **8**=1945–65; **9** post 1965.

Examples: $\dfrac{\text{H32}}{\text{115}}$ = a Victorian terrace of two-storeyed houses, with stone walls and roofs.

$\dfrac{\text{H52}}{\text{23b7}}$ = a detached, two-storeyed house, built of brick between the wars, and having a tiled, hip roof.

Fig. 143.—Mapping buildings by geographical fractions. There are various ways of mapping buildings in the field. They may be numbered on a map-tracing and details entered in a notebook, or—as here—their particulars may be inserted directly on to the map by some form of fractional notation. Following such fieldwork, a series of finished coloured maps may be prepared, *e.g.* one showing the distribution of houses, another the materials of which they are principally made, a third showing their approximate ages. Useful correlations may suggest themselves, and the tendency for a settlement to expand in a particular direction may become evident.

ing aspect, slope, height and land-form) and water (stream, spring, well and so on), and will give him a preliminary idea of its size, shape and form. Its situation may be judged from its communications with the surrounding area and from the public transport services which link it to a nearby town or towns.

There are, of course, many kinds of villages, *e.g.* agricultural, forestry, fishing, mining and quarrying, industrial. All have a distinctive setting and character. Here we shall in the main restrict ourselves to a considera- tion of a farm village though many of the suggestions put forward for field-work will apply equally well to other types.

The form of the village should be examined, at first, perhaps, on a large-scale map (6 inches to 1 mile), then on the ground. Whether the form is compact or loose-knit, square, cruciform, linear or amorphous, whether or not there is a green, what are the street widths and whether they are straight or winding (perhaps former field paths), whether the main street is used by long-distance traffic or not: all these are interesting details, and raise many questions for the geographer.

As with other settlements, a village is materially composed of many buildings, all of which have a particular size, age, shape, function and architectural style. These characteristics, along with the materials of which the walls and roofs are made, require detailed investigation, perhaps on the lines suggested in Fig. 143. The way in which several buildings are grouped together, the position and size of windows and the extent of the domestic gardens on a street side compared with those facing a field: all these have relevance to the study of buildings from both a social and an aesthetic point of view.

An examination of the approximate age of the buildings may provide some clue as to what extent and in what direction a village has grown. Supporting evidence for the past history of a village may be found in its place-name, in the Domesday Survey, in various tax returns (*e.g.* the 1379 Poll Tax) and in the dating of its oldest building (probably the church, but perhaps a castle or abbey). The existence of a very large church, an abbey or a castle may be taken as indicative of former defensive or religious significance, while the presence of a former market place or cross, or an unusual number of inns, will suggest a diminution in the importance of the settlement. If there is any evidence of recent expansion, the reasons for it should be considered: perhaps the village is becoming a dormitory for a large city, or it may be developing a singificant tourist function, or it may have been chosen as the site of a new factory.

It is worth while not only to map the functional use of each village building, but also to examine the services the village provides both for its own inhabitants and for those living in nearby hamlets or on farms within its ambit. How many shops are there and what do they sell? Do travelling shops call regularly? Is there a residential hotel? How many inns are there? Is there both a church and a chapel? Are there any other places of worship? Is there a school, county library and village hall, a post office and telephone kiosk? Is there a police office, a doctor or resident district nurse? Are there any street lights? What social clubs and societies does the village support? Are there adequate water, electricity and gas services?

How adequate are the village stores and the public transport services? Is there still an open railway station? Which is the most convenient town to visit for goods which are unobtainable in the village? Where do the villagers seek their entertainments and their cultural activities? In which town is the nearest secondary school located?

To find out more about the social geography of the village it will be necessary to conduct many interviews, *e.g.* with the vicar and publican, the shopkeepers, farmers and old inhabitants. Not only is the number of people living in the village of importance, but also their age structure, which should take account of the proportion of retired people who have recently come in from outside. The occupations of village workers, including craftsmen, and the number of people living in the village but working elsewhere are also significant.

Recent changes in village life brought about, for instance, by increasing road traffic, the reconstruction of old buildings, and the provision of new, the emigration of young adults, and the closure or impending closure of uneconomic schools, all have a part to play in the field programme.

Finally, as with farms, it is useful to compare the particular village under investigation with others in the region to see what differences there are in material structure, relations with town and country, social geography and so on. If the village is typical of the area, the time spent on field study is likely to be more profitable than if the village is for some reason atypical.

THE FIELD STUDY OF A TOWN

To make a field study of the whole of a sizeable town is a task too formidable for a single student, even with the help of 25- and 50-inch Ordnance Survey plans. It should, however, be possible to study the street pattern as a whole, to delimit the central area and to define in general the main functional zones, to gain some idea of the extent of the urban field, and to investigate some aspects of traffic flow, public transport facilities, urban decay and renewal, and the problems they bring. Maps and documents will help in the elucidation of the town's site and situation and their changing value in terms of physical and other features, though personal observation is needed if such features as breaks of slope, the existence of small knolls, used, perhaps by Norman castle builders, and the course of streams now culverted underground, are to be appreciated. For the rest, it is generally practicable only to attempt sample studies, *e.g.* by investigating the geography of an urban wedge starting from the town centre and broadening outwards, or by examining the features of a single residential area perhaps in relation to the neighbourhood unit concept.

FIG. 144.—Part of the Colne valley, Huddersfield. Here, near the western boundary of Huddersfield, the valley floor with its river and accompanying railway, roads and canal, is crowded with terraced houses and other close-set buildings, among which woollen factories, benefiting from water availability and the ease of transport, are prominent. The observer stands at a height of about 600 ft (180 m) and looks across the valley floor (300 ft (90 m)) to the horizon (600–750 ft (180–230 m)). The way in which the builders have followed the contours and made maximum use of the most gently sloping areas is common to settlements penned into rather narrow valleys such as this (*cf.* Fig. 106).

As explained in earlier chapters of this book, there are many different kinds of towns even in the same country or large region: old and new, planned and unplanned, industrial, commercial, mining, resort, dormitory, and so on. For field study purposes, each presents its own problems and opportunities, and its own economic and social characteristics. In an industrial town, for example, there are ample opportunities for investigating the distribution of factories in relation to site factors, water and power supplies, communications, and the source of raw materials and the means by which they reach the area (Fig. 144). Time can be profitably spent finding out the reasons for the importance of a single dominant industry, and studying the layout, siting, male and female labour supply and so on, of a single large industrial establishment. In the case of a holiday resort, attention has to be paid to the accommodation available for visitors (for example, hotels, boarding houses and caravan sites), the natural and man-made amenities, the attractions of the surrounding area, the town's accessibility to large centres of population, the places from which most visitors are drawn, the length of the average stay and of the holiday season, the problems of employment in the off-season, signs of expansion and contraction, and so on.

The Study of Urban Buildings

In a village, it does not take very long for two or three students to observe and record the age, function, size and other details about every building. Similar work may still be possible in a country market town, though it will, of course, take longer. In the case of a large city, it may be feasible only in the central area and in carefully selected sections of the

	Residential flat		
Caretaker's flat	Dept. store: storage	Architect	
Insurance broker	Dept. store: offices	Registrar	Wool merchant's offices
Finance company	Dept store: 2nd floor	Customs & excise	Accountant
Solicitor	Dept. store: 1st. floor	Accountant	Jeweller's workshop / Hair-dresser
Bank	Dept. store: ground floor	Chemist and photographer	Jeweller & watchmaker
Bank vaults	Dept. store: basement	Dark room	

R   O   A   D

Cinema	Confectioner	Furniture	Electrical goods		Women's clothing
Meeting-room	Café	Carpets	Workshop	Storage	Women's clothing
					Ladies' hairdresser

FIG. 145.—Field mapping of a multi-storeyed building block. In order to map the use made of each floor of multi-storeyed buildings, very large-scale base maps (preferably 1 : 1,250) are required. Even a map of this kind will require enlargement if the buildings are more than three or four storeys high, though space may be saved by employing symbols instead of words. Graph paper is very suitable. For presentation, several finished maps may be needed, say one for the first two floors, other for higher ones. Basements may be shown by extensions of buildings on to the pavements, as on the diagram shown above.

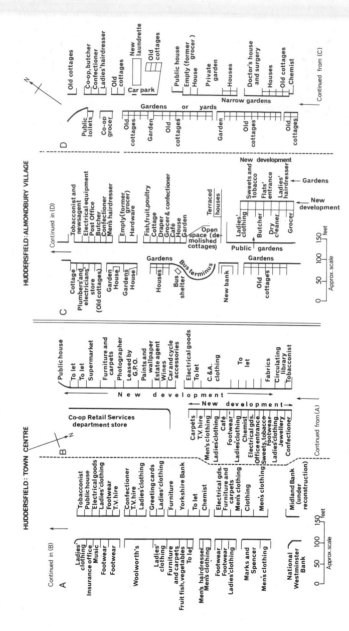

Fig. 146.—Huddersfield town centre and village shopping streets. These diagrammatic maps, based on a survey undertaken in January, 1970, illustrate the contrasts between the functional use of the ground floors of buildings fronting the southern half of the main shopping street of Huddersfield and those facing the main street in a village (Almondbury). The latter, although incorporated within the borough since 1868, still retains some of its individuality, and has its own range of shops and other service premises. While in the central area of the town 90 per cent of the shops are branches of multiple stores, those in Almondbury are almost entirely independently owned.

remainder of the built-up area, preferably in the form of wedges (as mentioned above). The results should illustrate, going outwards from the centre, the decreasing average height of the buildings, the changing forms of urban land use and the increasing youth of most of the buildings, except where recent urban renewal projects upset the theoretical pattern.

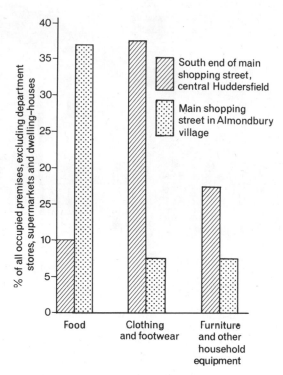

FIG. 147.—Huddersfield: analysis of town centre and suburban shops. These shop-analysis graphs, based on Fig. 146, are fairly representative of most central areas of towns and suburban villages. More than 60 per cent of Almondbury's retail businesses is concerned with the sale of foodstuffs, while over 70 per cent of central Huddersfield's shops deal in clothing, footwear and household goods.

The main problem encountered when investigating urban buildings is presented by the multi-storeyed structure, each of whose floors is used for a different purpose. However, diagrammatic representation, perhaps on graph paper, will enable this difficulty to be overcome (*see* Fig. 145).

In mapping a shopping area—which may perhaps be defined as one in which at least one in three of the buildings is a shop, at least on its ground floor—some method by which the different kinds of shops may be distinguished has to be devised so as to discover their relative frequency, and to see if shops retailing the same wares are grouped closely together or are well scattered. A comparison on these lines between the central shopping area and a range of shops in one or more city suburbs or in old villages now engulfed in the town will provide a rewarding subject of

FIG. 148.—A nineteenth-century terrace in a West Riding industrial town. Terraces such as the one shown in this photograph are common in the industrial towns of Lancashire and Yorkshire. They were erected in the nineteenth and early twentieth centuries for artisans near the factories where they worked. The row shown here is built of the local Carboniferous Sandstone, the roofs are of stone slats made from Coal Measure flags. Many of these houses have now degenerated into slums or have become substandard and are in course of demolition. The new lamp standard seems out of place.

study (*see* Figs. 146 and 147). Cartographically, the number of shops in a sub-centre may be represented by coloured circles of correspondingly different areas or diameters, while the main central shopping area may be simply outlined in the same colour.

When considering residential areas, stress should be placed on the age of the dwellings, the number of houses per acre, the average size of house and garden (a clue to the class for which the houses have been provided), the building materials, and the house-types (*e.g.* terrace, semi-detached, bungalow, flat-block or nineteenth-century back-to-back). Questions

FIG. 149.—Suburban sprawl. In contrast with the buildings shown in Fig. 148, these houses are not only newer and larger, but they have tiled roofs, some are built of brick and pebbledash, there is variety in their styles, and they have gardens at both back and front. Such dwellings are gradually spreading into the fields and woods of all urban outskirts.

concerning urban decay, renewal and sprawl, will obviously emerge even from a cursory survey of different kinds of residential areas (*see* Figs. 148 and 149).

Traffic Studies in Towns

Traffic studies must be based on traffic censuses. To be most useful, these need to be conducted by a number of students working as a team. A selection of points on busy roads and intersections, including bottlenecks such as bridges, on inner and outer ring roads as well as on through roads, on central and suburban carriageways, has to be carefully compiled before students begin to carry out their census. They must be prepared to work on a shift system, and to cover at least the whole of a working day. Results —compiled graphically—will show the number of different classes of vehicles (*e.g.* private cars, small vans, motor-cycles, pedal cycles, lorries, liquid tankers, coaches and so on) which move past a given point, in both directions, during different hours of the day. In the case of lorries and tankers, it will be found useful to note the goods carried, and, if possible, their place of origin. The increasing congestion and consequent traffic crawl observable during the morning and late afternoon rush hours will raise questions about the adequacy of urban transport atrangements in the minds of those undertaking a traffic census.

Opportunities for taking censuses of pedestrians along a selected number of streets in the central area of a town and beyond it should be seized. The number of pedestrians passing an observer on different sides of a shopping street at intervals of, say, five minutes in any one hour on a

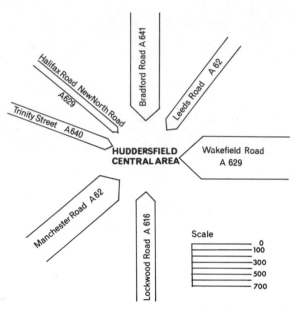

FIG. 150.—Public transport flow map for Huddersfield. This map, based on public service bus timetables (Monday–Friday, 1969) indicates the relative amounts of traffic on each of seven major roads as they converge on Huddersfield's central area. Further from the centre, of course, the traffic density is lighter, as fewer feeder roads, some of which carry motor buses, have entered these A roads. Over 2,500 motor buses enter Huddersfield, a town of about 130,000, every working day (the same number, of course, leave it each day).

Saturday morning may, for example, serve to show the advantage accruing to the retailer who has his shop on the popular side of the thoroughfare.

Traffic problems and problems of urban mobility, alluded to above, deserve close investigation, for so much attention is given by town-planners to schemes for their alleviation. Maps drawn to show one-way streets, car parks, the volume of traffic flow along busy thoroughfares, the roads used by public service vehicles and their frequencies, will help to reveal the extent of these problems, the adequacy of the town as an area of movement, and the accessibility of different parts of a town (*see* Fig. 150). The student may himself have some transport recommendations to offer as a result of such studies.

Towns in their Regional Setting

By using some of the criteria detailed in Chapter XIX, the extent of a town's urban field may be estimated and mapped. Census returns, backed up by personal investigation, may then be consulted in order to discover the approximate population of both the town and its sphere of influence: an important consideration in market research.

As a service centre a town has both shortcomings and advantages. It is up to the field investigator to find out in what respects a town falls short of the requirements expected of it both by its citizens and by the people outside it who depend upon it as their "town." He will have to ask whether the public transport facilities are adequate, whether there are enough parking spaces, whether there are sufficiently varied cultural and recreational facilities and what there is to entertain the young.

The reasons for expansion, stagnation or contraction—evident from successive census returns, and from the rapidity with which urban renewal is proceeding—reflect the character of the town itself, the degree to which the municipal government is enlightened, and also the nature of the region in which the town is located. In England, for instance, the population is now increasing more rapidly in the south-east region than in the north-east. Part of the geographer's task, especially if he is an urban geographer, is not only to ask why such a trend is taking place, but also to suggest some of the reasons. Some of the reasons will have come to his notice as a result of field observation, personal inquiries, recording, and cartographical and statistical analysis.

STUDY QUESTIONS

1. Draw a large sketch-map of the buildings of a farm in your vicinity. Indicate the materials of which they are made, what purpose each serves and, where possible, their approximate ages. How far do they reflect: (*a*) the size and prosperity of the farm holding; (*b*) the kind of farming carried on in the area?

2. Give an account of the maps you would draw to illustrate the geography of a small town or large village.

3. Write an account of the geography of any village with which you are acquainted. Base your account upon: (*a*) the study of the relevant Ordnance Survey and Geological Survey maps; (*b*) fieldwork and your own mapping; (*c*) interviews with selected inhabitants, *e.g.* the schoolmaster and vicar, a shopkeeper, and an old person who has lived in the village for a long time.

4. Explain carefully how you would undertake a land use survey of a village and the area round it.

5. How far is fieldwork in urban geography concerned with making additions to the data shown on Ordnance Survey maps?

6. Write an account of the town in which you live, or of the town nearest to your home if you live in a rural area. Use the following headings: (*a*) site and situation; (*b*) historical development; (*c*) principal functions.

7. Discuss some of the problems of mapping land use in urban areas.

8. (*a*) How would you delimit the central area of a town?

(*b*) Draw a map of the central area of your own, or nearest town, and mark on it the important public buildings, banks and shopping streets.

9. Compare the kinds and volume of traffic, both public and private, which use the main roads entering any town with which you are familiar. Note the destinations or places of origin of lorries, and, as far as possible, the loads they carry.

Bibliography

BOOKS

Alexandersson, G., *The Industrial Structure of American Cities*, Lincoln, Nebraska, 1956.
Arvill, R., *Man and Environment*, Penguin Books, 1967.
Barley, M., and Nuttgens, P., *Living in Towns*, B.B.C., 1966.
Beaujeu-Garnier, J., and Chabot, G., *Urban Geography*, Longman, 1967.
Beckinsale, R. P., and Houston J. M. (eds.), *Urbanization and its Problems*, Blackwell, 1968.
Berry, B. J. L., *The Geography of Market Centres and Retail Distribution*, Prentice-Hall, 1967.
Bonham-Carter, V., *The English Village*, Penguin Books, 1952.
Buchanan, C., *Traffic in Towns*, H.M.S.O., 1963.
Bull, G. B. G., *A Town Study Companion*, Hulton, 1969.
Burgess, E. W., and Bogue, D. J. (eds.), *Contributions to Urban Sociology*, University of Chicago, 1964.
Carter, H., *The Towns of Wales*, University of Wales, 1965.
Chabot, G., *Les Villes*, Armand Colin, 1948.
Chisholm, M., *Rural Settlement and Land Use*, Hutchinson, 1962.
Christaller, W., *Die Zentralen Orte in Suddeutschland*, 1933; first English translation, *Central Places in Southern Germany*, Prentice-Hall International, 1966.
Clayton, R. (ed.), *The Geography of Greater London*, Philip, 1964.
Coppock, J. T., and Prince, H. C. (eds.), *Greater London*, Faber, 1964.
Cornish, V., *The Great Capitals*, Methuen, 1923.
Cross, M. F., and Daniel, P. A., *Fieldwork for Geography Classes*, McGraw-Hill, 1968.
Cullingworth, J. B., *Town and Country Planning In England and Wales*, Allen and Unwin, 1967.
Dickinson, R. E., *City and Region*, Routledge and Kegan Paul, 1964.
Dickinson, R. E., *City, Region and Regionalism*, Routledge and Kegan Paul, 1947.
Dickinson, R. E., *The West European City*, Routledge and Kegan Paul, 1951.
Dilke, M. S., *Field Studies for Schools*, Rivingtons, 1965.
Duff, A. C., *Britain's New Towns*, Pall Mall Press, 1961.
Everson, J. A., and Fitzgerald, B. P., *Settlement Patterns*, Longman, 1969.
Forde, C. D., *Habitat, Economy and Society*, Methuen, 1934.
Freeman, T. W., *The Conurbations of Great Britain*, University of Manchester, 1966.
Geddes, P., *Cities in Evolution*, Benn, revised edition 1949.
Gilbert, E. W., *Brighton, Ocean's Bauble*, Methuen, 1954.
Gottman, J., *Megalopolis*, Twentieth Century Fund, New York, 1961.

Gruen, V., *The Heart of Our Cities*, Thames and Hudson, 1965.

Haddon, J., *Local Geography*, Philip, 1964.

Hall, P., *The World Cities*, Weidenfeld and Nicolson, 1966.

Hatt, P. K., and Reiss, A. J. (eds.), *Cities and Society*, New York, 1957.

Hoskins, W. G., *The Making of the English Landscape*, Hodder and Stoughton, 1960

Houston, J. M., *A Social Geography of Europe*, Duckworth, 1953.

Hoyt, Homer, *The Structure and Growth of Residential Neighbourhoods in American Cities*, Washington, 1939.

Johns, E., *British Townscapes*, Arnold, 1965.

Johnson, J. H., *Urban Geography*, Pergamon, 1967.

Jones, Emrys, *Towns and Cities*, O.U.P., 1966.

Jones, Emrys, *The City in Geography*, London School of Economics, 1962.

Knowles, R., and Stowe, P. W. E., *Europe in Maps*, Longman, 1969.

Madge, J., Smee, M., and Bloomfield, R., *People in Towns*, B.B.C., 1968.

Mayer, H. M., and Kohn, C. F., *Readings in Urban Geography*, University of Chicago, 1959.

Morgan, F. W., *Ports and Harbours*, Hutchinson, 1952.

Moser, C. A., and Scott, W., *British Towns*, Oliver and Boyd, 1961.

Mumford, Lewis, *City Development*, Secker and Warburg, 1947.

Mumford, Lewis, *The Culture of Cities*, Secker and Warburg, 1938.

Mumford, Lewis, *The City in History*, Secker and Warburg, 1961, Penguin Books, 1966.

Murphy, R. E., *The American City*, McGraw-Hill, 1966.

The New Towns Of Britain, C.O.I. Pamphlet, H.M.S.O., 1961 (and later).

Norborg, K. (ed.), *Symposium of Urban Geography*, Lund, 1962.

Park, R. E. (and others), *The City*, University of Chicago, 1923.

Pirenne, H., *Medieval Cities*, New York, 1940.

Pritchard, J. M., *Towns and Cities*, Dent, 1967.

Report on Greater London and Five Other Conurbations 1951 Census, England and Wales, H.M.S.O., 1956.

Robequain, C., *Malaya, Indonesia, Borneo and the Philippines*, Longman, 1954.

Sargent, A. J., *Seaports and Hinterlands*, Black, 1938.

Sauvain, P. A., *A Geographical Field Study Companion*, Hulton.

Schöller, P., *Aufgaben und Probleme der Stadtgeographie*, Erdkunde, 1953.

Seeley, I. H., *The Planned Expansion of Country Towns*, Godwin, 1969.

Self, P., *Cities in Flood*, Faber, 1961.

Senior, D. (ed.), *The Regional City: an Anglo-American Discussion*, Longman, 1966.

Sharp, T., *The Anatomy of the Village*, Penguin Books, 1946.

Sharp, T., *Town and Townscape* Murray 1968.

Sjoberg G., *The Pre-Industrial City*, Glencoe Free Press, 1960.

Smailes, A. E., *The Geography of Towns*, Hutchinson, 1953.

Smith, C. T., *An Historical Geography of Western Europe*, Longman, 1967.

Stewart, C., *The Village Surveyed*, Arnold 1948.

Storm, M., *Urban Growth in Britain*, O.U.P., 1965.

Taylor, Griffith, *Urban Geography*, Methuen, 1949.

Thomas, F. G., *The Village*, O.U.P., 1943.

Thorpe, D., *The Geographer and Urban Studies*, University of Durham, 1966.

Wright, F. Lloyd, *The Living City*, Horizon Press, New York, 1958.

Zipf, G. K., *Human Behaviour and the Principle of Least Effort* (Pt. II), Hafner, 1949.

SELECTED CHAPTERS FROM OTHER BOOKS

Archer, J. E., and Dalton, T. H., *Fieldwork in Geography* (Chap. 6), Batsford, 1968.
Beaujeu-Garnier, J., *The Geography of Population* (Chaps. 4 and 14), Longman, 1966.
Bowen, E. G. (ed.), *Wales* (Chap. 5), Methuen, 1957.
Briault, E. W. H., and Hubbard, J. H., *An Introduction to Advanced Geography* (Chaps. 29 and 30), Longman, 1957.
Brunhes, J., *Human Geography* (Chap. 3), Harrap, 1952.
Chorley, R. J., and Haggett, P., *Socio-Economic Models in Geography* (Chaps. 7, 9 and 10), Methuen, 1968.
Clarke, J. I., *Population Geography* (Chaps. 5–9), Pergamon, 1965.
Davis, D. H., *The Earth and Man* (Chap. 32), Macmillan, 1943.
East, G., *The Geography Behind History* (Chap. 5), Nelson, 1938.
Fleure, H. J., *A Natural History of Man in Britain* (Chaps. 11, 12 and 13), Collins, 1951.
Haggett, P., *Locational Analysis in Human Geography* (various chapters), Arnold, 1965.
Haggett, P., and Chorley, R. J. (eds.), *Frontiers in Geographical Teaching* (Chaps. 5 and 10–12), Methuen, 1965.
Jones, Emrys, *Human Geography* (Chaps. 6, 8 and 9), Chatto and Windus, 1964.
Mitchell, J. B., *Historical Geography* (various chapters), E.U.P., 1954.
Money, D. C., *An Introduction to Human Geography* (Chaps. 4, 6 and 7), U.T.P., 1954.
Moodie, A. E., *Geography Behind Politics* (Chap. 7), Hutchinson, 1948.
Perpillou, A. V., *Human Geography* (Chaps. 16 and 17), Longman, 1966.
Robinson, H., *Geography for Business Studies* (Chap. 26), Macdonald and Evans, 1965.
Stamp, J. D., *Applied Geography* (Chaps. 9, 12 and 13), Penguin Books, 1960.
Steers, J. A. (ed.), *Field Studies in the British Isles* (various chapters), Nelson, 1964.
Sylvester, D., *Map and Landscape* (Chaps. 12–15), Philip, 1952.

ARTICLES IN THE *GEOGRAPHICAL JOURNAL*

Baker, J. N. L., and Gilbert, E. W., "The Doctrine of an Axial Belt of Industry in England," Vol. 103, 1944.
Best, R. H., "Recent Changes and Future Prospects in Land Use in England and Wales," Vol 131, 1965.
Bird, J., "Seaports and the European Economic Community," Vol. 133, 1967.
Buchanan, C. D., "Britain's Road Problem," Vol. 130, 1964.
Carruthers, I., "A classification of Service Centres in England and Wales," Vol. 123, 1957.
Copland, B. D., "A Practical Application of the Theory of Hinterlands," Vol. 120, 1954.
Fawcett, C. B., "The Distribution of the Urban Population in Great Britain, 1931," Vol. 79, 1932.
Freeman, T. W., "Urban Hinterlands in Ireland," Vol. 116, 1950.
Freeman, T. W., "The Manchester Conurbation," Vol. 118, 1952.
Gilbert, E. W., "English Conurbations in the 1951 Census," Vol. 118, 1952.
Gilbert, E. W., "Oxford, 'Venice of the North'," Vol. 131, 1965.
Gilbert, E. W., "The Boundaries of Local Government Areas," Vol. 111, 1948.
Gilbert, E. W., "The Growth of Brighton," Vol. 114, 1949.
Gilbert, E. W., "The Industrialization of Oxford," Vol. 109, 1947.
Green, F. H. W., "Urban Hinterlands in England and Wales: an Analysis of Bus Services," Vol. 116, 1950.

Green, F. H. W., "Urban Hinterlands: Fifteen Years On," Vol. 132, 1966.
Holford, Sir W., "Brasilia: the Federal Capital of Brazil," Vol. 128, 1962.
Kalab, M., "A Study of a Cambodian Village," Vol. 134, 1968.
Moser, B. and Tayler, D., "Tribes of the Piraparana," Vol. 129, 1963.
Pounds, N. J. G., "Port and Outport in North-Western Europe," Vol. 109, 1947.
Scott, P., "The Population Structure of Australian Cities," Vol. 131, 1965.
Stamp, L. D., "The Common Lands and Village Greens of England and Wales," Vol. 130, 1964.
Stamp, L. D., "The Future of London," Vol. 130, 1964.
Sylvester, D., "The Hill Villages of England and Wales," Vol. 110, 1947.
Thomas, D., "London's Green Belt: the Evolution of an Idea," Vol. 129, 1963.
Willats, E. C., and Newson, M. G. C., "The Geographical Pattern of Population Changes in England and Wales, 1921-51," Vol. 119, 1953.

ARTICLES IN *GEOGRAPHY*

Agnew, S., "Rural Settlement in the Coastal Plain of Bas Languedoc," Vol. 31, 1946.
Allen, M. C., "Broken Hill, New South Wales," Vol. 39, 1954.
Andrews, J. H., "The Development of the Passenger Ports of South-East England," Vol. 35, 1950.
Brice, W. C., "The Anatolian Village," Vol. 40, 1955.
Bull, G. B. G., "Field Work in Towns: a Review of Techniques for Sixth Forms and Technical Colleges," Vol. 49, 1964.
Cole, J. P., "The Million Cities of Latin America," Vol. 47, 1962.
Dickinson, R. E., "The Development and Distribution of the Medieval German Town," Vol. 27, 1942.
Dickinson, R. E., "The Distribution and Functions of the Smaller Urban Settlements of East Anglia," Vol. 17, 1932.
Dickinson, R. E., "The Regional Functions and Zones of Influence of Leeds and Bradford," Vol. 15, 1930.
Dickinson, R. E., "Town Plans of East Anglia," Vol. 19, 1934.
Dwyer, D. J., "The City in the Developing World and the Example of Southeast Asia," Vol. 53, 1968.
Edwards, K. C., "The New Towns of Britain," Vol. 49, 1964.
Everson, J., "Some Aspects of Teaching Geography through Fieldwork," Vol. 54, 1969.
Fleure, H. J., "The Life of Europe," Vol. 19, 1934.
Fogg, W., "The Suq: A Study in the Human Geography of Morocco," Vol. 17, 1932.
Gray, D., "Farming in Western Norway," Vol. 23, 1938.
Green, F. H. W., "Town and Country in Northern Ireland," Vol. 34, 1949.
Hamdan, G., "The Pattern of Medieval Urbanism in the Arab World," Vol. 47, 1962.
Hilling, D., "Tema: The Geography of a New Port," Vol. 51, 1966.
Hunt, A. J., and Moisley, H. A., "Population Mapping in Urban Areas," Vol. 45, 1960.
Johnson, J. R., "Population Growth and Urbanization in Australia, 1961-66," Vol. 52, 1967.

Jones, Emrys, "Settlement Patterns in the Middle Teify Valley," Vol. 30, 1945.
Karmon, Y., "Ashdod: A New Mediterranean Port," Vol. 51, 1966.
Keating, H. M., "Village Types and their Distribution in the Plain of Nottingham," Vol. 20, 1935.
Keeble, D., "School Teaching and Urban Geography: Some New Approaches," Vol. 54, 1969.
King, H. W., "Canberra Grows Up," Vol. 39, 1954.
Lawton, R., "Problems of Population Mobility in Contemporary Britain," Vol. 49, 1964.
Leakey, E. A., and Rounce, N. V., "The Human Geography of the Kasulu District, Tanganyika," Vol. 18, 1933.
Learmonth, A. T. A., and A. M., "Aspects of Village Life in Indo-Pakistan," Vol. 40, 1955.
Lewis, G. J., "Commuting and the Village in Mid-Wales," Vol. 52, 1967.
Linton, D. L., "Millionaire Cities Today and Yesterday," Vol. 43, 1958.
Lodge, O., "Villages and Houses in Yugoslavia," Vol. 21, 1936.
Mellor, R. E. H., "The Population of the Soviet Union," Vol. 42, 1957.
Meston, Baron, "The Geography of an Indian Village," Vol. 20, 1935.
Milne, G., "Some Forms of East African Settlement," Vol. 28, 1943.
Mountjoy, A. B., "Million Cities: Urbanization and the Developing Countries," Vol. 53, 1968.
Pounds, N. J. G., "The Ruhr Area: A Problem in Definition," Vol. 36, 1951.
Prentice, Anne, "Islamabad: A New Capital City," Vol. 51, 1966.
Robinson, H., "The Influence of Geographical Factors upon the Fine Arts," Vol. 34, 1949.
Savory, H. J., "Farming in North Trøndelag," Vol. 39, 1954.
Smailes, A. E., "The Analysis and Delimitation of Urban Fields," Vol. 32, 1947.
Smailes, A. E., "The Urban Hierarchy in England and Wales," Vol. 29, 1944.
Spate, O. H. K., and Deshpande, C. D., "The Indian Village," Vol. 37, 1952.
Stedman, M. B., and Wood, "Urban Renewal in Birmingham," Vol. 50, 1965.
Swainson, B. M., "Dispersion and Agglomeration of Rural Settlement in Somerset," Vol. 29, 1944.
Swainson, B. M., "Rural Settlement in Somerset," Vol. 20, 1935.
Swinnerton, H. H., "The Biological Approach to the Study of the Cultural Landscape," Vol. 23, 1938.
Thorpe, H., "Some Aspects of Rural Settlement in County Durham," Vol. 35, 1950.
Watstaff, J. M., "Traditional Houses in Modern Greece," Vol. 50, 1965.
White, H. P., "New Ports in Dahomey and Togo," Vol. 46, 1961.
Wise, M. J., "Problems of Planning for a Changing Britain," Vol. 49, 1964.
Wise, M. J., "Reforms in Local Government in Britain," Vol. 49, 1964.

ARTICLES IN THE GEOGRAPHICAL MAGAZINE
Abraham, J., "The Changing Face of Paris," Vol. 41, 1968.
Brown, E. H., and Salt, J., "A New City on the Oxford Clay" (Milton Keynes), Vol. 41, 1969.
Chisholm, M., "Have English Villages a Future?", Vol. 35, 1962.
Crease, D., "Brasilia Becomes a Capital City," Vol. 41, 1969.
Doutré, N. H., "Kano: Ancient and Modern," Vol. 36, 1964.

Fisher, C. A., "Japan's Great Cities: Nearing 'Standing Room Only'," Vol. 39, 1966.
Grantham, Sir A., "Housing Hong Kong's 600,000 Homeless," Vol. 31, 1959.
Grondona, L. St. C., "The Romance of Broken Hill," Vol. 38, 1965.
Gussman, B., "Shanty Towns in Southern Africa," Vol. 25, 1952.
Harrisson, T., "The Kelabits of Borneo," Vol. 24, 1951.
Jamoud, L., "Islamabad—The Visionary Capital," Vol. 40, 1968.
Lawton, R., "Putting People in Their Place," Vol. 41, 1969.
Marquis, R. V., "London's New City within the Old," Vol. 31, 1959.
Milner, D., "Calcutta—A City in Despair," Vol. 41, 1968.
North, G., "Gargantuan Rotterdam," Vol. 40, 1968.
Panjabi, R. M., "Chandigarh: India's Newest City," Vol. 21, 1958.
Pritchard, G. B., "New Town in the Far North" (Inuvik), Vol. 37, 1964.
Robertson, V. C., "Settlers in the Rain Forest" (Malaysia), Vol. 40, 1968.
Stead, R., "The 'New Villages in Malaya'," Vol. 27, 1955.
Stedman, M. B., "Birmingham Builds a Model City," Vol. 40, 1968.
Taylor, E. R., "The World Wide Growth of Cities," Vol. 22, 1950.
Thurston, H., "France Finds a New Holiday Coast," Vol. 41, 1969.
Wilkinson, H. R., "Humberside," Vol. 38, 1965.
Wise, M., "The Pull of the South-East" (Two parts), Vol. 37, 1964.

ARTICLES IN OTHER JOURNALS

Aurousseau, M., "The Arrangement of Rural Population," *Geographical Review*,
    Vol. 10, 1920.
Berry, B. J. L., Simmons, J. W., and Tennant, R. J., "Urban Population Densities,"
    Geographical Review, Vol. 53, 1963.
Bracey, H. E., "Towns as Rural Service Centres," *I.B.G.*, Vol. 18, 1952.
Demangeon, A., "L'habitation Rurale en France," *Annales de Géographie*, Vol. 29,
    1920.
Fleure, H. J., "Some Types of Cities in Temperate Europe," *Geographical Review*,
    Vol. 10, 1920.
Gottman, J., "Megalopolis," *Economic Geography*, Vol. 33, 1957.
Green, F. H. W., "Bus Services in the British Isles," *Geographical Review*, Vol. 41.
    1951.
Harris, C. D., "A Functional Classification of Cities in the United States,"
    Geographical Review, Vol. 33, 1943.
Harris, C. D., and Ullman, E. L., "The Nature of Cities," *Annals of the American
    Academy of Political and Social Science*, Vol. 242, 1945.
Jefferson, M., "Great Cities of the United States," *Geographical Review*, Vol. 23, 1933.
Jefferson, M., "The Distribution of the World's City Folks," *Geographical Review*,
    Vol. 21, 1931.
Jefferson, M., "The Law of the Primate City," *Geographical Review*, Vol. 29, 1939.
Lee, D. H. K., "Thoughts on Housing for the Humid Tropics," *Geographical Review*,
    Vol. 41, 1951.
Murphy, R. E., and Vance, J. E., "Delimiting the C.B.D.," *Economic Geography*,
    Vol. 30, 1954.
Nelson, H. J., "A Service Classification of American Cities," *Economic Geography*,
    Vol. 31, 1955.

Robertson, I. M. L., "The Occupational Structure and Distribution of Rural Population in England and Wales," *Scottish Geographical Magazine*, Vol. 77, 1961.

Smailes, A. E., "The Urban Mesh of England and Wales," *I.B.G.*, Vol. 11, 1946.

Various articles on urban geography, *Scientific American*, September 1965. (Published in Pelican Books, 1967.)

Ward, B., "The Surge to the Towns," *Unesco Courier*, September 1964.

Whittlesey, "Kano: A Sudanese Metropolis," *Geographical Review*, Vol. 27, 1937.

OTHER SOURCES

Bus and rail timetables

British Association local handbooks

Census volumes, England and Wales, 1951 and 1961

Current town development plans

Encyclopedia Britannica yearbooks

Local newspapers and museums

Ministry and Economic Planning Reports (*e.g.* *The South-East Study, 1961–81* (H.M.S.O., 1964), and *Huddersfield and the Colne Valley* (H.M.S.O., 1969))

Ordnance Survey maps (various editions, and scales)

Philip's annual *Geographical Digest*

The Times and *The Guardian*

Town guides and directories

Town maps (historical and current)

Index

Bremerhaven, 182
Brenner Pass, 139
Breslau, 90
Brest, 138, 148, 189, 204
Brice, W. C., 57
Brick dwellings, see Dwellings
"Brick villages," 24
Brick-making, 26
"Brick-nogging," 24
Bridgwater, 130
Brighton, 109, 149, 210, 211, 212, 214, 215, 289
Brill, 47
Brisbane, 264
Bristol, 93, 101, 124, 131, 165, 175, 181, 223, 300
Britain, 68, 89, 103, 104, 158, 184, 195, 214, 232, 242, 246, 248, 249, 252, 258, 268, 288, 304
British Columbia, 136
Brittany, 158
"Broadacre City," 306
Broken Hill, 146, 197
Bronze Age, 38, 87, 194
Brooklyn, 262
Bruges, 89, 175, 184, 215
Brunhes, Jean, 30, 49
Brussels, 155, 156, 220, 263, 277, 312
Buchanan, Colin, 274
Buckinghamshire, 47
Budapest, 130
Buddha, 207
Buenos Aires, 97, 175, 182, 218, 220, 276
Buildings, 29, 108
  age of, 328
  cultural environment and, 26
  Elizabethan, 29, 53
  forms of and architectural styles, 28
  functional use of, 328
  Georgian, 29, 53, 251, 253
  Gothic, 57
  Jacobean, 29
  mapping, 332, 333
  materials of, 21, 328
  neo-Gothic, 29
  Queen Anne, 29
  timbered, 31
  Turco-Oriental, 32
Buffalo, 231
Bull Ring, 226
Bunbury, 188
Bunter Sands, 74
Burgess, E. W., 238, 239
Burnley, 300

Bury, 225
Butte, 146
Buxton, 109, 211
Byblos, 87
"By-pass variegated," 29

C

Cadbury, George, 289
Caerleon, 89
Caernarvon, 71, 90
Cairo, 30, 100, 172, 237
Cairo (U.S.), 132
Calais, 136, 190, 192
Calcutta, 94, 98, 154, 175, 176, 192, 220, 237, 252, 258
Calder, River, 226
Calgary, 139
California, 210, 218
Cambridge, 10, 130, 131, 149, 165, 209, 215
Canada, 81, 104, 105, 121, 142, 159, 162, 183, 262
Canadian Prairies, 61, 74, 75
Canaries, 214
Canberra, 148, 155, 158, 160, 302
Cannes, 149
Canterbury, 206, 207, 209
Canton, 98, 175
"Cape Coloured," 265
Cape Town, 99, 100, 175, 177, 192, 265
Capitals, 117
  as strongholds, 157
  characteristics of, 155
  compromise, 158
  forward, 160
  national, 154
  political, 154
  regional, 154, 163
  situations of, 155
  within a federation, 162
Caracas, 173, 220
Carboniferous Limestone, see Limestone
Carcassonne, 148, 204
Cardiff, 124, 155
Carlisle, 90, 165
Carlsbad, 93, 149
Carmarthen, 71
Carpathians, 66
Carthage, 88
Catskill Hills, 268
Catterick, 148, 204
Causses, 65
Census,
  (1851), 121
  (1951), 223

Northern Michigan University

3 1854 000 840 887

EZNO
HD111 H85
A geography of settlements